PRIVATE LIVES MADE PUBLIC

Medieval & Renaissance Literary Studies

Originally titled the *Duquesne Studies: Philological Series* (and later renamed the *Language & Literature Series*), the **Medieval & Renaissance Literary Studies Series** has been published by Duquesne University Press since 1960. This publishing endeavor seeks to promote the study of late medieval, Renaissance, and seventeenth century English literature by presenting scholarly and critical monographs, collections of essays, editions, and compilations. The series encourages a broad range of interpretation, including the relationship of literature and its cultural contexts, close textual analysis, and the use of contemporary critical methodologies.

PRIVATE LIVES
MADE PUBLIC

THE INVENTION OF BIOGRAPHY
IN EARLY MODERN ENGLAND

ANDREA WALKDEN

DUQUESNE UNIVERSITY PRESS
Pittsburgh, Pennsylvania

Copyright © 2016 Duquesne University Press
All rights reserved

Published in the United States of America by
DUQUESNE UNIVERSITY PRESS
600 Forbes Avenue
Pittsburgh, Pennsylvania 15282

Library of Congress Cataloging-in-Publication Data

Name: Walkden, Andrea, author.
Title: Private lives made public : the invention of biography in early modern
    England / Andrea Walkden.
Description: Pittsburgh, Pennsylvania : Duquesne University Press, [2016] |
    Series: Medieval & Renaissance literary studies | Includes bibliographical
    references and index.
Identifiers: LCCN 2016021714 | ISBN 9780820704821 (cloth : alk. paper)
Subjects: LCSH: England — Biography — History and criticism. |
    Biography — Social aspects — England — History — 17th century. |
    Biography — Political aspects — England — History — 17th century. |
    Biographers — England — History — 17th century. | Biography as a literary form —
    History—17th century. | Authors, English—Biography—History and criticism. |
    English literature — Early modern, 1500–1700 — History and criticism. |
    England — Intellectual life — 17th century. | England — Social conditions —
    17th century. | Great Britain — Politics and government — 1603–1714.
Classification: LCC CT34.G7 W35 2016 | DDC 920.042 — dc23
LC record available at https://lccn.loc.gov/2016021714

∞ Printed on acid-free paper.

An earlier version of chapter 2 was published as "The Servant and the Grave
Robber: Walton's *Lives* in Restoration England," in *Writing Lives: Biography and
Textuality, Identity and Representation in Early Modern England,* ed. Kevin Sharpe
and Steven N. Zwicker (Oxford: Oxford University Press, 2008), 319–36, reproduced by permission of Oxford University Press, www.oup.com. Part of chapter 4
appeared under the title "Parallel Lives and Literary Legacies: Crusoe's Elder Brother
and Defoe's Cavalier," in *English Literary History* 77, no. 4 (2010). I am grateful to
Johns Hopkins University Press for permission to reprint this material here.

For John

Contents

ACKNOWLEDGMENTS

My research has been generously supported by an Osborn Fellowship from the Beinecke Library at Yale University and a Whiting Fellowship. A research leave given by Queens College and grants from the PSC-CUNY Research Foundation and Faculty Fellowship Publication Program at CUNY helped me bring the project to completion. I am grateful for the kind support of the English department chair, Glenn Burger, and for the friendship and inspiration of my colleagues at Queens College, especially Carrie Hintz, Caroline Hong, Duncan Faherty, Talia Schaffer, Amy Wan, Gordon Whatley, and, offering insight and advice on countless occasions, Richard McCoy.

David Quint oversaw the earliest beginnings of this book and has continued to follow its progress with unflagging support and encouragement. Janice Carlisle, Blair Hoxby, Lawrence Manley, Annabel Patterson, Steve Pincus, and Elliott Visconsi were also generous mentors who helped me find my feet at this formative stage. I have benefited immensely from sharing my work with Allison Deutermann, Gavin Hollis, András Kiséry, Vimla Pasupathi, and James Matthew Zarnowiecki, all now also wonderful friends. I am thankful, too, for the friendship and intellectual conversation across many different fields of Christopher Bond, Jo Briggs, Maria Fackler, Alexandra Gajda, David Miguel Gray, Thomas Karshan, Alexis Kirschbaum, and Jennifer Sisk. As an erstwhile colleague, lively interlocutor, and the most irrepressible of friends, I owe a special thanks to Eric Song.

It is my great good fortune to have had the steadying counsel and encouragement of Rebecca Totaro and Susan Wadsworth-Booth at Duquesne University Press. I am also indebted to the anonymous readers who offered many constructive insights, and to Kathy Meyer for editing my manuscript with such care.

My parents, Maureen and Barry Walkden, have supported all of my intellectual endeavors for as long as I can remember. My stepdaughters, Lily and

Adeline Rogers, have welcomed me into their lives even as I continued to wrestle with the lives in this book.

Finally, my dedication is to my husband, John Rogers. For all the best moments that a life can give.

INTRODUCTION

IN LATE 1651 or early 1652, a volume of church lives appeared on the Interregnum bookstall with the title *Abel redevivus; or, The dead yet speaking.* Its entries were ordered chronologically, offering a version of ecclesiastical history from Berengar of Tours in the eleventh century (famous for his writings against the doctrine of transubstantiation) to William Whately of Banbury in Oxfordshire, a Puritan preacher whom "God tooke away a little before the Civill Wars began" in 1639.[1] If not quite A to Z, then B to W, the volume's biographical wares were entirely typical, varying little from those in other comparable collections. The majority of its entries, together with their accompanying portrait miniatures, had, in fact, appeared in another biographical collection, Samuel Clarke's *Marrow of Ecclesiastical Historie,* just the year before.[2] A prolific editor and compiler of lives, Clarke was not slow to point out this flagrant thievery: "There is lately come forth a Book called *Abel Redivivus,* or *The Lives of Modern Divines,* wherein there are threescore and nine Lives Printed *verbatim* out of my first Part of *The Marrow of Ecclesiastical History,* and divers more, with very little variation; which I thought fit to give the Reader notice of, that so he may not be deceived in buying the same thing twice."[3] Clarke's proprietary stance, his professed concern that unsuspecting readers — *his* unsuspecting readers — not squander their money on a virtually indistinguishable collection, testifies both to a reliable demand for ecclesiastical biography and a protectionist desire to create brand loyalty and preserve market share. It speaks also to the inertia and conservatism of a genre that routinely re-editorialized and repackaged traditional lists of lives, a practice that had been going on at least since Jacobus de Voragine's thirteenth century collection of medieval saints' lives, the *Legenda aurea,* or *Golden Legend,* and continued with John Foxe's *Acts and Monuments,* better known as the *Book of Martyrs,* a vast, illustrated compendium of martyr stories from the early church to the Tudor present, which supported a veritable industry of updatings, abridgements, citations, and augmentations across the seventeenth century.[4] These lives may thrill but they also foreground the familiar, the warmer pleasures of encountering stories that are always the same and already known.

The editor-compiler of *Abel redevivus* was Thomas Fuller, a churchman, historian, and former "cavalier parson," or chaplain in the royalist army. A decade later, he would publish, posthumously, another volume of lives, *The History of the Worthies of England* (1662), a county-by-county description of all the notable people throughout England's history. The physical strain caused by the scale of this massive, one-man undertaking is vividly described in a contemporary life of Fuller attributed to John Fell. It reports how after Fuller "had laid a while dead, an eruption of blood burst from his Temples, which was conjectured to have been long settled there, through too much study, in the methodizing and compleating those various Pieces in his WORTHIES GENERAL." The life also recounts how Fuller compiled much of the topographical and historical research for his collection while traversing the country as an army chaplain, pursuing his "marching Observations" wherever his regiment happened to take up quarters. Styling his research as "a kind of Errantry," a retreat from the uniform array of the battlefield into the singularities of antiquarian romance, Fell's life represents the totalizing achievement of the *Worthies* as the extraordinary, compensatory labor of Fuller's sense of uprootedness and dispossession during the civil war years.[5] At a time when the country had been carved up ideologically into armies and parties and factions and geographically into camps and billets and battlefields, Fuller had conceived of a biographical collection coextensive with the nation itself.

Abel redevivus and *The History of the Worthies of England* are both works of biography — what were known during the period as "lives" — but when considered from a modern perspective it is their differences, not their similarities, that appear to be most striking. The one lays claims to something old, a rehash of existing materials in the lineage of Foxe's martyrology or Eusebius's ecclesiastical history, while the other heralds something new, a possible precursor to the *Dictionary of National Biography (DNB)*, compiled between 1885 and 1900 under the general editorship of Leslie Stephen and Sidney Lee, and to the revised and expanded *Oxford Dictionary of National Biography (ODNB)*, with Colin Matthew as its founding editor, launched online in 2004. Upon what grounds, then, might these two volumes of lives be considered together? How, and why, did Fuller bring about a harbinger of a new mode of writing, the national biographical dictionary, out of his old-fashioned editorial practices? Is there a line of continuity to be traced between the tired Interregnum volume and the pathbreaking Restoration text?

An answer to these questions requires that we turn our attention from the unpromising content of *Abel redevivus* to its radical context: the crisis in church and state relations that took hold in 1641–42 and continued to intensify over the following decade. Heirs to Foxe, if not also aspirants to the same heights of cultural celebrity, Samuel Clarke, a reform-minded Puritan who favored a Presbyterian system of government, and Thomas Fuller, a defender of moderate orthodoxy and of the episcopal Church of England, shared at this time a common antagonist. Both men stood opposed to the Independents or Congregationalists, so called because pastors in Congregationalist churches are not appointed by a centralized hierarchical body as are both Anglican and Presbyterian parochial ministers but are chosen by their congregations. Never a united community and only ever a fractious political coalition, the Independents mobilized around a platform of liberty of conscience for themselves and a stricter separation of church and state.[6] Many dense works of polemical prose were written on just these relations of the church to the civil magistrate, including, among Anglicans, Henry Hammond's *Of the power of the keyes* (1647), Jeremy Taylor's *Treatise of Episcopacy* (1648), and John Bramhall's *A Fair warning to Take Heed of the Scotish Discipline* (1649); among Presbyterians, Thomas Edwards's *Gangraena* (1646), Samuel Rutherford's *A Survey of the spirituall antichrist* (1648) and *A Free disputation against pretended liberty of conscience* (1649); and among Independents, John Owen's postregicide sermon *Righteous Zeal encouraged by Divine protection* (1649), Henry Danvers's *Certain quaeries concerning liberty of conscience* (1649), and *Zeal examined* (1652), attributed to Henry Vane.[7] Between the execution of Charles I on January 30, 1649, and the installation of Oliver Cromwell as Lord Protector on December 16, 1653, the Independent party and its ideological adherents held much of the political initiative. The future of a national church, controlled and maintained by state power and compelling some form of religious uniformity, appeared under imminent and violent threat.

Abel redevivus is a work of political reaction to these new emergency conditions. Self-consciously positioned, "in the interstitium betwixt two Disciplines and give me leave," writes Fuller in his epistle to the reader, "to terme Discipline the Armour of the Church *Episcopacy* put off, and another Government not as yet close buckled on," it seeks to rally the public's support for a national church not by mounting an intellectual defense of its institutions, doctrine, or liturgical ceremonies but by convening an ancestral ministry.[8] The members of this ministry are brought into agreement by being brought into the collection: all are hailed as forebears, creating the fiction, cast backward in time and carried forward to the present, of an unbroken spiritual accord. Fuller's metaphorical license, his figuration of "discipline," the outward governance and practice of the church as the suit of armor that not only protects but also marks the identity of its wearer, introduces the defensive and genealogical duties that his volume, too, will perform. In the absence of a functioning ecclesiastical polity, there may yet remain a constitutive unity of persons, a variation on the secular model of political sovereignty represented by the frontispiece to Thomas Hobbes's *Leviathan* (1651) in which the people consent to cover, and so to create, the enlarged figure of the king, plating his body with their smaller bodies. In his capacity as editor-compiler, Fuller forthrightly assumes the centralizing, ordaining powers of the bishop or presbyter over this assembled polity: his collection of lives needn't argue for an established church because it already functions as one.

The political intelligence behind Fuller's biographical practice is again in evidence in *The History of the Worthies of England*, published in the aftermath not of the abolition of the Stuart monarchy but of its triumphal restoration. It, too, is a work of reaction to changing circumstance, a collection for the new, postwar world ushered in by the return of Charles II. Its title alludes to the medieval theme of the Nine Worthies, a pantheon of legendary warriors drawn equally from biblical, classical, and romance history. The superheroes of their day, the Worthies were a staple of English popular culture, featured in ballads, chapbooks, mummers' plays, and pageants, and depicted on the painted cloths that hung on the walls of humbler households.[9] Fuller not only nationalizes this finite canon, he also liberates it from its rule of fixed numbers, extending it to people of all stations in what amounts to a radical redistribution of renown. Declaring his disinterest in the violent disagreements of the preceding decades and assigning the description of people an unchallenged privilege over the presentation of beliefs and ideas, Fuller seeks to divest the nation from ideological struggle or argument. In its vastness, chorographical arrangement, and greater inclusiveness, his *Worthies* may appear to offer an alternative vision to *Abel redevivus,* but both are motivated by a single insight: that the ability of biographical writing to depoliticize the pursuit of its own political aims and interests is what makes it so effective a form of public speech. This insight, together with the quarrels and consequences arising from it, is the subject of this book.

Much of the period's controversial prose presumes a specialist or, at the least, an exceptionally invested and practiced reader. Exegetical energy is required to master its terms of art or to keep track of its often fastidious, sometimes playful, twists and tangles, ripostes, rejoinders, and rebuttals, even if we assume a reader familiar with polemical encounters and their generic conventions. Biographies, by contrast, tend to be narratives without closely articulated positions, still less unfettered arguments; they don't demand a reader of any considerable education or insider expertise, and they reach out to a broad literate public as well as to smaller interest groups. This distinction, between the textual difficulty, political tribalism, and open belligerency of polemic, on the one hand, and the simplicity and self-idealization of life stories, on the other, is helpful for explaining the remarkable level of popularity that biographies achieved during the later seventeenth century. Focused primarily on printed works that enjoyed large sales, fast sellers as well as steady sellers that accumulated recognition over a long run, my study explores why contemporaries were motivated to interpret their century through the lens of the life or collections of lives.[10] It further considers the consequences of this biographical reorientation of public discourse away from open polemical engagement and toward a less threatening conversation about the unfolding of an individual's life.

Private Lives Made Public is not intended to be a comprehensive survey of all of the biographical writing in print across the later seventeenth century.[11] Instead, it concentrates on an interconnected group of writers, ghostwriters, and editors, John Milton, Izaak Walton, Samuel Clarke, John Gauden, Thomas Fuller, John Aubrey, Edward Hyde, the Earl of Clarendon, and Daniel Defoe, who were variously involved in producing works of biography or exercised by their effects on a rapidly changing political culture. The consideration of these is set, in turn, in the context of broader life-writing traditions: lives of saints and martyrs, the medieval and Tudor *de casibus* or fall-of-princes collections, classical lives of heroes and statesmen by Plutarch and of philosophers by Diogenes Laertius, and an emergent trend toward prefatory lives that recognized and helped to advance the prestige of the individualized author. Throughout, my purpose is to show how the period's biographies sought to replace violent disagreement with life stories whose affecting celebrations of the individual were designed to distract and detract from argumentative discussion. Profiling persons rather than taking positions and diverting opinion into transparent testimony, the writers of lives, by avoiding outright conflicts of views, were able to present their work as external to the debates they were seeking to influence. The success with which the biographical narrative is able to disown the argumentative energies that animate its telling made it, so I argue, such a flexible discursive mode during the postrevolutionary era in England.

The depoliticizing strategies of biography are neatly exemplified in Fuller's midcentury collections. Both claim an ideal inclusiveness, universalizing the interests of a cohesive group, class, or national community. In both, too, Fuller presents himself not as an author but as an editor and compiler, drawing on a stockpile of knowledge derived from older, established genres: martyrology and ecclesiastical history, in the case of *Abel redevivus;* chorography and chronicle, in the case of the *Worthies*. This unapologetic practice of lifting and reframing existing material explains how biographical compilations could be put together quickly and with a short lead time, adapting to the needs of a particular crisis, news cycle, or historical moment. Indeed, the responsiveness of the biographical collection to current events is most interesting precisely for the ways in which it takes what is topical and passes it off as something timeless. By lining up lives behind a present-minded political position, the collection performs its work of reassuring readers that what might appear to be contentious and contingent is, in fact, just the opposite: the received or received-again wisdom of a virtuous majority. That the lives themselves aren't new — in the sense of having already been written as well as having already been lived — is what gives the impression that the political position is nothing new. It is for this reason that collections are more appropriately edited than authored, the chief responsibility of an editor being to cite and recharacterize what is already understood to be on record. Finally, and most importantly, lives demonstrate rather than argue. In the *Worthies,* especially, Fuller takes pains to declare his discomfort with more adversarial or openly disputatious forms of writing, forwarding the view that the violence of the civil wars must be answered by a new way of thinking, centered upon the endeavor and industry of individuals and not upon the partisan appraisal of beliefs and ideas.

I am not, of course, suggesting that all, or indeed any, of these characteristics are necessarily unique to seventeenth century lives. Stories of saints and rulers, the learned and illustrious, had long proved themselves to be among the most adaptable, dynamic, instructive, best-selling, and enduring of literary works. But I do want to suggest that these characteristics are made newly salient by the widespread culture of public discussion that prevailed during the revolutionary and postrevolutionary era in England. Under these wartime and postwar conditions, biographical writing served as a proxy political discourse, securing legitimacy by setting itself apart from contestable argument. That this ostensible use of biography to diffuse controversy itself proved to be highly controversial, upending the conventions of public political debate, further evinces both the form's ideological value and its success as a cultural enterprise.

We can sharpen our sense of the kinds of inclusiveness that the biographical collection was able to postulate by attending to the different logic at play in the engraved frontispiece to *Abel redevivus* and in the *Worthies*'s opening metaphor. Drawn by Robert Vaughan, who that same year would be indicted by the Commonwealth authorities for publishing a portrait print of the executed king, the frontispiece captures the collection's claim to perform a textual resurrection that precedes, and perhaps enables, a future spiritual one (fig. 1). It depicts a funerary monument with a sprightly skeleton, its flesh picked clean, laid out inside. The skeleton declaims the Horatian tagline, "Mors ultima linea rerum est," or "death is the finishing line of all things."[12] Books, standing upright on shelves, their spines inward and fore-edges displayed, form the tapering roof of the monument, the clasps or straps of their bindings hanging loose in a manner reminiscent of burst open graves. Their material shelf life above counters the sententious skeletal wisdom below, transcending the physical limit of the death of the body through the accumulations of print.[13] By following their upward trajectory, the eye arrives at the apex of the roof, where a single book is poised, its pages spread wide like an open mouth. This is the Book of Life, the heavenly registry of the names of the faithful announced in the book of Revelation and from whose pages the names of Milton's fallen angels will be a conspicuous absence, "blotted out and razed" by their act of rebellion (*PL* 1.362).[14] On the frontispiece, the shelves of books build up toward and are finally to be subsumed within this one book, a bibliographical path to salvation.

Yet the open book perched at the tip of the textual pyramid need not be the heavenly Book of Life but its earthly deputy, a book of lives, perhaps the very book of lives that the potential reader weighs in his or her hand. A less exalted epitome, to be sure, the book of lives holds out a more practical promise of summation, digesting the contents of the intimidatingly loaded shelves beneath it into a single volume. On this account, the binding clasps of the books are untied because their contents have been released into the one book that stands open invitingly above them. The shelves are scalable if you start at the top. There may be a clear affinity between collections of lives and what Ann Blair describes as the practices of pre-modern "information management," but the knowledge such collections aggregate, and the totality toward which they orient the reader, is of a particular kind.[15] The logic of summarization found in a book of lives is often accompanied by a complementary logic of substitution or elision: not just one book in place of many but a personal life story or stories in place of a corpus of published writings, a corpus that, in the case of these venerable ecclesiastical Abels, would include sermon books, commentaries and annotations, theological treatises, and thousands upon thousands of closely argued pages of ecclesiological controversy.

With the *Worthies,* the ecumenical focus of *Abel redevivus* changes to a civic one. The organizational structure of the pyramid, its plotted ascent from the graveyard to the posthumous print archive to the biographical collection and its vicarious substitutions — the life for the works; the book of lives for the higher, heavenly Book of Life — are replaced by a different conceptual framework. Now the task confronting Fuller entails schematizing hierarchies within a single model of national inclusion. For this project of totality he turns to an enduring metaphor, describing England as a house, its shires or counties as rooms, and its people and commodities as the furniture inside those rooms.

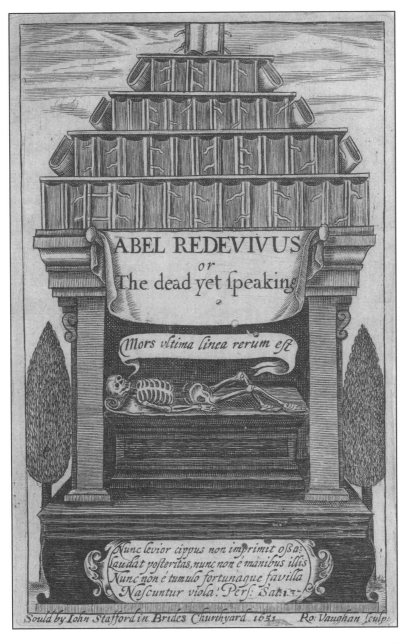

ABEL REDEVIVUS
or
The dead yet speaking

Mors ultima linea rerum est

Nunc levior cippus non imprimit oßa:
laudat posteritas, nunc non e manibus illis
Nunc non e tumulo fortunaque favilla
Nascuntur viola: Perſ. Sat.

Sould by Iohn Stafford in Brides Churchyard 1651   Ro: Vaughan ſculp:

Fig. 1. Thomas Fuller, *Abel redevivus; or, The dead yet speaking* (1652), title page, engraved by Robert Vaughan. By permission of the Folger Shakespeare Library.

> England may not unfitly be compared to an House, not *very great,* but *convenient,*
> and the several Shires may properly be resembled to the *rooms* thereof. Now, as
> learned Master *Camden* and painful Master *Speed* with others, have discribed the
> *rooms* themselves; so is it our intention, God willing to discribe the *Furniture* of
> these *rooms;* such Eminent Commodities, which every Country doth produce,
> with the Persons of Quality bred therein, and some other observables coincident
> with the same subject.[16]

Acknowledging a debt to the cartographic and chorographic representations of William Camden's *Britannia* (1586) and John Speed's *Theatre of the
Empire of Great Britaine* (1611), Fuller extends his governing comparison to
include an economic geography of natural, manufactured, and human goods.
"Persons of Quality" are equally inventoried as products bespoken to a particular county, part of the furnishings of a national domestic interior whose
proportions are notably modest, "not *very great,* but *convenient,*" closer to a
middle-class dwelling than to the splendors of an aristocratic estate. Con-
ceiving of the nation as a house, Fuller dedicates the *Worthies* to the royal
householder, Charles II.

    Fuller's English interior around which the reader is invited to perambu-
late as one would the rural landscape of a country-house poem is also, in Ian
Donaldson's analysis, a house of memory, both in the strict sense intended by
classical treatises on the memorial arts — a storehouse of materials inventoried by location for mnemonic safe-keeping — and in the looser sense of a site
of commemoration, a durable record of wonder, sites of natural beauty, and
monuments of human distinction.[17] In the reference categories that Fuller
devotes fully 80 pages to elaborating, classes of persons far exceed classes of
things. One of these categories stands out from the others, designating not an
occupational group or status-based identity but the kind of person who qualifies for inclusion simply for being "memorable"; that is, for not needing to be
artificially recalled or consciously summoned to remembrance. Elaborating
on his ancillary category of "Memorable Persons," Fuller declares,

> The former *Heads* [category headings] were like *private Houses,* in which persons
> accordingly *Qualified,* have their several habitations. But this last Topick is like
> a publick *Inn,* admitting all Comers and Goers, having any *extraordinary* (not
> vitious) *Remark* upon them, and which are not clearly reducible to any of the for-
> mer *Titles.* Such therefore, who are *over, under,* or *beside the Standard* of Common
> persons; for *strength, stature, fruitfulnesse, Vivacity,* or any other observeable

eminence, are *lodged* here under the *Notion* of *Memorable Persons*, presuming the pains will not be to Me so much in *marking*, as the pleasure to the *Reader* in *knowing* them.

Under this *Title* we also repose all such *Mechanicks*, who in any *Manual Trade* have *reached a clear Note* above others in their *Vocation*. (*Worthies*, 40)

Fuller's string of prepositions — "over, under, or beside" — plots a cultural logic of deviation, identifying persons nonjudgmentally by their difference. To these, he appends a further preposition, "above," transposing a variance that is multidirectional and exists in the realm of the congenital or natural, denoting distinctions of longevity, fecundity, feat, or feature, to one that is unidirectional and exists in the realm of socioeconomic labor, denoting distinctions of expertise, technical accomplishment, or entrepreneurial skill.

The conjunction of these two criteria strains not only Fuller's subject category of "Memorable Persons" but also his governing metaphor of the house of England. A communal national residence is here replaced by a grid of "private houses," each separately occupied by eligible property holders. By contrast, Fuller's "publick Inn" welcomes "all Comers and Goers," a space of contact and exchange and of mobility — social as well as geographic — although it is also a space whose occupants are itinerant, divested of the real estate of the kingdom in which, under the terms of Fuller's opening metaphor, they owned an equal share. As an instance of metaphorical reorganization, Fuller's inn tests the limits, perhaps, of an idea of identity dependent upon where one lives, of people as located and locatable, fixtures that reliably stay in place. It also attests to the developing idea of the private, and of the private and the public as separate geographies within the national imaginary. Fuller is remarkable not least because he attempts to elucidate these categories, to rewrite the metaphors, as it were, in the process of using them.

In occupying itself with mechanical labor and, more broadly, with the localized distribution of manufactured goods and natural resources, the *Worthies* might plausibly be ranked alongside such data-driven projects as John Graunt's population study of London, *Natural and Political Observations...Made upon the Bills of Mortality,* or William Petty's fiscal assessment of Ireland, *A Treatise of Taxes and Contributions,* both also published in 1662. These early forays into what Petty would later classify as "political arithmetic," the pragmatic attempt to maximize indefinite assets by quantifying and redistributing them, takes the same conscious turn away from argument, although here in the direction of mathematical enumeration rather than biographical description. That record-keeping, population studies, and statistical analysis might be the best precaution against a return to civil warfare is an idea at the heart of the Restoration's practice of political economy, and of the steady centralization of government power, which has been variously described by Joyce Appleby, Mary Poovey, Andrea Rusnock, Steve Pincus, and Peter Buck.[18] To what degree the *Worthies* should be equated with this more general reorientation of statist thinking—to what degree, that is, its collectivities of persons reflect less a form of knowledge removed from ideological dealings than an emerging ideology of government — must here remain as an open question. Certainly, Fuller's aims are pragmatic, attempting to give coherence to the nation so as to make it appear habitable, and cohabitable, again after the divisions and conflicts of the preceding decades.

Fuller's strategy for negotiating what he delicately refers to as "our Civil Distempers" is to cordon them off in their own category, "Of Modern Battels," where their damage can be descriptively contained:

> These *Battels* are here inserted, not with any intent (God knows my heart) to perpetuate the odious Remembrance of our mutual Animosities; that *Heart burnings* may remain, when *House burnings* are removed, but chiefly to raise our Gratitude to God, that so many *Battels* should be fought in the bosome of so little a Land, and so few *Scars* and *Signs* thereof extant in their visible Impressions. Such, who consider how many men we have lost, would wonder we have any left, and such, who see how many we have left, that we had any lost. In a word, as it is said of the best Oyl, that it hath no *Tast,* that is, no *Tang,* but the pure Natural Gust of Oyl therein, so I have indevoured to present these *Battels* according to plain Historical truth, without any partial Reflections. (*Worthies,* 52)

Fuller does not perform the humanist's exercise of *in utramque partem,* or arguing on both sides of an issue, but he does perform the empiricist's exercise of *observing* on both sides of an issue. The demographic balance sheet supports two different assessments depending on which body count — those lost or those left — is presently being taken. Characterizing this evenhanded treatment as a kind of gustatory blandness, Fuller invokes the analogy of the finest oil whose superiority resides in its absence of excrescent flavor — no tang and no taste. What the oil does have is "pure Natural Gust," an innate or inherent flavor, a quality proper to itself and therefore not subject to the powerful vagaries of disagreement or dislike. Resorting to figurativeness, as he habitually does when intervening in his organizing categories, Fuller declares his intention to deliver an impartial record without the sour admixture of partisan commentary to offend the palate of his reader.

One admittedly partial measure of the success of Fuller's biographical strategy comes from the diary account of the indefatigable naval administrator and man-about-town, Samuel Pepys. After his first futile thumbing through the volume at the bookstall, searching for any reference to his own family, Pepys records other occasions when he picked up "Dr. Fuller's book." Struck down with a cold on his twenty-ninth birthday, he takes the day off work, "pleasing myself with my dining-room, now graced with pictures, and reading of Dr. Fullers *worthys*." Two years later, on Easter Sunday 1664, and struggling with flatulence, he forces his wife Elizabeth to stay home from church with him — "though much against her will…for she had put on her new best gown" — placating her by finding in the *Worthies* the record of the Clifford family, her distant relations who, unlike the Pepyses, had made it in.[19] The most illuminating entry sees Pepys again at the booksellers, in funds and in two minds about what to buy. Tempted by "books of pleasure, as plays, which my nature was most earnest in," he opts instead for Fuller's *Worthies,* classifying the collection among works "of good use or serious pleasure" — a mixed category combining enjoyment and improvement.[20] Absolving Pepys from the guilt of knowing that he should be reading something better while not denying him his fix of entertainment, the *Worthies* occupies an ideal position in the literary marketplace, partway between the diverting and the serious.

Pepys cared deeply about what he read and how his reading might support his aspirational social performance. His diary entries offer a privileged vantage onto a phenomenon we can call "biographical populism," where populism as opposed to the simply popular refers to a style of address that does not require — and may even push aside — a narrowly elite or specialist class of readers. This usage aligns with the second of two strands of populism that Margaret Canovan has developed with reference to contemporary Western politics, where the term describes not solely "the confrontational politics that mobilizes ordinary people against the establishment" but also "a classic tactic available to insiders: a kind of 'catch-all' politics that sets out to appeal to the people as a whole...playing down divisions along the lines of party, class, or ideology."[21] Behind Canovan's second kind of populism, the politician's expedient art of unite and conquer, stands the early modern understanding of "popularity," a term derived from the Latin *popularis* ("of or belonging to the people"), but whose meaning narrowed during the Elizabethan period to describe a style of politics that sought to gain favor with ordinary people. Initially, popularity was the creation and concern of a ruling class, a new style of elite politics that had the potential to challenge the monarch's monopoly over the loyalty and affections of her people. Indeed, Raymond Williams points out that this early use of "popular" as a "term of policy" stalks its modern use as a "term of condition": to be identified as popular means to be "widely favoured or well-liked," but it comes "with a sense of calculation that has not quite disappeared."[22]

As the seventeenth century progressed, and as the periodic and occasional publicizing of political and religious debates became a more regular occurrence, appeals to popular opinion developed into a recognizable, and finally permanent, dimension of national public life. By the later Stuart period, according to Steve Pincus and Peter Lake, "public rationality appeared as an ideal to be aspired to"; according to Mark Knights, who explores the anxiety and alarm these new means of political communication occasioned, "the capacity of the people to make informed, rational, political judgements" had itself become a topic of incessant public discussion.[23] In this context, and with this new understanding of the people as inexperienced but inescapable arbiters of a participatory public culture, the phenomenon I call biographical populism — the use of life stories to reinforce conservative values and positions — is able to perform its most powerful and influential work.

So far, I have been using the older term "life" and the newer term "biography" interchangeably, without stopping to examine or to historicize their relation. By far the largest share of the period's biographical writing falls under the looser rubric of the "life," an Anglo-Saxon word whose meaning is double, referring both to the record of a life and to the simple fact of living.[24] Biography, by contrast, is more restrictive, referring only to the written narrative of a life that is separated out from its lived existence. Its polysyllabic form is composed of two Greek elements: the Hellenistic noun *bios,* denoting a particular way of living, as distinct from purely animal or organic life; and the suffix *-graphō,* meaning to write, draw, or record.[25] In the minds of most scholars, John Dryden deserves credit for transporting the word "biography" into English in his *Life of Plutarch* (1683) when he was commissioned to preface Jacob Tonson's new edition and translation of Plutarch's *Lives* (1683–86). As we shall see, Dryden employs the word with a high degree of critical self-consciousness, setting out to describe, and so prescribe, the features of an identifiable genre. His marking of the difference between biography and other kinds of historical writing has retained its privileged position in part because it anticipates so brilliantly the now classic account of the intellectual life of the period developed by Jürgen Habermas, in which an idea of public reason comes to replace the ostentation of sovereign power.[26] Certainly, there is uncanniness to the way Dryden identifies grand narrative history with the representation of rank and distinction before an assembled audience, and biography with the motivated subversion of rank and distinction before an indefinite public of readers. His biographically shaped consciousness of public life was inherited by the eighteenth century, and it laid the theoretical foundations for Samuel Johnson's call for life stories of comparable — as opposed to incomparable — individuals in his essays for the *Rambler* and the *Idler* during the 1750s.[27]

Yet when we look closely at the semantic history of the word "biography," and, especially, at the very earliest examples of its English usage, the authority of Dryden's remarkable account, its monopoly over our understanding of biography's progressive membership within the modern literary system starts to seem less certain. These early usages are valuable, I want to suggest, because they show how the "life" is not simply to be understood as the pre-modern progenitor or precursor to the modern "biography" but as its untheorized alternative: a form of antibiography, committed to leaving intact and unexamined the conventions that biography avows and self-consciously presents to our view. Working backward from Dryden, reaching behind the Whiggish narrative he inaugurates, we will be in a better position to assess the impact of lives and collections of lives on the public culture of later Stuart Britain.

In the best-known passage from the *Life of Plutarch,* Dryden defines biography or *biographia* as a subgenre of history, distinguished by its "descent

into minute circumstances, and trivial passages." Developing this opposition
between the narrative scope of history and the more intimate approach of
biography, he continues:

> There you are conducted only into the rooms of state; here you are led into the pri-
> vate Lodgings of the Heroe: you see him in his undress, and are made Familiar with
> his most private actions and conversations. You may behold a *Scipio* and a *Lelius*
> gathering Cockle-shells on the shore, *Augustus* playing at bounding stones with
> *Boyes;* and *Agesilaus* riding on a Hobby-horse among his Children. The Pageantry
> of Life is taken away; you see the poor reasonable Animal, as naked as ever nature
> made him; are made acquainted with his passions and his follies; and find the
> *Demy-God* a *Man.*[28]

In the first stage of biographical observation, the hero is rejuvenated, returned
to a childlike condition. These initial scenes are sunlit, carefree, and full of
movement. They are also fleeting, held captive to a further regressive movement that takes the hero back to a more primitive developmental state. With
the addition of the adjective "poor" to Aristotle's definition of natural man
as a rational animal, the biographical drama takes a turn to the tragic: "poor"
here not only in the sense of to be pitied but to be socially impoverished,
stripped of the trappings that confer and maintain greatness. Dryden surely
intends the faint but perceptible echo of King Lear's words to Poor Tom
on the storm-swept heath; a recognition scene that ends with Lear impa-
tiently tearing the clothes from his own body, the better to recognize himself:
"Unaccommodated man is no more but such a poor, bare, forked animal as
thou art. Off, off, you lendings! Come unbutton here" (3.4.98–101). In this
telling, biography is the heir to tragedy, invested with all of its grandeur and
possessed of all of its cruelty.

But while biography for Dryden obeys the stern and rigorous logic of
tragedy, its leveling action is plotted not simply vertically, from high to low,
but horizontally, from the public "rooms of state" to the hero's "private
Lodgings" or dwelling place. This spatial distinction is absent from Plutarch's
Life of Alexander, cited by Dryden as his source text. In Plutarch, the different routes taken by biography and history are exemplified in the contrast
between throwaway speech and devastating action: "sometimes a word, or a
casual jest, betrays a Man more to our knowledge of him, than a Battel fought
wherein ten thousand Men were slain, or sacking of Cities, or a course of

Victories."[29] Plutarch's point is that hugely significant outcomes tell us very little about the human beings who achieve them. Reframing Plutarch, Dryden omits the battlefield slaughter and plundered cities so as to isolate a public identity that is not heroic but ceremonial, constituted not by deeds but by display. It is the removal or forfeiture of this speciously manifested worth — what Dryden refers to as "the Pageantry of Life" — that creates the unique viewing conditions of the biography. Under these conditions, the beholder discovers that the singled-out personhood of a great man belongs, for better or for worse, with the mass of universal humanity.

The idea that biography achieves the vulgarization of the great by returning them to the precivil state of the natural human, a state characterized as much by infantilism and negative feelings ("passions" and "follies") as by an innate capacity for reason, may appear quasi-Hobbesian rather than proto-Habermasian. Indeed, the biographical imagination, in Dryden's view, is one in which the state of nature persists both as a hidden interior condition and as an empirical reality behind the scenes, pending our discovery and, perhaps, our disappointment. Nonetheless, his sense of biography as crossing a boundary between the public and the private does contain an emancipatory potential for the understanding of ethical practice. In his sweeping analysis of the new public relevance of private life in the later seventeenth and eighteenth centuries, Michael McKeon argues that biographical exemplarity "underwent a revolution," unseating the lofty and installing the lowly in their place. This sociopolitical change is significant because it transforms the domestic into an independent site of self-improvement: private behavior need no longer refer to a grander public history in order to be considered morally instructive, having become ethically and epistemologically meaningful in its own right. Traditionally, the cultural power of biography had depended upon the importance of its private disclosures to a public world of state government and power. Only in the eighteenth century, McKeon insists, did biography become fully domesticated, uncoupling itself from the *grand récit* of history and achieving ethical possibility exclusively within the private realm.[30] In this way, the humanization of the great cedes its priority to the greatness of the human, sealing the fate of Dryden's already fallen demigods.

McKeon narrates the progressive destiny of biography through its choice of examples: lives that contribute to political histories of nation and empire are ultimately found to be less instructive, less relevant or richly expressive, than lives that remain within the everyday social landscape of domestic sympathies and familial affection. This newly "private" world of biography participates in and is made possible by a broader reevaluation of the private realm of intimate life — and corresponding devaluation of the public realm of political life — as the arena of our most significant moral choices and actions. Embracing McKeon's thesis, we can see how already in its Drydenian incarnation the biography is prescient of, and a participant in, these broader cultural shifts, not only separating out the natural being from his or her political existence but also drastically attenuating the terms of that existence by reducing it to mere "Pageantry," the empty display of authority and power.

This stirring cultural history is persuasive and perhaps inescapable as a way of explaining the future and the advent of modernity. Yet it is inadequate as a detailed explanation of the historical relation between the early modern form of lives and the genre of biography that developed alongside it. In the decades before Dryden, it was, in fact, *biography* that was relegated to an undesirable past. This we can see by examining how the word "biography" started to gain a more dubious currency two decades before Dryden published his *Life of Plutarch,* appearing in a cluster of lives printed in the immediate aftermath of the Restoration. Thomas Fuller uses the word only once in his *Worthies* (1662) when he discusses the far-fetched miracles and other sensational happenings reported in Catholic saints' lives, regretting the "*Want of honest hearts,* in the *Biographists* of these Saints, which betrayed their Pens to such abominable untruths." The life of Fuller (1661) refrains from "giving a particular account" of Fuller's published writings because their "sure and perpetual Duration needs not the Minutes of this Biography." In the opening paragraphs of his life of the Elizabethan theologian Richard Hooker, also published in 1661, John Gauden launches a scathing attack, presumably aimed at Samuel Clarke, on those who having "warped from the Church of *England*" have "ventured to be (*Biogrrphers*) writers of the lives of some English *Divines* (as some of late have done during the *Ataxy* or *Anarchy* of *Presbytery* and *Independency*)." Finally, the epistle to the reader that opens James Heath's best-selling life of Oliver Cromwell, *Flagellum* (1663), argues that Cromwell's rise to power was not only unprecedented but divinely permitted. To persuade the reader on both these counts is, it declares, "the design of this Biography."[31]

What might be said about these early usages of the word "biography" and its collective agent nouns, the parenthesized "*Biogrrphers*" (presumably a misprint on the part of a compositor negotiating a new and unfamiliar word) and "*Biographists*"? Fuller, Fell, Gauden, and Heath were all committed supporters of the king, and it is possible that the word carried a distinctly royalist inflection when it was first introduced into print in the early 1660s. Certainly, the success of the scurrilous *Flagellum,* running through five expanded editions between 1663 and 1672, would have helped maintain its association with a tendentious royalism. But if "biography" did function as a coterie word, defining an emerging field of study, then its connotations largely appear to have been negative ones. Fuller and Gauden both use it to discredit rival religious traditions, associating the term, on the one hand, with a discredited Catholic hagiography, full of outright lies and exaggerations and, on the other, with a separatist movement egregiously rewriting church history. Even in the examples from Heath and Fell, where biography functions as a form of generic self-designation, it does so in contexts that suggest overt belligerence or modest belittlement. Earlier, I observed that one advantage of the word "biography" resides in its capacity to distinguish the written life from the life of personal experience. Yet it is possible also to imagine how this distinction might bring with it a certain discomfort, inviting the examination of the writer's aims and motives that the older term "life," where the relation between the lived life and the narrated life remains unacknowledged, does not. It is because biography opens itself up to the analysis of the difference between experience and discourse that it is able to function critically in these examples, setting in place and even obliging certain conditions of judgment. But it is for this same reason, it could be argued, that, these early royalist adopters notwithstanding, the label is not more generally favored or sooner taken up.

This brief, and somewhat unpropitious, history of the word "biography" suggests how we might reframe the trumping claims that Dryden makes two decades later on its behalf. It shows not only how the modern biography was to extend and pursue methodological aims that had long been implicit in the pre-modern life, but equally, and just as importantly, how the life persisted with a less regularized, and less consciously theorized, understanding of its narrative form. The political utility of the life is bound up with this ability to circumvent analytical inquiry, I want to argue, cultivating an ambiguity of reference that is capable of holding in a kind of precritical suspension the correspondence of the life written with the life lived. By refusing to problematize its form, lives create the pretense of their own lack of pretension, professing to communicate directly with and to the reader. As we will see, the pre-"biographical" life appeals to and works silently toward the cultivation of a kind of conformity that is almost always polemical, a version of pastoral in the Empsonian sense both of making the complex simple and of courting a popular authority mediated by elites and supportive of their values and interests.[32] I stress here the provisional distinction between "biography" and "life" in order to draw out this crucial aspect of the life's polemical value. Nonetheless, I have chosen to follow convention and deploy the words interchangeably, except in cases where I draw special attention to one or the other's use.

In making the populist ethos of best-selling, printed life stories so central to its account of public discussion, this book distinguishes itself from the literary historical examination of "life-writing" as it has developed from the 1980s forward. An omnibus label, life-writing encompasses biography, autobiography, memoirs, letters, diaries, journals, family histories and genealogies, survivor, refugee, witness, and travel narratives — in fact, just about any kind of written record that might be taken to represent selves or incipient selfhoods. The academic study of life-writing first developed in the context of a desire to make visible a broader range of texts from different social groups and postcolonial constituencies, raising questions of canonical representation within the academy and political representation, empowerment, and advocacy outside it. The term "life-writing" was self-consciously adopted for its emancipatory energies, freeing the enterprise of recovering lives from the entailments of the Western humanist tradition and its dominant model of liberal subjectivity.[33] Less a unified field than a set of methodological and ideological commitments uniting its practitioners across disciplinary boundaries, life-writing studies won full academic legitimacy from the Modern Language Association (MLA) in 1991 when the division Autobiography, Biography and Life Writing broke away from the more general rubric Nonfiction Prose Studies. Marking the 20-year anniversary of the division in 2011, Sidonie Smith delivered that year's MLA presidential address, notable for its official adoption of the more expansive rubric, "life narration." Lyrically celebrated in the exordium to Smith's address, "life narration" signals a determination to move beyond the confines of literate culture, assembling and analyzing selves constructed from oral performance and testimony as well as from other visual and digital media and archived materials. The term is also asked to carry an increased burden of ethical responsibility, coined for a new century of internationalism, migration, and terror.[34]

In the field of early modern studies, life-writing has acquired a double valence, designating a commitment not solely to recognizing and reclaiming marginalized figures but also to capturing the diversity of forms and venues in which life stories were staged in the pre-modern period. In this way, the politics of identity that motivated the term's more general academic adoption have been combined with a historicism that cautions against imposing anachronistic order on either the possible subjects or the putative forms of early modern lives.[35] This approach has proved to be necessary and enormously productive, bringing to the fore an astonishingly vital and absorbing archive of personal writing and, especially, writing by women.[36] The recovery of this neglected body of work, much of it in manuscript form, remains ongoing, although recent scholarship has directed attention away from sociological and confessional categories of identity toward the mixed circumstances, material practices, and linked styles of telling that organize a broader cultural geography of life-writing. This new direction has also sought to resist, if not entirely renounce, a model of identity predicated upon inwardness or psychological depth, on the one hand, or upon the power and effects of a self-authorizing agency or autonomy, on the other. Instead, this approach construes selves socially, economically, and materially through possessions, objects, environments, and performative displays of eloquence.[37] These reorientations are exemplified by Adam Smyth's study, which analyzes four kinds of autobiographical text — the annotated printed almanac, the financial account, the commonplace book, and the parish register — that fill up local archives but defy any standard or finite categorization of their function and form.[38] Alongside other accounts of the period's life-writing, such as those by David Booy and Meredith Anne Skura, Smyth's research affirms the abundance of archival materials available to literary scholars and issues a call for them to stop curtailing their investigations and start looking for lived experience in new places and in an ever more innovative fashion.[39]

My study steps back from this rich material imagining of how early modern individuals recorded their lives, returning instead to the best-selling, printed biographies that so thoroughly conditioned, in still unrecognized ways, the period's broader life-writing culture. Within the field of early modern studies, these works might now be said to occupy a doubly unprivileged position. Written for wide dissemination, to amass lucrative sales and command broad assent, they possess none of the coruscating brilliance of the best polemical writing of the period, a level of difficulty that makes it more amenable to the kinds of alert analysis that are the literary scholar's stock in trade (the "Brief Lives" of John Aubrey being a special case here). Yet while early modern printed biographies suffer the artistic disadvantages of their lowbrow inclusiveness, in another sense, of course, they appear all too exclusionary, compiling class-bound and masculinized canons of greatness: military generals and soldiers; poets, philosophers, and experimentalists; bishops and godly ministers; kings, aristocrats, and landowners; courtiers, politicians, and statesmen. There are many lives that never find their way into the pages of a biography, and it is precisely these lesser-known figures that the more flexible category of life-writing has been successful in recovering. It is only by pressing beyond the question of biography's social exclusions, however, taking up the lives that are represented instead of regretting those that are missing, that questions of biography's relevance to a newly configured public realm can productively be raised. By reading and recuperating the politics of this deliberately depoliticized genre, we will be in a much better position to see how much cultural knowledge has been overlooked in the name of our own politics of identity and inclusion.

Indeed, it is these printed and widely consumed lives, I argue, that now have the potential to unsettle the prevailing scholarly consensus, providing a resonant contrast to the unruly pleasures of the archive and defying the pattern of our own progressive preoccupations with what life-writing is and how, as a field of study, it should work. Ideologically conservative, intolerant, and absolutist in their political leanings, immensely popular printed works such as the *Eikon Basilike,* Walton's *Lives,* and Clarendon's *History of the Rebellion* are clearly inimical to the democratic values that impel the contemporary study of early modern life-writing. Yet a history of biography that avoids discussion of these widely consumed works is denied an appreciation of the period's progressive struggle with the political ramifications of the biographical populism they manifest. John Milton and Daniel Defoe, the crucial, dissenting commentators who chronologically frame my study, both labored to confront the cultural threat they identified in the runaway trend of their cultures' generation of seemingly depoliticized biographies of political and religious figures. Milton and Defoe were both complexly aware of the orchestrated use of biography as a counter-response to a participatory political culture. It is their critique of the implicit politics of biography that we as scholars of the form would do well to emulate. This study argues for the inclusion of their dissenting perspective within the ever more inclusive stories we are moved to tell about how early modern men and women wrote, read, and understood their lives.

In developing this argument, I have been fortunate in my access to previous studies of early modern biography that powerfully illuminate its historiographical contexts and multigeneric forms. The descriptive accounts of Donald Stauffer and, more recently, Allan Pritchard, catalogue and impose order upon the enormous range of biographical materials in print across the seventeenth century in England, while a collection of essays edited by Thomas Mayer and Daniel Woolf situates the English example within traditions and practices developing across Europe.[40] Aspects of the wider terrain these studies survey have been finely detailed by other scholars, including Richard Wendorf, who fruitfully compares the evolving techniques of biographical writing to those of the arts of portraiture; Jessica Martin, who demonstrates how exemplary biography evolved in relation to the Protestant funeral sermon; and Ian Donaldson, Keith Thomas, and Kevin Sharpe and Steven Zwicker who, writing in the aftermath of the 2004 launch of the revised and extended *Oxford Dictionary of Natural Biography,* emphasize a tradition of biography that is collective and nationalistic in its contours and motivations.[41] To these must be added Judith Anderson's exploration of the "deliberate and creative shaping of fact" in early modern biographical representations and Kevin Pask's study of the development of the "life of the poet" and its formative role in fashioning a vernacular literary tradition.[42] In many and various ways, these studies attest to how the literary form we comfortably recognize as biography had yet to coalesce into a distinct genre within the early modern literary system. And they valuably trace a general movement away from the exemplary and toward the particularized, thus explaining what they characterize as the "rise" or "birth" of the modern biography out of long-standing everyday practices, rhetorical traditions, and records of subjective expression. I draw on many of the conclusions reached in these studies and I take as a premise the now inarguable point of the generically inchoate literary form of most of this early period's biographical writing. But I also push the analysis of early modern biographies in a direction that these previous academic works have largely declined to move. My study insistently asks not just *what* the early biography is but *why* it is. The hitherto neglected question of the motivating energy behind this nascent form, and of the social, cultural, and political purposes to which widely circulating, popularly inclined biographies could be put, emerges as the urgent, even primary, concern of my study. Nor does this book take the democratically enlightened destiny of biography for granted; rather, it shows how within the period and coincident with its rise, biography was perceived as a consequential and potentially destructive development for public life.

I begin this book with what might perhaps be termed the publishing event of the century: the *Eikon Basilike,* or the "King's Book," a pseudo-autobiographical memoir of Charles I that began selling in the London streets within hours of his death on the scaffold and which would go on to outsell practically all other books across the later Stuart period. The royalist team who ghosted Charles I's private writings had pulled off a media coup, but they had also found a way to diffuse the political controversy surrounding the monarchy, appealing to the language of the psalms, a language that had less to do with the political philosophy of monarchy or republicanism than it did with the common sufferings of life. My story about biography opens with a fake autobiography because it was through the success of the *Eikon Basilike* that biography was first to establish its eligibility not as a humanist discipline or fund of moral example but as a populist form of political discourse. Its galvanic appearance coincided with Milton's publication of his *Tenure of Kings and Magistrates,* a work of political philosophy (specifically, of constitutional resistance theory) from which all personal reference had studiously been stripped and which hit the bookstalls at spectacularly the wrong moment to exert influence over a reading public whose imagination had been caught by the pseudo-soliloquizing of their dead king.

Toward the end of the year, Milton published a second tract, *Eikonoklastes,* answering the *Eikon* point-by-point. In it, he forwarded a political reading of the *Eikon's* literary form, insisting upon its relation to the theatrical melodrama of *de casibus* tragedy in order to suggest not only that the king's life story constituted an attempted exercise of absolute power, but that biographical narrative itself had the capacity to figure forth absolute rule. Milton's formalist opposition to biography was not uncomplicated. His account of the *Eikon* would have been surprising, even shocking, to anyone familiar with his own fiery antiprelatical writings from earlier in that decade, which, following the practice of forensic and laudatory oratory, make a habit of turning to personal prayer and testimony so as to ethically instantiate their arguments. But however ad hoc to its occasion, Milton's repudiation of the "King's Book" forced him to think radically about the power of biography to organize a new popular politics. Chapter 1 interprets his alarmist account not as another polemic against royalism but as the first polemic against biography — a manufactured and marketed political product that seemed poised to take over the discourses that for Milton were constitutive of national public life.

Chapter 2 tests the populist appeal of biography — what Milton saw as its competitive advantage over other, more critically demanding, varieties of political interpretation — by following the path of Izaak Walton's hugely influential series of lives from their inception in 1640 to their completion in 1678. The protracted period of the lives' composition, revision, and republication placed them in spiritual competition with other long-running anthologies of godly lives, most notably those compiled by Fuller's biographical foil, Samuel Clarke, which were re-edited and reconfigured in conformity with current needs and preoccupations both during and after his lifetime. The competition in collective biography was further intensified by the return of the monarchy and of a uniform national church after 1660, and by the resurgent crises over theology and loyalty in the years that followed. Walton wrote and published his lives to gain popular support for an Anglican ecclesiology and devotional literary tradition, inventing a primitive English church for his modern Restoration moment. In recent times, the polemical presentmindedness of Walton's writings has come under more exacting critical examination. One of the claims of this chapter, however, is that the lives possess a broader significance, functioning not simply as identifiable interventions in particular religious debates but also as attempts to reorient the political sphere in the direction of a perennial populism based not upon argument but upon a kind of infallible, straightforward sense of what is true. What the lives imagine, what they work with whatever degree of self-consciousness to shape, is a cultural phenomenon I call the "silent public sphere." To substantiate this claim, chapter 2 traces Walton's patient choreography of a series of self-inscribing servant figures — inspired first by Plutarch's *Parallel Lives,* then by the Gospel narratives, and finally by the national nightmare of the English civil wars — which exalts the lowly biographer to a position of priestlike importance within the memorial culture of Protestant England. Walton's lives indubitably perform the function that Milton was most afraid of: encouraging readers to embrace politicized allegiances without needing to think critically, or even explicitly, about them. Yet they also, I argue, forward a new and emotionally compelling understanding of biography as the ground on which a richer, simpler, communal public life might be built.

My third chapter turns to the English antiquary John Aubrey, whose manuscript collections of lives assembled between 1680 and 1692 and now commonly known as his *Brief Lives,* present a compendium of public figures from among his contemporaries and the century past. The potential for biography to evacuate the political, a potential Walton's lives depend upon to cloak their political agenda, is radicalized by Aubrey, who writes anecdotal accounts of public persons in which ideological motives compel no interest and in which politics happens elsewhere, outside the intimate space of the biography. Any reader of Aubrey must confront the dashed-off, chaotic, and incomplete state of his manuscripts, which are comprised of an assemblage of textual pieces, or what Aubrey refers to dismissively, and disarmingly, as "minutes" — rough copies, notes, or memoranda, but also, etymologically, small things. Taking its cue from this term of choice, chapter 3 treats Aubrey's habit of "minuting" alongside his propensity to miniaturize, scaling down the heroic figure so as to house him (and only occasionally her) inside a domestic, interior space that was itself undergoing cultural redefinition and revalorization during Aubrey's lifetime. The connections between these admittedly haphazard experiments in form and the particular contents of the *Brief Lives* support a new interpretation of Aubrey's work, which is seen almost to go so far as to disarticulate entirely the political from the public life.

The final chapter of my study aligns its own revisionist account of postwar biographical writing to the brilliant critique of early modern English biography that fills the pages of Daniel Defoe's pseudobiography, *The Memoirs of a Cavalier* (1720). In this eighteenth century fabrication of a seventeenth century soldier's memoir, Defoe runs amok through the treasured myths of royalist biography and historiography. He takes particularly pointed aim at Clarendon's *History of the Rebellion,* a Tory blockbuster composed over a 25-year span from 1646 to 1674 but first printed posthumously and for party political advantage between 1702 and 1704. The history lesson Clarendon delivers is one of conspiracy. Through a sequence of exquisitely composed character portraits, he explains how, under the guise of constitutional principle, an elite faction of courtiers and advisers provoked a national rebellion to address their personal grievances against the crown. By focusing on characterological forms of explanation, Clarendon's *History* succeeds in marginalizing ideological conflict, a historiographical strategy that reproduces, in a different register, the shift from political arguments to life stories that the earlier chapters of this study have been concerned to trace. And so Defoe's attack on Clarendon also takes the form of a life story, interweaving the micro-plot of the no-name Cavalier with the Tory macro-plot of seventeenth century history and, thus, inviting his readers to review an entire period through the lens of a single, simulated life. Defoe doesn't so much invent the figure of the Cavalier, however, as resurrect him from the opening pages of his bestseller, *Robinson Crusoe* (1719). There he had killed off Crusoe's elder brother, the old world Tory soldier, in the process of launching his entrepreneurial hero, the new world conqueror and colonizer, on his global adventures. Investigating Defoe's self-conscious adoption of a biographical approach toward the biography, chapter 4 unpicks the narrative interlace that links the life of Defoe's most famous protagonist to that of his now forgotten fraternal counterexample. Its aim is not to rehearse the literary-historical narrative from lives to fictional lives to the form of the early novel, a trajectory that underlies much critical thinking today. Biography's role in the development of that most familiar form of prose narrative is far more complex, uneven, and persistent than that: as I demonstrate, what we have misrecognized as the origin of the novel is actually, in Defoe's hands, a cultural and political history of biography. And so this book is doubly situated: the intellectual descendant both of Milton's tragic anticipation and of Defoe's shrewd historicization of the social, ideological, and cultural conditions that gave rise to the life's newfound prominence.

CHAPTER ONE

A YEAR IN THE LIFE

MILTON AND THE KING'S BOOK

IN THE OPENING paragraph of his prose tract *Eikonoklastes,* written to answer the *Eikon Basilike,* the posthumous prayers and meditations of Charles I and by far the year's best-selling book, Milton makes the following observation: "Kings most commonly, though strong in Legions, are but weak at Arguments; as they who ever have accustom'd from the Cradle to use thir will onely as thir right hand, thir reason always as thir left. Whence unexpectedly constrain'd to that kind of combat, they prove themselves but weak and puny Adversaries."[1] The habituated biases of kingship are laid before the reader in binary fashion: coercion is opposed to persuasion; warfare to diplomacy; the will of the practiced right hand to the reason of the inexpert left.[2] Ostensibly, Milton is lowering our expectations of the king's abilities, but he is lowering our expectations of his own performance, too, warning us that the fight is too lopsided, the odds too much in his favor, his opponent too unworthy for their contest to be meaningful. By phrasing his remark as a general proposition, he suggests that this imbalance holds true not just for this particular contest but for all such contests. Once the skill of arguing replaces the possession of armies, kings everywhere will have no choice but to fight on unequal — because equalized — terms with their erstwhile subjects.

Yet Charles, and the collaborative team of writers, editors, and stationers responsible for guiding his book into print, had not honored the new rules of combat as they were laid out by Milton. Despite Milton's setting up of the terms that Charles is constrained to follow as belonging to argument, the *Eikon Basilike* declines to offer a philosophical justification or proof of the necessity of monarchy, offering instead a collection of prayers interwoven with a passionate account of the burdens, disappointments, and trials that occasioned their utterance. No longer backed by armies nor equipped with arguments, the king enters the lists of public discussion with the story of his life, or at least of its last turbulent and ultimately tragic decade. Measured not in points scored but in the numbers of copies sold and seized and secreted away, his was a resounding victory. This chapter will draw out the stakes of this victory, the means by which it was accomplished, and its effects (or what Milton feared were to be its effects) upon the nation's public political culture.

1

The *Eikon Basilike* made its galvanic appearance within hours of the king's execution on January 30, 1649. Copies of the first octavo edition circulated privately in the days leading up to the beheading and began to be hawked on the street in its immediate aftermath. They became available in bookshops on or before February 9, the day of the king's funeral, when Milton's neighbor George Thomason purchased and dated his copy.[3] Published by the prominent royalist bookseller Richard Royston, whose name defiantly appears on the first privately circulated issue of the first edition, the book became an instant best seller and quickly went through two more editions, the type hastily reset as press runs sought to keep pace with the public's demand.[4] Recounting his efforts to purchase a copy in Cambridge at the end of February, Richard Holdsworth complained to his patron William Sancroft about the *Eikon*'s exorbitant asking price: "The King's bookes are so excessive deare, that I believe you would not have soe many of them at their prices. Morden sells the worse impressions for 5^s.... If they be Roystons they will be above six shillings. They are sold for 6-6 in London. The other sort are dully printed in dull paper. I shall get one of the best printed for you, if there be any come."[5] Holdsworth resolves to buy his patron a "Royston," not settling for one of the cheaper substitutes, which by late February had started to enter an inflated market. These included five editions of minute size, adopting the duodecimo format customary for inexpensive copies of the Psalter and the (now proscribed) Book of Common Prayer.[6] By the middle of March,

21 English editions of the *Eikon* had left the press; by the end of the year, 35 English editions would be printed, with multiple others appearing on the Continent, translated into Latin, French, Dutch, Danish, and German. Nicholas Ferrar, together with his nieces Mary and Virginia, bound over 200 copies with the intention of exporting them to Virginia.[7]

When the *Eikon* made its debut, it was a less encumbered volume than it would later become, consisting of 28 chapters prefaced only by a title page, a table of contents, and a double-page engraving showing the king on his knees at prayer. The volume's English subtitle, *The Povrtraicture of His Sacred Maiestie in His Solitudes and Sufferings,* turns on two senses of the preposition "in": the one expressing a condition of physical persecution and imprisonment, the other of mental isolation and duress. An equivalent distinction between outward circumstance and inward experience organizes the chapters, which are divided into two parts: a short autobiographical essay followed by a transcribed prayer. The essays recall the political crises of the preceding decade beginning with Charles's convening of the Long Parliament in November 1640 and progressing in loose chronological sequence to the Vote of No Addresses in January 1648, which publicly cut off all further negotiations between Parliament and the king. The prayers, which are marked off typographically by the change of type from roman to italic, string together quoted or half-revised verses from the book of Psalms, including the penitential psalms traditionally attributed to King David. By means of this twofold arrangement, each prayer is dramatized as the sometimes anguished, sometimes indignant response of the king to a critical moment from his public life, a self pressed into speech by the burdens and misadventures of political government.[8]

Turning the leaf from the table of contents, readers of the first privately circulated issue would have encountered an engraved portrait of the king, tipped in between the first and second quarto gathering. Designed by William Marshall — who five years previously had engraved the portrait frontispiece of Milton for his 1645 *Poems* — it shows Charles alone, kneeling in profile in the front plane of a partially enclosed building (fig. 2). A martyr's crown of thorns is held extended in his right hand; his left delicately touches his neck as though feeling where the stroke of the executioner's axe will fall. With the tip of his foot Charles pushes a bejeweled earthly crown away from his suppliant

Fig. 2. *Eikon Basilike* (1649), fold-out portrait of Charles I after first gathering. By permission of the Folger Shakespeare Library.

body, lifting his eyes to the radiant eternal crown seen through the window behind and above. Two diagonal beams of light, the one descending from the amassed storm clouds in the top left, the other ascending to the eternal crown framed in the window at top right, externalize the drama taking place inside Charles's head, which tilts back at an angle that continues the left diagonal to the tip of his stiletto beard. The beams cut across the binary division of the portrait into exterior and interior scenes: on the left, a purgatorial land-scape; on the right, a tapering room. The landscape's emblems stand in for the king — a palm tree unbowed by the weights attached to its branches, a rock steadfast against a heaving sea — but his back is turned, seemingly impervious to their objective representation of his subjective endurance. Speech scrolls write over this impassive scene of crowning, materializing the royal voice for the first time in the volume.[9]

The ingenuity of the *Eikon's* earliest editions — printed clandestinely, at speed, and for an audience the size and breadth of which surpassed all expec-tation — still appears remarkable, a feat of market forces and commercial opportunism, of mass fervor and immense personal risk. Yet in March or April, still only weeks after Charles's execution on January 30, they found themselves competing with a repackaged and expanded edition of the *Eikon* that claimed to release new and unseen documents from the final hours of the martyred king's life. Printed by William Dugard for the bookseller Francis Eglesfield, this latest edition contains the prayers Charles recited during his captivity, and which he carried with him to the scaffold, as well as a reported account of his affecting words of farewell to his two younger children, the thirteen-year old Princess Elizabeth and the eight-year old Prince Henry. Also included were the speech Charles had prepared, but which he was not permitted to deliver at his trial, to the High Court protesting its legality; a last letter from his son and heir, the future Charles II, written in exile from the Hague; and two further narrative "relations" of the family farewells promised by Princess Elizabeth to her condemned father during their final, tear-filled moments together. Dugard felt sufficiently emboldened to include his initials in the imprint to the edition's rubricized title page: "Printed by W. D. in R. M. Anno Dom. 1649" — the second set of initials, R. M., or "in Regis Memoriam," replacing, as Kathleen Lynch observes, the con-ventional place of publication with a vow of remembrance.[10] Commercially,

Dugard's additions triumphed: retroactively inserted into unsold copies of earlier editions and the majority of later ones, they quickly assumed canonical, although never uncontroversial, status in the contents of the "King's Book."[11] Politically, they provoked swift reaction: on March 16, the day after Dugard's latest edition began selling, the House of Commons ordered the sergeant-at-arms "to make Stay of, and seize at the Press, all those Books now printing or printed under the Name of the Book of the late King." James Cranford, the Presbyterian cleric and licensor of *His Majesties Prayers Which He Used in Time of His Sufferings,* was removed from office.[12] Dugard himself was taken into custody.[13]

Dugard's additions not only expanded the authorized text of the *Eikon,* they also focused its plot more tightly around the melodrama of Charles's death, incorporating the testimony of intimate bystanders, most notably the royal children. At the same time as he was playing up these family farewell scenes, Dugard was busy filling out the volume with verses: an explanatory epigram to go beneath the Marshall engraving, which had already been moved to face the title page; a panegyric; and a closing epitaph. In her important examination of the *Eikon*'s material history, Laura Lunger Knoppers assesses the impact that Dugard's and other subsequent additions may have had upon its early readership. She argues that by extending the volume's representation of the royal household, the additions could only have weakened its political effects, encouraging readers to engage its domestic scenes not as a spur to public agitation and activity but as a version of what would later come to be known as sentimental fiction.[14] Knoppers describes how readers, many of them female, transformed copies of the *Eikon* into household objects, recording their own life histories — births, baptisms, marriages, deaths, and burials — in the flyleaves and margins, and so moving the work out of the "sphere of rational debate and critique" entirely. One Restoration reader even inscribed Eve's swooning lines to Adam from Dryden's *State of Innocence* (1677), his operatic adaptation of *Paradise Lost:* "And when your eyes lookt languishing on mine / and wreathing arms did soft embraces joyne."[15] This annotation is, indeed, remarkable, recognizing an affiliation between the *Eikon* and the heroic drama that bypasses political debate — and the notorious poet Milton — altogether. Taking the *Eikon* into their homes, according it the status of a family Bible, forgetful of its polemic history, these early readers display an attachment remarkably free from the obligations of controversion or argument.

Knoppers is surely right to emphasize *Eikon*'s bold departure from the kinds of "representative publicity" that Jürgen Habermas identifies as the preserve of the ceremonial monarch or sovereign figure. She notes how this departure was coercively achieved before it was strategically embraced; how the Parliament's redacting and publishing of Charles's private letters to his wife, Henrietta Maria, in *The Kings Cabinet Opened* (1645) invented "a new language of royal domesticity" for the *Eikon,* appearing just four years later, to seize hold of and reappropriate.[16] For Knoppers, this language proves prescient of a literary future in which genres of intimacy such as the family melodrama and the sentimental or domestic novel assume control of an expanding middle-class marketplace. In the case of the *Eikon,* however, this literary future is glimpsed at the expense of a more immediate political one, as readers, deaf to the political registers of its domestic language, engaged with the text on a purely affective level, in the private "realm of imagining," not in the public realm of action.[17] Having found a place in the hearts and homes of so many, the *Eikon* could then be recommitted to the story of popular political support for the Stuart monarchy once its restoration had been accomplished, recrossing, and so blurring, the lines of sentimental and political allegiance.

There is much that is compelling about this thesis, and my own reading of the *Eikon* is indebted to it in numerous ways, not least for its recovery of how early readers inscribed and interacted with their copies of the text. I remain, however, less convinced than Knoppers that the *Eikon*'s depoliticization of the consciousness of its readers was an undesirable and inadvertent consequence of its domestic fiction-making rather than this fiction-making's calculated, and highly political, effect. That is, I want to consider the possibility that in divorcing the king's words from the burden of their immediate context, the *Eikon*'s earliest readers weren't misrecognizing the volume's political agenda but fulfilling it.

That the *Eikon* doesn't appear to have succeeded all that well in mobilizing the types of behavior we typically group under the category of the political — as, for example, public discussion, petition, protest, demonstration, organized resistance, riot, and the taking up of arms — should not surprise us since these are all portrayed negatively in its pages.[18] The chapter titled "Upon the Insolency of the Tumults" declaims, for example, that "nothing was more to be feared and less to be used by wise men, than those tumultuary confluxes of mean and rude people, who are taught first to petition, then to protect, then to dictate, at last to command and overawe the Parliament."[19] In the *gradatio* of this sentence, the people are shown learning their political lessons all too well as they progress from addressing and defending Parliament to claiming despotic powers over its proceedings, imperiling the foundations of responsible government. Famously, Milton would protest the king's borrowing of the Greek word "demagogue," from *agogos* (leader) and *demos* (people), to name the organizers of popular protest, pronouncing it "this Goblin word," an abuse of plain English, and proposing to replace it with "good Patriots," an appropriately nationalistic term of praise.[20] "Who were the chief Demagogues and Patrons of Tumults, to send for them, to flatter and embolden them, to direct and tune their clamorous importunities," asks the king conspiratorially (*Eikon,* 61). Used here for the first time in English in an unfavorable sense, "demagogue" captures the royal attitude toward this new and foreign, hurly-burly political culture. The public political sphere, as the *Eikon* represents it, is far from being an occasion for the expression of rational thought or the realization of liberal individuality. It is a field of confrontation, insecurity, turmoil, intimidation, and threat.

Importantly, the royal speaker is divided from the political sphere not solely by principle but by feeling—feeling more, feeling differently, and feeling before, for, and with his subjects. His is a survival story, as all martyr stories finally are, yet the stakes of survival are not so much ideological or doctrinal as they are emotional, calling upon the reader's sympathy and compassion. It matters, therefore, that the king is not a member of (indeed, is routinely baffled by) the political community represented in the *Eikon*'s narratively vague accounts of actual historical episodes. These accounts are generally plotted as critiques of bad people, of malicious intention or simply misguided impulse—the generic "some men" and its variant elaborations, "some men's distempers" (*Eikon,* 51); "some men's rigour or remissness" (52); "some men's Hydropic insatiableness" (70), and so on—but they are also organized more forcefully against the involvement of the English public, a public to which the *Eikon* directly appeals, asking its members to resist the process of their own politicization.

What, then, might the *Eikon* propose to offer in exchange for the kinds of popular political participation it seeks to denigrate and dissuade readers from pursuing? The radical promise of the *Eikon* is unprecedented access: access to the king's innermost thoughts, his sorrows and sufferings, petitions and confessions; also his extraordinary powers of perseverance, trying and trying again as each chapter fails, and succeeds, by repeating the pattern of the one before. Indebted both to the genre of the poetic complaint and to the dramatic soliloquy, the king's self-representation has been taken to reflect and so to intercept a broader epistemological shift toward what Katharine Eisaman Maus names the "unexpressed interior" — an intimate realm governed, on the one hand, by the passions, and, on the other, by conscience.[21] It is this privatized, as opposed to merely private, self that the *Eikon* claims to make public, and this chapter takes a closer look at how this self is editorially constructed. Yet the volume's equally important and less reported task is to make the king's soliloquies not only persuasively personal but also persuasively general, voicing not just the kinds of things a king might say but the kinds of things anyone might say if they were to find themselves in his predicament.[22] Even as it reveals the innermost workings of the royal mind, the *Eikon* commits itself to the idea that the most personal language is a language that is held in common, widely shared and deeply known.

The common language that the *Eikon* speaks comes from the book of Psalms. As Barbara Lewalski and Ramie Targoff valuably demonstrate, the Psalms furnished English Protestants, as they had so many Jewish and Christian communities before them, not only with the liturgical forms of thanksgiving, praise, petition, and contrition, the public recitation of which supplied the rhythms of the church service and the church year, but with a mapping of their own emotional lives especially in their most intensely charged moments of joy, gratitude, preservation, affliction, desperation, and loss.[23] In her study of how public prayer shaped habits of private devotion, Targoff quotes the fourth century theologian Athanasius and the Jacobean Puritan divine Richard Bernard, both of whom articulate the power of the Psalms to confer self-recognition upon those who encounter them: "Whosoever take this book in his hande, he reputeth & thinketh all the wordes he readeth ... to be as his very owne wordes," writes Athanasius, while Bernard pronounces, "there is no condition of any in prosperity or adversity, peace or warres, health or sickness, inward or outward distresse, with many particular causes in all these kinds, but he shall find some Psalmes, which he may thinke almost to have beene composed upon his owne occasion."[24] In her wide-ranging account of how the book of Psalms was received, imitated, and adapted as a compendium of lyric forms across the seventeenth century, Lewalski cites John Calvin's starker summation of what the Psalms know on our collective behalf: "all the trubblesome motions wherewith mennes mindes are woont to be turmoyled."[25] Following Saint Augustine, Calvin attributes ultimate authorship of the Psalms to the Holy Spirit, but there remained strong interest among Protestant exegetes and commentators in David as their human — and kingly — composer, and in the circumstances of David's biography as providing them with a definite history, the particular occasions that prompted his recourse to prayer and song.

We can see, therefore, how the Psalms already fulfilled the double commitment that the *Eikon* was anxious to honor, serving both as a record of singular experience and as a shared lexicon for the expression of idiosyncratic feeling. While critics have enjoyed some success in analyzing the *Eikon*'s borrowings from individual psalms — and especially from Psalm 51 (*Miserere mei Deus*), the most important of the seven penitential psalms whose verses the king pronounces after confessing his guilt in the execution of the Earl of Stafford — it is not, primarily, in the citation and workings of specific scriptural allusions, so I will argue, but in its broader enactment of psalmic forms of expression that the volume is able to mount a compelling defense of kingship.[26] For if in post-Reformation England the book of Psalms was valued not thematically but functionally, for the effect it had on the faithful who were able to find themselves in its verses and so come into their own powers of personal expression, then the *Eikon* aligns itself and its royal speaker with this experience of individualism, an individualism embedded not in the achievement of rights and freedoms through the kinds of privatized political activity — petition, discussion, and protest — that we see the *Eikon* denouncing, but in the structures of common feeling that unite a people, a church, and a nation. It is true that *Eikon* never comes close to a logical articulation of the opposition it constructs between these two models of individualism. But despite its fuzzy presentation, it does manage implicitly to convey a sense of distinction between a collective individualism and a political one — the former dramatized implicitly through the raw and naked language of the Psalms and the other attacked explicitly through the recounting of its devastating and misguided effects upon the course of national events. Through its adept location of the origin and force of psalmic expression in the biblical line of kings that starts with David and extends to Charles, the *Eikon* is able to align this wisdom-seeking self with the monarch's voice. On this account, individualism affirms and is affirmed by sacral kingship.

2

That the persuasive burden of the *Eikon* will have little to do with its appreciable contents — the reasons and beliefs it gives for the king having acted in a particular way at a particular time — is (dismayingly) clear from its first sentence:

> This last Parliament I called, not more by others' advice, and necessity of My affairs, than by My own choice and inclination; who have always thought the right way of Parliaments most safe for My Crown, and best pleasing to My People: And although I was not forgetful of those sparks, which some men's distempers formerly studied to kindle in Parliaments, (which by forbearing to convene for some years, I hoped to have extinguished) yet resolving with My self to give all just satisfaction to modest and sober desires, and to redress all public grievances in Church and State; I hoped by My (freedom and their moderation) to prevent all misunderstandings, and miscarriages in this: In which as I feared affairs would meet with some passion and prejudice in other men, so I resolved they should find least of them in My self; not doubting, but by the weight of Reason, I should counterpoise the overbalancings of any factions. (*Eikon*, 51)

Descriptive accounts of the king's prose have noted its fondness for doubling a word with an alliterative synonym ("misunderstandings and miscarriages"; "passion and prejudice"), for paralleling phrases ("not more by others' advice, and necessity of My affairs, than by My own choice and inclination"; "most safe for My Crown and best pleasing to My People"), and for deploying natural metaphors ("those sparks, which some men's distempers formerly studied to kindle in Parliaments"). As Steven Zwicker observes, such scrupulous artistry "allows prose to make the man," conveying a cast of mind that is confirmed, settled, and measured, correcting the imbalances it encounters out in the world.[27] As the pages unfold, so the sentences pile up in elegant variation, but they give few concrete details. As a reader, it is hard to keep them distinct from one another. Exasperated, Milton would declare the text lacking in "any moment of solidity" (*Eikonoklastes,* YP 3:339), and it is true that the *Eikon* never descends to names or facts, holding to the higher ground of gauzy abstractions and vaguely pleasing prose.

Less immediately clear is that every chapter of the *Eikon* will move in the same direction, from narrative to prayer. In the narratives themselves, this movement is anticipated by the invocations and asides that punctuate the king's retelling of historical events: "God knows" (63, 66–67, 77–78, 81–82, 85–86, and so on); "which God knows" (58); "and that very unwillingly God knows" (56); "I thank God I know" (67). Reiterating these phrases or variants upon them, the king is, by turns, emphatic and reactive as he struggles to mark off knowledge that is absolute, beyond the reach of rhetorical posturing or maneuver. When functioning as asides, such phrases are often enclosed in parentheses, another distinguishing feature of the *Eikon*'s deliberately indeliberate prose. The standard early modern use of parentheses is to bracket subordinate or relative clauses, as in the first paragraph of the *Eikon* quoted above. But the royal speaker uses them in other ways, too: to self-report — "(as I think)" (66); "(I say)" (134); "(I hope)" (56, 161, 173, 185, 196); "(as I hold this to be)" (131); "(for so it was to Me)" (55) — or to close off injury and allegation — "(which some have highly calumniated against me)" (105); "(whatever my Enemies please to say, or think)" (106); "(as some have suspected, and uncharitably avowed)" (71). Sometimes two different usages combine and one set of parentheses nests within another: "(as they confidently but (God knows) falsely divulge)" (67).[28] One way to interpret the use of parentheses is to think of them as places where the king — as a dramatic character — gives himself away, where emotion and outrage pool and he tries too hard or wants to be heard too badly. Another way would be to consider them as signs not of distress but of anxious affectation, roughing up sentences that might appear to flow too smoothly were their progress not worried from within. Read in light of the overall movement of the chapters, however, the parentheses come repeatedly to mark a point of impasse or epistemological limit where a gulf opens up between what the king knows and what he is convinced of convincing us to know. Two arms thrown up, whether in consternation or surrender, the parentheses become a kind of dramatic signposting, pointing the reader in the direction of the prayer to come. In the narrative portion of the chapter, the divine is parenthetical to the earthly, but this relation exists to be reversed in the chapter's second half when the speaker gives himself over entirely to God.

By their form and grammar, therefore, as much as by their contents, the chapters instruct us in how they are to be read, not necessarily in sequence and with an understanding that the narrative parts are preliminary, and so in a way provisional, creating the need for the prayers to follow. Additionally, there is a third, nonauthorial element to each chapter: the italicized headnotes that announce its occasion, referring to the royal speaker in the public third person — "the King," "the KING," "his Majestie," "his MAJESTIE" — so as to mark their distance from and deference to his personal voice. Contentwise, the headnotes are redundant, repeating the same information that the chapters establish at their outset. Chapter 1, for example, carries the headnote *"Upon His Majesty's calling this last Parliament"* and begins, *"This last Parliament I called"* (51), while chapter 8, "Upon the Queen's departure, and absence out of England," opens with "Although I have much cause to be troubled at My Wife's departure from Me, and out of My Dominions" (73). Kathleen Lynch observes that their third-person references "strike such a jarring note" because they are so evidently gratuitous, violating the decorum of a volume that appeared, in its original incarnation, with "no dedications, no prefatory letters by booksellers or pastors, no marginal scriptural notations — no overt fussing with proof, methodology, or authentication."[29] Yet it is precisely by taking exception to this rule, performing so obtrusively and indecorously the kind of extrinsic labor that the volume elsewhere does not prioritize, that the headnotes offer themselves as visible evidence of an editorial practice postdating the king's own thoughts and prayers. As with the inherent theatricality of the portrait conceit of the volume's title, so the headings confirm that the king's words are being staged, but they transfer all knowledge of their staging from the royal speaker to his readership. In this way, I would argue, the volume's overt construction underwrites the fiction of the king's radically unconstructed prose.

Beyond their contribution to the volume's visual iconography and its editorial framing, the *Eikon*'s third-person headnotes assume, I believe, a still more important function of imitating the *tituli* or superscriptions placed before individual psalms in the Hebrew Bible. The biblical titles ascribe authorship and give directions for musical scoring and performance, but some also name the historical circumstances behind a psalm's composition. Of the psalms attributed to David (Pss. 3–41, 51–71, 86, 101, 103, 108–10, 138–45), 13 carry superscriptions that connect the psalmist's words to a critical moment or event in his life story (Pss. 3, 7, 18, 34, 51, 52, 54, 56, 57, 59, 60, 63, 142). Psalm 3, for example, carries the title, "A Psalm of David, when he fled from Absalom his son"; Psalm 34, "A Psalm of David, when he changed his behavior before Abimelech; who drove him away, and he departed"; Psalm 63, "A Psalm of David, when he was in the wilderness of Judah." Scholars agree that these biographical superscriptions were a later midrashic addition, introduced by Hebrew editors and retained in the Latin Vulgate where they are routinely Christianized, casting the character David as a type of Christ.[30] In the King James Bible, the titles are marked with a pilcrow (¶) and set distinctly apart, not being counted among the psalm's numbered verses.

In *The Whole Booke of Psalmes* (1562), the metrical Psalter commonly known as "Sternhold and Hopkins" and used widely in English churches, the Hebrew titles are not merely retained but amplified into paragraph-long prose arguments, placed before each psalm and marked sometimes with a pilcrow, sometimes with a manicule or pointing hand. As Beth Quitslund demonstrates, the arguments derive from, and often reproduce verbatim, those in the Geneva Bible, although John Hopkins makes his own editorial emendations to the arguments of psalms he translated.[31] The argument that prefaces Psalm 3, for example, comes directly from the Geneva Bible and is typical in its two-part structure, leading with the psalm's narrative context before unfolding its dramatic arc from fear and threat to rescue and relief: "David being persecuted, & driven out of his kingdome by his owne sonne Absalom: was greatly tormented in minde for hys sinne against God: and therefore calleth upon God, and waxeth bolde through hys promises, against the great terrors of his enemies: yea, and againste deathe it selfe, whyche he saw present before hys eyes. Finally he rejoyseth for the good successe and victory, that God gave hym and all the Churche over hys enemies."[32] Through the conjunctive adverb "therefore," the argument emphasizes the causal relations among David's personal experience, his internal state of contrition, and the content of his devotional song.

This exegetical tradition of interpreting the Psalms as the personal prayers of David, keying particular psalms to historical episodes related in the book of Samuel so that song and situation gloss and explain each other, was imaginatively and intensively rethought by Thomas Wyatt in his lyric sequence, *Certayne psalmes chosen out of the psalter of David,* printed in 1549. Modeling his sequence after poetic paraphrases of the seven penitential psalms by Dante and Petrarch and borrowing closely from a 1534 prose paraphrase by Pietro Aretino, *I Sette salmi de la penitentia di David,* Wyatt not only offers his own versions of the Psalms but sets them within a narrative framework, interpolating poems that supply dramatic scenarios for their lyric expression. The sequence narrates the events of 2 Samuel 11–12 — David's adultery with Bathsheba, his arrangements for the murder of her husband, Uriah, and his denunciation by the prophet Nathan — which lead him to cast aside "his crown of gold / His purpirll pall" (46–47) and withdraw "into a dark Cave" (60), harp in hand.[33] David composes all seven psalms (Pss. 6, 32, 38, 51, 102, 130, 143) during his sojourn in the cave, returning to the world to restore peace to Israel and confront the rebellion of Absalom, his favored son.

Given the speech prefix of "The Auctor" in the 1549 printed edition, Wyatt's narrative poems are clearly marked off from the Psalms they introduce, not least by their being written in stanzaic ottava rima rather than in the terza rima reserved for David. Their narrator frequently shows himself to the reader, placing a particular construction on David's words, indulging his fondness for similes, or interjecting an "I say," sometimes testily, for rhetorical emphasis. At moments, he approaches the talkative and opinionated narrator of a more playful poem like Marlowe's *Hero and Leander,* although the limits of his omniscience are generally staged for stronger and more serious effect.[34] Here, for example, are his lines introducing and commenting upon David's voicing of Psalm 51, coming at the end of the fourth prologue, and the beginning of the fifth, respectively:

> Stertyng like hym whom sodeyne fere dismays,
> His voyce he strains, and from his hert owt brynges
> This song that I not wyther he crys or singes. (424–26)

> Off diepe secretes that David here did sing,
> Off mercy, off fayth, off frailte, off grace,
> Off goddes goodnes and off Justyfying,
> The grettnes dyd so astonne hymselff a space,

As who myght say who hath exprest this thing?
I synner, I, what have I sayd, alas?
That goddes goodnes wold within my song entrete,
Let me agayne considre and repete.

And so he doth, but not exprest by word:
But in his hert he tornith and paysith
Ech word.   (509–19)

Introducing the psalm, the narrator admits that the abruptness and extremity of David's outburst have left him at a loss, incapable of supplying reliable stage directions as to the manner of its vocal expression. His response afterward opens with a list of genitive nouns, the "deep" contents of the psalm that David has sung straight out, taking himself so much by surprise that he is struck to stone. Here the narrator pulls away from the striken psalmist; the reported speech of the next four lines is not in David's voice but in that of an imagined proxy, "As who myght say who hath exprest this thing." The answer ("I synner, I") and question ("what have I sayd, alas?") that follow in such quick and emphatic succession are similarly suspended between identification and alienation, self-assertion and self-betrayal, their speaker expressing immediate dismay at his unwilled and therefore unworthy speaking in the first person of what God has chosen to speak through him. Only by repeating the words of the psalm under his own volition is David able to recover himself, a rite of recitation as opposed to an act of creative authorship. "And so he doth" — the four, confirming words that come after the stanza break return us to the solid iambic ground of external narration. That they are immediately followed by a double adversative, plunging us back into the inner world of the royal speaker, is part of what makes Wyatt's sequence so exhausting and exhilarating a reading experience.

There is nothing as bold as this in the *Eikon Basilike,* but Wyatt's orchestration of the penitential psalms is helpful, nonetheless, for understanding what the royalist team that assembled the volume may have had in mind. Earlier, I suggested that the *Eikon*'s third-person chapter headings operate in a manner analogous to the titles or superscriptions found in nearly all versions of the book of Psalms, repurposing not simply the actual verses of the Psalms, but the practice of nominating the biographical occasion for which each prayer was composed. Now we are in a position to see how the two-part structure of the *Eikon*'s chapters, a narrative prologue that introduces and sets a psalm prayer in context, is designed to recreate the conditions under which the Psalms were traditionally spoken, sung, studied, and read. Like the prose arguments of the Geneva Bible and the Sternhold and Hopkins Psalter, and even more like the diffuse poetic prologues of Wyatt's psalm sequence, the *Eikon* contextualizes its prayers at considerable length, expanding the titles or chapter headings into elaborate disquisitions upon recent historical affairs. Its distinction is to have placed these contextualizations not in the third-person voice of the biblical editor or poetic narrator, however, but in the first-person voice of the royal singer so that Charles, unlike David, represents his own understanding of the occasion that provokes his recourse to song.

Comparisons of Charles to "the sweet psalmist of Israel" were an established feature of royalist propaganda of the later 1640s (2 Sam. 23:1). Henry Lawes dedicates his musical settings, *Choice Psalmes* (1648), to the imprisoned king, noting regretfully how "much of Your Majesties present condition, is lively described by King *David's* pen." Drawn by William Marshall, the frontispiece to the 1647 and 1650 reprintings of Robert Ashley's translation of Virgilio Malvezzi's *Il Davide perseguitato* goes further, transposing Charles's face onto an image of David, sitting enthroned in the foreground and poised to sing.[35] In one sense, then, the *Eikon Basilike* was doing nothing new by representing the king as a psalmist, his suffering consecrated by words that originate with a king and belong to the sacred institution of kingship. But the *Eikon* was doing nothing new in a more novel way too, or so I have tried to suggest. For what the king is represented as doing is what every congregant is implicitly invited to do when reading or reciting or hearing the Psalms: to encounter the expression of deep personal feeling, and to experience that expression as though the feelings that shaped it were one's own. The autobiographical narratives that occasion the king's prayers, motivating and shaping them in the same way that David's historical situation was imagined to have motivated and shaped the Psalms themselves, are doing something in common with their readers, enacting the conditions under which a shared language is agreed to be personal and so available to everyone. This is an old way of holding the world together, achieved by consensus (which in a different political register would be called obedience) and attachment and deep familiarity. By making this language accessible to a wide reading public, at once proposing it as an alternative to the tumult of public discussion and reinscribing it within the bounds of sacral kingship, the *Eikon* endows it with its own seemingly apolitical, and so actively political, force.

3

If readers were lucky enough to find a copy of the *Eikon Basilike* left in the bookstalls, they may well have found a tract by Milton right alongside it, *The Tenure of Kings and Magistrates* which went on sale on or before February 13, during the first wave of the *Eikon*'s popular success. A defense of the people's natural and arbitrary right to depose a sitting monarch or governing magistrate, the treatise is known among scholars of Milton for being the first of the poet's writings to lack the flights of heroic self-representation that had distinguished the prose of his early polemical career.[36] The sentences of the *Tenure* are stripped down, unadorned, detached from personal revelations or promises of greater things to come.[37] Yet at the very moment when Milton had pledged himself to sobriety and the sufficiency of argument, the royalists were pulling off their greatest stunt against it, promoting a personal history that sought to diffuse the philosophical claims being leveled against kingship. At this most divisive moment of the century, a political opposition had calcified into a literary one. The ideological standoff between Parliament and monarchy was now embedded within a formal distinction between arguing an impersonal claim and telling a personal story.

It would be in another tract, published late in 1649 and appearing as the commissioned response of the commonwealth government to the *Eikon Basilike*, that Milton would assemble and array his arguments against a text so conspicuously and strategically lacking in them. In that tract, titled *Eikonoklastes* after "the famous Surname of many Greek Emperors, who in thir zeal to the command of God, after long tradition of Idolatry in the Church, took courage, and broke all superstitious Images to peeces," Milton sought publicly to deny the *Eikon* its exemption from argument (YP 3:343). His approach is analytical in the strict etymological sense, taking apart the *Eikon*'s sentences so that they lose their fluency and lightness of impression. As scholars have described Milton's manner of attack, adopting, as Daniel Shore points out, his own language of iconoclastic zeal, so they have also described how the tract's unsparing scrutiny becomes its own excruciating exercise, a cautionary tale of how depressing close reading can be.[38] "It were an endless work to walk side by side with the Verbosity of this Chapter," complains Milton at one point, pantomiming his weariness (YP 3:433). As with the metaphor of single combat with which the chapter began, so this metaphor of the foot journey represents the egalitarian relation of the former subject to his sovereign under the newly instituted commonwealth. Their relation is construed laterally as opposed to hierarchically, "side by side." No sooner are Milton and Charles placed in equal relation, however, than Milton is forced to labor under the burden of his evident superiority. In this new and uncomfortably close relationship, it is he who is obliged to check his pace.

The metaphor is meant as a quip, a jab at the *Eikon*'s expense. How dreary, Milton seems to be sighing, it is to plod alongside this slowest of kings. To the disheartened reader, already eight chapters and over a hundred pages into the tract, the question of who is delaying whom can only seem to be spectacularly the wrong one to be posing. Ill-timed, the quip is also more telling than it intends. For one thing, to refute or animadvert (a contraction of *animum advertere,* to turn one's mind toward, to refer) is not to walk "side by side" but to follow after, to be subservient to the direction taken by a prior text. For another, Milton's complaint, by comically insisting upon the wide difference in ability between the struggling king and himself, mischaracterizes the nature of the challenge posed by their mismatched texts. Within the logic of the metaphor, this challenge is not a difference of style or literary genre, merely a difference of argumentative skill.

In fact, Milton does moot the possibility of answering Charles in the genre that Charles offers in the *Eikon,* although only for the slenderest of moments, in a dependent clause that takes up the first half of the first sentence of his long, long tract: "To descant on the misfortunes of a person fall'n from so high a dignity, who hath also payd his final debt both to Nature and his Faults, is neither of it self a thing commendable, nor the intention of this discours" (YP 3:337). Opening with a commission and ending with its refusal, the sentence rounds upon the idea of mourning the royal death as a tragic event. It pronounces stiffly, grandly, but also impersonally. There is no identifiable speaker, for Milton has yet to step forward, and no identifiable figure to mourn. The indefinite article — "a person fall'n" — indicates that the death could be of any disgraced dignitary who meets the requisite criteria. Denying the regicide its claim to exceptional status, Milton sententiously assigns Charles's death to the fixed scheme of *de casibus* ("fall of princes") storytelling, a lowbrow plot awaiting its next highborn victim. By refusing to furnish Charles with another such narrative, he establishes his own argumentative practice in relation to what it excludes: the cheap arts of the tragic biography. From this moment forward, Milton forces the *Eikon*'s prose to present itself as though it were written in his genre, a genre of critical analysis.

The distinction between an argumentative and a biographical engagement with the *Eikon*'s materials is at once declared and richly overdetermined by Milton's choice of verbal infinitive, "to descant." Derived from the Middle English verb "descanten" (from the Latin; prefix *dis-,* asunder or apart, and *cantus,* song) the common meaning of "descant" is straightforwardly given by the Elizabethan composer and organist Thomas Morley as "singing a part extempore upon a playnesong," plainsong being the music to which the prayerbook liturgy was sung.[39] However intricate their workings, such variations were typically improvised on the spot — impromptu exercises in vocal mastery and skill. Nicholas Temperley explains how this technique of singing one tune over another was adapted to the practice of psalm singing in parish churches following the Elizabethan religious settlement. In this congregational setting, psalms were typically sung before and after the sermon and to one of a handful of common tunes. The tunes were often slowed down to accommodate the weakest singers, with the parish clerk or more musical members of the parish improvising descants, note for note, above them. In some instances, Temperley notes, the descants — which, for simplicity's sake, tended to diverge from the main tune only in places — ended up being sung by the congregants themselves, supplanting the original tune entirely.[40] This rougher form of choral music was far different from the four-, five-, sometimes six-part settings of metrical psalms more frequently used by cathedral or college choirs and in private households, including Milton's childhood home in Bread Street, London. A gifted musician and amateur composer, Milton's father contributed four-part settings for six of the psalms in Thomas Ravenscroft's collection, *The Whole booke of psalmes* (1621).[41] Milton himself, according to his early biographers, "had a delicate, tuneable Voice" and "an excellent Ear, and could bear a part both in Vocal & Instrumental Music."[42]

Taking the inaugural infinitive "to descant" in this choral sense, Milton is declaring his refusal to harmonize with, or sing a tune over, the *Eikon Basilike*'s fraudulent liturgy. In the context of the congregational psalm singing that Temperley describes, the verb may already identify the *Eikon* more narrowly as a book of psalms. The generic identification is made explicit a few pages later when Milton refers to the prayers directly, as a "privat Psalter," and, more disparagingly, "a kind of Psalmistry" (YP 3:360). In this last expression, the king's individual voice is canceled out by the Latin suffix "-ry," referring to a characteristic or collective type and thus denigrating his personal compositions to an instance of prelatical groupthink, a kind of a kind of song. That Milton declines to improvise a supporting descant, moving note for note against the royal melody, is hardly surprising, although the musical practice approximates (perhaps too well) the actual procedures of his textual criticism. His refusal is sharpened, I would argue, by his already public association with another royalist Psalter that doubled as a martyrology, the *Choice Psalmes put into Musick, for Three Voices* (1648), published by Humphrey Moseley and assembled by Henry Lawes. Lawes dedicates the *Choice Psalmes,* we remember, to the imprisoned Charles. The volume ends with a group of musical settings by Lawes's younger brother and fellow composer, William, who had died three years earlier at the siege of Chester. These final settings are introduced by a stately procession of elegies, each written by a different musician who mourns his fallen companion.[43] The elegies intrude midway through the volume, dividing the living from the dead. Their intrusion is anticipated by a sequence of four commendatory poems placed at the head of the volume, including a friendship sonnet addressed affectionately to Lawes by Milton.

Milton's sonnet was written several years before the publication of *Choice Psalmes* — in the volume it is flanked by poems that address more squarely the work's tragic fraternal occasion.[44] But we know that in the spring of 1648, Milton had taken up his own practice of metrical psalm composition, painstakingly translating psalms 80–88 from the Hebrew into English verse. Milton's sequence remained unpublished until the 1673 edition of the *Poems,* one year before his death. It appears there with an explanatory headnote, "*Nine of the Psalms done into Metre, wherein all but what is in a different Character, are the very words of the Text, translated from the Original.*"[45]

Scrupulously marking in italic type any words and phrases of his own embellishment, Milton raises exactness and technical rigor above vague and splashy effects. Avoiding even the suspicion of self-expression or autobiographical indulgence, his private labor of psalm composition was undertaken around the time that Charles with his royalist team of writers and editors was composing the *Eikon*'s prayers. There is personal affront as well as artistic disdain in Milton's public resistance to supplying a "descant" for the king's psalms, to assuming the role of a congregant whose crude and uninspired harmonization participates in the Anglican prayerbook service, a prescriptive rotor of prayer.

Outside of this liturgical context, two critics have already begun a fruitful debate about the secular senses that accrue to the word "descant" and what these might tell us about how Milton conceived of his polemical task. In his important study of the imbrications of aesthetic and political authority, Steven Zwicker casts Milton's "work assign'd" as a descent from heaven, arguing that the poet felt compelled by the false artistry of the *Eikon Basilike* to disown his own higher poetic gifts and sojourn in a Stygian world of prose (YP 3:339). Zwicker permits speculation as to the psychological trauma of this act of disownment and, following the theological logic of the atonement, celebrates its extraordinary compensation: the "deepest work of the imagination" that Milton was able to embrace later when he composed *Paradise Lost* (1667). On this account, Milton's use of the verb "descant" is valedictory, a reluctant yet dutiful departure from the embrace of lyric song.[46] In response, Nicholas McDowell counters that Milton, far from renouncing his allegiance to literature, exploits the resources of a national literary tradition in *Eikonoklastes,* reframing Shakespeare's plays as political case studies in the workings of idolatry and tyranny. On his account, *Eikonoklastes* does not simply take up and turn about a tradition of humanist advice literature, offering itself as a handbook not for the prince but for the people, and with exemplars drawn from the most celebrated of English playwrights; additionally, it seeks to restore theater to the originary role it had enjoyed in the Athenian *polis,* making it central to the political well-being of the republican nation. To clinch his reading, McDowell calls attention to the Shakespearean echo activated by the verb "descant," which recalls the opening scene of *Richard III* when a soliloquizing Richard claims a license to "descant on mine own deformity."[47] Why would Milton have invested all the power and undiminished possibility of his exiled art in a verb that summons to memory the most infamous tyrant ever to tread the English stage?[48]

Rather than adjudicating between these two positions, I want to add my own voice to them by proposing some further examples of early modern usage of the term "descant" and its cognates. I am interested, in particular, in tracing what will turn about to be the word's double migration: from song to speech, and from the realm of uncensored feeling to the public culture of argument. Thomas Blount's mid-seventeenth century dictionary *Glossographia* (1656) supplies evidence for the first of these movements, describing how the verb came to figure the free play of spoken language: "*Descant (discanto),* to run division, or variety with the voyce, upon a musical ground, in true measure;…Transferred by metaphor to paraphrasing ingenuously upon any affective subject."[49] Blount's definition is precise: the speaker's equivalent to the singer's "musical ground" is a subject that is "affective," belonging to the world of feelings and emotions and amorous desires. Thus, Shakespeare's Richard exempts himself from the sex games of the Yorkist court — the capering and strutting, courting and pleasing — only to exempt himself from that exemption, making love to his own body by "descanting" upon its ugliest features as a Petrarchan poet would run variations upon his lady's face (1.1.10–31).

The affective domain of the spoken "descant" is key to understanding how the word manifests itself in political discussion during the seventeenth century. In this context, the verb names a manner of speaking that is agitated, impassioned, inopportune, undaunted, needlessly effusive, seemingly pointless, politically illiterate, or, more simply, free. A term of abuse, its practitioners are portrayed as possessing a weak-minded understanding of the political, allowing strong and instinctual feelings — panic, zeal, pity, anger, envy, grief, love — to disrupt the philosophical or rational process of argument. Addressing the House of Lords in 1628, the parliamentary member (and future regicide) Henry Marten spoke against the passage of an amendment to the Petition of Right, fearing that it would provoke unrestricted discussion: "For the Petition being a Thing that concerneth every Man so nearly, it will run through every Man's Hands, and every Man will be reading of it. In perusing whereof, when they shall fall upon this additional Clause of the King's Sovereign Power, presently they will run descant upon these Words, What Sovereign Power is? what is the Nature of it? what the Extent? where the Bounds and Limits? whence the Original? what is the Use?"[50] Delivered rapidly, presumably at the speed with which the Petition will "run through every Man's Hands," Marten's stream of questions threatens not so much a re-signification as an unstoppable oversignification of the rendered words, "sovereign power." Milton's own pronouncement, added to the 1644 edition of his *Doctrine and Discipline of Divorce,* that the endeavoring man of "a discount'nanc't truth" must expect to "be boorded presently by the ruder sort, but not by discreet and well nurtur'd men, with a thousand idle descants and surmises," likewise uses "descant" (here as a noun) to characterize disruptive, multitudinous, and unsubstantiated speech (YP 2:224).[51]

A final example of usage from later in the century, and across the Atlantic, clarifies these derogatory connotations. It comes from an anonymous pamphlet discussing the 1689 uprising against the colonial government of Edmund Andros in the Massachussetts Bay Colony. The pamphlet opens with an expression of regret: "It is the Unhappiness of this present Juncture, that too many Men relinquish their Stations of *Privacy* and *Subjection,* and take upon them too freely to descant upon affairs of the *Publick.*" Michael Warner cites this passage as evidence that "expressly political publications" remained exceptional events in the colonies before 1720.[52] Of interest here, however, is the pampleteer's adoption of the verb "to descant" to cast opprobrium upon the preponderance of self-forwarding discussion he reports. The verbal descant is harmful not just for what it is (a vulgarly affective manner of speaking imbued with feeling and passions that escapes the channels of rational self-control), but also for where it is being used — in the public realm where it does not, and should not, be allowed to belong.

These examples of usage are instructive because they show that, with *Eikonoklastes,* Milton is thinking beyond the immediate political occasion, positioning the *Eikon Basilike* as simply one instance, or symptom, of the opening of public discourse and of the popular polemical consciousness to affectively driven modes of personal expression. Milton makes the act of elaborate and passionate public speaking, assuming the mode of the verbal or choral descant, his object of contention in the opening sentence of the tract. At the same time that he is working to name or characterize the category of public speech that Charles is using, he is also working to derogate its status, representing it not as emergent but as timeworn and outdated, as obsolete as the monarchy itself. To gain a fuller understanding of these two tasks — of nomination and of derogation — it will be helpful to step back to the medieval genre of biographical storytelling with which Milton associates the *Eikon,* the narrative of the "misfortunes of a person fall'n from so high a dignity," the fall of princes or *de casibus* tale.

4

The English *de casibus* tale descends from Boccaccio, whose collection *De casibus virorum illustrium* (written between 1356 and 1360 and issued in a revised version in 1373) was translated and reworked by John Lydgate, via Laurent de Premierfait's French translation, *Des cas des nobles* (1409), into the vernacular *Fall of Princes* (c. 1432–38). Before Lydgate, the most famous fan of *de casibus* fiction is Chaucer's Monk, who launches into a sequence of such tales, of which he claims to have 100 at the ready in his cell. The Monk is only permitted to finish 17 tales, however, before the Knight interrupts him, discomforted by the genre's tragic insistence, "for litel hevynesse / Is right ynough to muche folk, I gesse." The Knight's intervention carries a suspicion of class interest, conjecturing a general intolerance for a narrative form that brings down its noble subjects with such metronomic zeal. His objection is immediately seconded by the Host, who claims to speak for "al this com- paignye" in adjudging the tales to be not unremittingly tragic but tediously soporific: if it weren't for the "clynkyng" of the bells hanging from the bridle of the Monk's horse, he "sholde er this han fallen doun for sleep," toppling into the mud in a stupor.[53] Ignoring the edifying lesson of the Monk's *de casibus* fiction-making, the Host threatens a literal reenactment of its tragic pattern: no more falls, or he'll end up falling too. Who gets the last laugh, however, is uncertain. For like the Knight — although not, importantly, like Chaucer himself, who interpolates scenes of *de casibus* storytelling into several of the other tales — the Host badly misjudges the appeal of a genre equipped with a ready supply of famous, forever-falling victims. Paul Strohm notes that "The Monk's Tale" was one of the most frequently anthologized of the *Canterbury Tales* in the fifteenth century, anticipating the popularity of *de casibus* stories with an emerging print readership in the century to follow.[54]

The history of the printed *de casibus* collection properly begins with Richard Pynson's illustrated folio edition of Lydgate's *Fall of Princes* in 1494, reissued in 1527. But it was during the 1550s, a decade in which the English crown changed hands no fewer than four times, that the *de casibus* collection truly imposed itself upon the popular imagination. New editions of Lydgate, funded by the printer Richard Tottel and by his competitor John Wayland, appeared in 1554. They were joined at the end of the decade by the first edition of *A Mirror for Magistrates,* a *de casibus* collection edited by the enterprising printer-writer William Baldwin.[55] The 1559 *Mirror* consists of 19 first-person narratives connected by prose links in which the assembled "cumpany" debates their edifying lessons and decides who should next take a turn. Baldwin explains the rules in his preface to the reader, describing how his cowriters "al agreed that I shoulde vsurpe Bochas rowme, and the wretched princes complayne vnto me: and tooke vpon themselves euery man for his parte to be sundrye personages, and in theyr behalfes to bewayle vnto me theyr greuous chaunces, heuy destinies, & wofull misfortunes." In this way, Baldwin becomes the designated addressee of a series of theatrical impersonations, each originated by one of the assembled writers. He is an audience of last resort, both because his more illustrious predecessors, Boccaccio and Lydgate, are no longer available and, more fundamentally, because the undeserving dead (of whom, Baldwin reports with mock-patriotic reproach, there were so many "of our nacion" that he can't think why Boccaccio had neglected to include them) are so distressfully in need of someone to whom they "might make their mone."[56] Initially the national tale-telling game of *A Mirror* worked squarely, if never unplayfully, in the tradition of political advice literature, although critics remain divided over just how radical were its intentions.[57] Over the next half-century the collection would appear in various new iterations and expansions and under four different editors, a reliable best seller whose popular appeal came to reside less in its purported political wisdom than its remarkable body of stories and their truths, high and low, about the hapless, culpable business of living.[58] They are ghost stories narrated by a fallen elite who return from the postpurgatorial dead ghastly and bloodied over — "full of woundes, miserably mangled, with a pale countenaunce, and grisly looke" — to report their case aright.[59] As Meredith Anne Skura persuasively argues, *A Mirror* constituted one of the most readily available, recognizable, and imitable collections of autobiographical — or pseudo-autobiographical — life stories assembled during the early modern period in England.[60] And its influence was only further extended by the ready migration of its narratives of princely falls and follies to the mass entertainment of the public stage. In the final act of *Richard II* (1595), Shakespeare, perhaps with a knowing nod to Baldwin, who had made Richard's reign the historical starting point for his English *de casibus* tradition, shows the deposed king scripting himself to his grieving wife as the subject of just such a *de casibus* tale.[61]

The cultural ubiquity of the *Mirror*'s brand of tragic biography must have made it seem all but inevitable that Charles would be scripted this way to his posthumous admirers. In fact, the royalist team at work on the *Eikon* did put out an exploratory pamphlet testing the dramatic techniques of the *Mirror* by voicing the then-living Charles in the manner of one of its distraught and desperate ghosts. Titled *The Religious & Loyal Protestation,* written by John Gauden, the ghostwriter of the *Eikon Basilike,* licensed by James Cranford, and produced in Richard Royston's printing house, the pamphlet went on sale on January 10, 1649, the day after the sergeant at arms, Edward Dendy, rode into the Great Hall at Westminster and formally announced that the king was to be put on trial. It purports to make public a private letter Gauden had sent five days earlier to the leaders of the New Model Army, appealing to them to intervene and stop the trial from going ahead. But the real drama happens in an additional letter that Gauden addresses directly to his readers and that breaks off midway through, interrupted by an unexpected visitor:

> *Me thinks I heare His Majesty in His Agony, solitude, and expectation of an enforced death, calling to me, and all other His Subjects,* You that never believed My Life was sought after in the bottome of this Warre but My safety and Honour, you that never fought for me yet professed to abhorre the fighting destinately against Me, or destroying of Me; Cannot you, dare not you now speak one word to save My Life, and your own Soules? shall your silence seem to encourage and make up their suffrages, who therefore pretend they may, and will destroy Me, because it pleaseth you, and the generality of My people?[62]

Gauden's "Me thinks I heare" unmistakably recalls the dream accounts and frame stories that introduce the ghostly speakers of *A Mirror for Magistrates.*

In one such prose link, Baldwin (in character) falls asleep while skimming the chronicle histories in search of fresh material:

> Methought there stode before vs, a tall mans body full of fresshe woundes, but lack-yng a head, holdyng by the hande a goodlye childe, whose brest was so wounded that his hearte myght be seen, his louely face and eyes disfigured with dropping teares, his heare through horrour standyng vpryght, his mercy cravying handes all to bemangled, & all his body embrued with his own bloud. And whan through the gastfulnes of this pyteous spectacle, I waxed afeard and turned awaye my face, me thought there came a shrekyng voyce out of the weasande pipe of the headles bodye, saying as foloweth.[63]

Baldwin's mental paralysis is dramatized in the pair of impersonal construction — "methought there stode," "methought there came" — as though he has lost control of the grammar of happenings inside his head. By contrast, Gauden's "Me thinks I heare" retains its first-person initiative, moving the dream report into the present time of writing, a dramatic height-ening that is still unreal but remains part of the conscious waking world of the speaker. Unlike the lurid pair, later identified as Richard, Duke of York, and his son, the Earl of Richmond, whose opened bodies and gaping wounds Baldwin describes so painfully, Charles is not returning from the dead, although he is an imprisoned soul for all that. His cry is stricken, thrown out to his subjects, a self-exempting majority guilty of silently condoning his murder. This is a mirror monologue in prospect not retrospect, a foreboding that is not yet the stuff of nightmares. And its message is clear: act now to stop the king joining the procession of *de casibus* ghosts.

Ceding his letter to the voice of the monarch, Gauden discovers in this pamphlet a way to dramatize, and potentially remedy, the political speechless-ness of the king by having him speak directly to the reader. Yet, as we have seen, the *Eikon* pulls away from this technique of dramatic impersonation, present-ing Charles as the most credible witness to his own tragedy, but without ask-ing the nation to confront his returning ghost. Committed to a more mimetic rendering of the king's final thoughts and prayers, the *Eikon*'s writers reject the artificial framing devices and theatricalized complaints of the *Mirror*'s ghostly monologues, turning instead to the biographical template of the Psalter for their model of personal expression. Yet it is just this genre, the tale of the fall of the prince as related by the prince's ghost himself, to which Milton labors to attach the *Eikon* in the opening sentence of *Eikonoklastes* and more generally across his regicide tracts. In the *Pro populo Anglicano defensio* (1651), a Latin defense addressed to the whole of Europe, he makes the connection between Charles's soliloquies and the stagey stories as perfected by Baldwin and his crew embarassingly clear, reporting how the king "rose from the grave, and in that book published after his death tried to cry himself up before the people with new verbal sleights and harlotries."[64] *Eikonoklastes* makes no equivalent reference to a returning royal ghost, but it, too, writes the king into the long-running series of *de casibus* tragedies all cut from the same eternal pattern and obedient to the same underlying laws of fault and fate. If the descant names a type of political speech mobilized and maintained by emotion, then the *de casibus* tale valorizes a reading of political history through the lens of personal tragedy, romanticizing the fate of the individual at the expense of a more capacious and collective scrutiny of the historical record. Milton's association of the soliloquizing king with the ventriloquized and garish ghosts of *A Mirror* succeeds in turning the regicide into the latest version of a predictable story, but it also exposes this story as a kind of refuge, or last resort, for absolutist kingship. To get rid of the king, one needs to get rid of the story too.

In his final literary work, the 1671 closet drama *Samson Agonistes,* Milton returns to the scenario he rules off-limits at the opening of *Eikonoklastes*: the act of descanting over a fallen figure. While I am in no way suggesting that Milton is giving us in the story of the Hebrew champion an allegorical reading of the events of 1649, I am interested in how the concerns of the regicide tract recur in this late poem, how Milton revisits the scene of combat and, more crucially, the problem of the life story and the ease with which it claims cultural attention. These connections can be seen most clearly in an extrabiblical encounter Milton scripts between Samson, the fallen deliverer of the Israelites, and Harapha, the "tongue-doughty" giant of Gath.[65] Goaded by Harapha, Samson claims a prerogative of violence, declaring his act of mass murder (the slaughter and stripping of 30 men) divinely covenanted and outside the form of natural law. This declaration follows hard on Samson's affirmation of his divinely infused strength, two claims whose legitimacy still divides Milton's critics but whose proximity has been consistently interpreted as a turning point in the drama: as one strong man speaking to another, Samson is finally able to cultivate his distinction in the terms prescribed by the poem's orthodox and troubling theology, proclaiming himself the instrument of an arbitrary and overwhelmingly powerful God. Yet the interview between Samson and Harapha only proceeds at all under the pressure of Harapha's refusal to advance or accept a challenge to single combat, agreeing to what for Samson would clearly be a more satisfying form of differentiary proof. Reluctant to keep their encounter at the level of argument and eager to fall back upon simple force, Samson, even at the interview's end, is spoiling for a fight:

> Cam'st thou for this, vain boaster, to survey me,
> To descant on my strength, and give thy verdict?
> Come nearer, part not hence so slight informed;
> But take good heed my hand survey not thee. (1227–30)

Samson — and the poem more generally — casts Harapha in the role of the braggart-soldier, "vain boaster," or "his giantship" (1244), as the Chorus crows after he exits ignominiously from the stage. Such insults highlight Harapha's dramatic pedigree; the Philistinian giant is not so far removed from Shakespeare's Falstaff or Ben Jonson's Captain Bobadilla, a stage history of heroic imposture relocated to Gaza from the London streets.[66] But there is a more specific and unnoted echo secreted inside Samson's contemptuous overture to his adversary, and it carries a quite different resonance. Functioning within Samson's speech as an amplification of the verb "survey," "to descant" — that is, to enlarge or comment at length on a subject — recalls the opening words of *Eikonoklastes*. There, as we remember, Milton launched his attack on the king's book by issuing an absolute, seemingly arbitrary, prohibition against such expansive speech.

It is possible, of course, that Milton did not intend this echo in Samson's mouth of his polemical voice; that the self-quotation is too momentary, too peripheral to the drama's larger concerns, to be acknowledged by Milton or to be worth acknowledgment from his readers. But in a poem whose plot hinges on an act of "shameful garrulity" (491), Samson's disclosure of the secret of the source of his strength, even a slip of the tongue may carry revelatory interest, especially a slip that is itself concerned with too much talking, with the wrongful occasion or prolongation of speech. Straining to grapple with flesh and muscle, Samson is forced to attack instead the discursive fascination that his body publicly elicits and excites.

Samson's accusation that Harapha has come to look but not to touch, to
talk but not to fight, might well be taken as a complaint against the closet
drama itself, which, up until this point, has delivered little more than its
own extended exercise in descanting, producing countless variations on
the story of the fallen folk hero and the tabloid-style display of his broken
body. Sharon Achinstein has analyzed the various narrative constructions
that different characters attempt to place upon Samson's life history, declaring the drama to be "nothing if not a performance of political memory."[67]
This contest of stories is complicated by a phenomenon that Linda Charnes
terms "notorious identity": the indentured relationship of the belated literary character toward his or her already written story.[68] Charnes confines her
study to Shakespeare's dramatic characters, but Milton's Samson displays the
same prescient awareness of his coming notoriety, blaming Dalila for what he
predicts will be a humiliating afterlife among the ranks of duped and emas-
culated husbands, "by quick destruction soon cut off / As I by thee, to ages
an example" (764–65). Samson is not wrong in his prediction. It is, after all,
this familiar version of his story that appears in the "book of wikked wyves"
from which Jankyn reads "every nyght and day" to the Wife of Bath; and it
appears, too, in the tragic narratives of the medieval *de casibus* tradition in
which the Hebrew champion routinely holds a place in the lineup of mighty
men brought low by misfortune.[69] Of the 100 tales in the tragic library of
Chaucer's Monk, Samson's is the third to be narrated.

In its final moments, Milton's closet drama ironically confirms the advent
of this legendary Samson when Manoa fantasizes about the mourners who
will one day visit the monument he plans to erect in memory of his slaughtering son. Segregated from the "valiant youth" who precede them (1738), the
virgins are imagined strewing Samson's "tomb with flowers, only bewailing
/ His lot unfortunate in nuptial choice, / From whence captivity and loss of
eyes" (1742–44). Presumably intended by Manoa as a collective penance for
Dalila's singular treachery, this all-female lament isolates the marriage plot
(which had played no part in the original Judges story) from the larger heroic
narrative of Samson's life. The demands of the Father God are similarly excised
from this redacted version, replaced by the operations of a secular Fortune,
the strong woman of the moment. From "intimate impulse" (223) to "the
lot unfortunate," at the end of a drama aggressively based on Greek tragic

models, Manoa thrusts his son's story into the populist idiom of medieval *de casibus* tragedy.[70] As Samson had feared, it is this version of his story that will become a durable cultural document for the after-ages to read and work their own descants upon.

I am not suggesting that the troubling political and theological questions that Milton attaches to Samson's life and death should in any way be subordinated to the drama's failure to escape the vulgar biographical ending of *de casibus* tragedy. What I am suggesting, however, is that Milton is gesturing in these lines toward a popular version of Samson's story that so clearly runs counter to the dominant discursive energies in the poem. What remains when we consider only Manoa's account of the affective narrative future he scripts for his son the fallen hero might well be construed as more moving, and in its domestic love drama more culturally familiar, but it is no longer political or arguable in the way that Milton's closet drama is constructed to be. In *Eikonoklastes,* Milton had resisted the biographical framing of the monarch, naming it a weak strategy to insulate him from polemical argument. Here in his last reflection upon the role of the biographical mode in public life, a reflection that stands uncorrected by the close of the play, he seems resigned to the entry of his biblical hero into the canon of *de casibus* legends. We might choose to interpret this resolution ironically, but that need not prevent us from seeing Milton almost convinced that the task he had set for himself in 1649 was insuperable. For as we will see in subsequent chapters, the affective telling of a life story to diffuse controversy and claim allegiance had only become more pervasive in the two decades since Milton had refused the tragic commission of descanting upon the king's misfortunes.

CHAPTER TWO

A SERVANT'S LIFE

IZAAK WALTON, THE PARISH, AND THE SILENT PUBLIC SPHERE

OVER 20 YEARS AFTER the appearance of *Lyrical Ballads* (1798), the great work of his radical youth, William Wordsworth published *The Ecclesiastical Sonnets* (1822), a history of the national church in the form of a lyric sequence beginning with the arrival of Christianity to Britain and flowing forward to the present day. In the third and final part of the sequence appears a sonnet titled "Walton's Book of Lives":

> There are no colours in the fairest sky
> So fair as these. The feather, whence the pen
> Was shaped that traced the lives of these good men,
> Dropped from an Angel's wing. With moistened eye
> We read of faith and purest charity
> In Statesman, Priest, and humble Citizen:
> O could we copy their mild virtues, then
> What joy to live, what blessedness to die!
> Methinks their very names shine still and bright;
> Apart — like glow-worms on a summer night;
> Or lonely tapers when from far they fling
> A guiding ray; or seen — like stars on high,
> Satellites burning in a lucid ring
> Around meek Walton's heavenly memory.[1]

The image of the stray feather, dislodged from the angel's wing by the delicate weighting of Wordsworth's reversed first foot (line 4), presents divine

60

inspiration as a gift uncalled for, conferred without claim or expectation, perhaps even without the knowledge of its heavenly giver. In its second quatrain, the sonnet convenes the priests and statesmen — John Donne, Henry Wotton, Richard Hooker, George Herbert, and Robert Sanderson — who are the subjects of Waltonian biography, and it surely intends Izaak Walton as the "humble Citizen" who follows modestly behind. Unnamed, these men are not representative of themselves but of the social order that the *Lives* celebrate and eternalize. The moral and theological virtues of faith and charity together with the behavioral arts of living and dying require only that we "copy their mild virtues" — an oxymoron that softens what might otherwise appear as unseemly, an individuating show of strength.

The governing metaphor of the *Ecclesiastical Sonnets* is the "holy river" (1.1.10) winding its way emblematically through the English landscape, flanked on either side by the sweet "flowers, and laurels" which the poet gathers and arranges in his lyric florilegium (1.1.11). In its evocation of this pastoral setting, the sequence remembers an earlier, far more famous, ecclesiastical riverbank, immortalized by Walton in his *Compleat Angler*, at once a literary dialogue, fishing handbook, and poetic anthology voiced by Piscator and his fellow Anglican outdoorsmen. First published in 1653, enlarged in 1655 and 1661, reissued in 1664, and reprinted in 1668 and 1676, *The Compleat Angler* turned Walton, a London tradesman and linen draper, into a "virtuoso" of the English countryside.[2] At the age of 84, writing what was to be his final "life," of the celebrated casuist and Restoration bishop Robert Sanderson (1587–1663), Walton returned to *The Compleat Angler* with an episode that not only adopts the pastoral setting of his commonwealth best seller but also reclaims its charmed circle of companionship. The episode starts out in Interregnum London, in a narrow street dominated by booksellers. Walton and Sanderson meet by chance, and when the weather turns stormy they take shelter in a "cleanly house" where they enjoy a good fire and a hospitable board of bread, ale, and cheese.[3] The scene combines the country inn of *The Compleat Angler* — "an honest Alehouse, where we shall find a cleanly room, Lavender in the windowes, and twenty Ballads stuck about the wall" — with the lyric topos of the Cavalier winter, most famously expressed in Richard Lovelace's ode "The Grasse-hopper. To my Noble Friend, Mr. Charles Cotton" (1648).[4] Like the anglers of Walton's fishing handbook and the "best of *Men* and *Friends*" of Lovelace's poem, Sanderson and

Walton spend their retreat quite cheerfully, delighting in their secure haven from the storm raging outside the inn's culturally soundproofed, ballad-papered walls. Their encounter is brief, the solace of the riverbank and festivities of the Cavalier drinking poem contracted to an hour's conversation, but the fondness of its recollection supplies the pretext for the life of Sanderson that Walton was to write many years later, long after Sanderson's death. This is a scene that comes straight out of the golden age playbook, rallying old-time readers to feel nostalgia for what was already a work of nostalgia, a disappearing habit of vision. Walton trades on this nostalgia to offer a final, valedictory portrait of the biographer as angler, combining his two literary personas into a single, self-mythologizing figure.

The Walton represented in the opening paragraphs of this chapter, the Walton Wordsworth puts forward for our tearful emulation and who, I'm suggesting, Walton had already invented as a fictional character within his biography, has now been consigned to his own precritical riverside past. Wordsworth's sonnet would be reproduced in the endless editions of Walton's *Lives* that appeared during the nineteenth and early twentieth century, but the story told by his larger sequence was outdated almost from the moment of its first publication. In 1828–29, Parliament passed the Sacramental Test Act and Roman Catholic Relief Act, repealing the Corporation Act of 1661 and the Test Acts of 1673 and 1678, which had made it illegal to employ Catholics and Dissenters in any civil, military, or corporate office.[5] Walton was not only a member of the exclusionary Anglican church that this legislation finally dismantled but also its eager promoter and propagandist, complicit in its state-assisted oppression of dissenting communities of belief.

The centrality of Walton's lives to the Anglican propaganda campaigns that followed the Restoration religious settlement has long been recognized, but it has been brought to the fore in recent scholarship dedicated to anatomizing the political and religious divisions of the later seventeenth century. Following in the path of the nineteenth century Nonconformist historian Benjamin Hanbury, Diarmaid MacCulloch has written amusedly of Walton's 1665 *Life* of the Elizabethan theologian Richard Hooker (1554–1600) as a "feline" production that deliberately misleads readers into picturing Hooker dressed in "humble country garb," a rustic saint preaching in the wilderness and proclaiming the Restoration settlement to be at hand.[6]

If Hooker invented Anglicanism, then it is Walton, MacCulloch observes, who must take credit for inventing the Anglican Hooker.[7] With rather more severity, Sharon Achinstein argues that Walton's 1670 *Life* of the Jacobean minister and poet George Herbert (1593–1633) needs to be returned to its exact political context in the spring of 1670 when the successful passage of the Second Conventicle Act through Parliament further tightened the punitive conditions under which Dissenters were being forced to live and worship. Achinstein argues that "the political context of Walton's publication within the history of debates over Restoration Anglican persecution has not been adequately understood," and she resituates the churchmanship of the *Life of Herbert* within these debates, showing how its bland postures of commonality helped to institutionalize "ideologies of exclusion."[8] Both these politically sharpened interpretations trace their descent from David Novarr's seminal 1958 study, *The Making of Walton's Lives,* which collated variants across successive editions, tracked down Walton's acknowledged and unacknowledged sources, and fact-checked his biographical information. With some reluctance, Novarr pronounces Walton guilty of multiple counts of omission, distortion, misquotation, conflation, and manipulation, although he attributes at least some of these lapses to Walton's pre-Enlightenment poetics rather than to his advertent political maneuvering.[9] In all cases, however, the scholarly consensus has been to take down the constellation that closes Wordsworth's sonnet, the brightly shining names: "like stars on high, / Satellites burning in a lucid ring / Around meek Walton's heavenly memory" ("Walton's Book of Lives," 12–14). The celestial bodies of Hooker and Herbert and Donne have been freed from orbiting their biographer. And the Walton at their center, the "meek" man who inherits the heavens, has been brought down to earth once more.

Such critical reassessments are bracing and, to the extent that they have focused upon the narrower timeframes and immediate agendas motivating particular lives, may still understate the value of Walton's writings to the Restoration ecclesiastical establishment that adopted and sponsored him. Certainly, Walton's relations with his longstanding patron, George Morley (1598?–1684), support a more comprehensive account of his obligations and commitments than even these recent studies have shown. Walton had an exceptionally close and enduring relationship with Morley, a Calvinist clergyman and member of the royalist intellectual circle at Great Tew, who briefly attended Charles I in his captivity before going into exile. Upon his return, Morley became a leading figure in the Restoration high church party led by the Lord Chancellor Edward Hyde, the Earl of Clarendon, and Gilbert Sheldon, bishop of London (1660–63) and later archbishop of Canterbury (1663–77). Despite his initial support for a comprehensive religious settlement, Morley cut an uncompromising figure at the Savoy Conference of 1661, clashing with the Presbyterian divine Richard Baxter over the wording of the revised prayerbook. Afterward, he banned Baxter from preaching within his diocese, which included Baxter's former parish of Kidderminster. Between 1661 and 1662, Walton served as Morley's steward at Hartlebury Castle, his episcopal residence outside Worcester. When Morley was elevated to the see of Winchester in 1662, Walton and his family moved with him to Farnham Castle where they lived as permanent members of the bishop's household until close to Walton's death, one year before Morley's own, in 1683.

On his visits to London, Walton often stayed at Winchester House, Morley's episcopal headquarters in Chelsea. It is from there that he supervised the collected edition of the *Lives* through the press in 1669–70. From 1662, Walton also held the lease on a church property in Paternoster Row, a gift from Gilbert Sheldon in his capacity as bishop of London, which Walton would bequeath to his daughter Anne and son-in-law William Hawkins in his will. In 1665, the year that the *Life of Hooker* was published, Morley appointed Walton's brother-in-law Thomas Ken to be his domestic chaplain; in 1678, the year that the *Life of Sanderson* was published, he arranged for Walton's son, also named Izaak Walton, to occupy the same position under Seth Ward, bishop of Salisbury. Through his writings, Walton was able not only to maintain himself as a client of the Anglican establishment but also to provide for and promote the ecclesiastical careers of members of his family.[10]

I present these patronage arrangements, which show Walton to have been acting in close concert with Morley and the Anglican leadership from 1660 onward, as the broadest contextual frame for a political reading of the *Lives.* They show how the bishops recognized the value of Walton's popular celebrity after *The Compleat Angler* and were eager to capitalize further on his vision of the Anglican good life with its unspoken notions of common decency and hospitality, of frank and familiar relations among all men under the great social tent of the English sky. The reorganization of this perennial vision into a sequence of life stories enables Walton to give it a historical existence, fabricating a primitive English church for his modern Restoration moment. At the same time, the immediate circumstances of Walton's biographical production, the polemical occasions that call each life into existence, are routinely suppressed, smothered in an array of sociable attachments that personalize all political relations. Biography supports itself on "happy affinities" (where "happy" suggests not only favor but also the accidental vagaries of good fortune), not on the structural antagonisms associated with controversial divinity.[11]

Documented by John Spurr for the 1660s, by Mark Goldie for the 1670s, and perhaps best known to literary scholars from the opposition writings of Andrew Marvell, John Locke, and the Shaftesbury circle, the Anglican propaganda machine was adept at turning out polemical works to order and at an unrelenting pace. It was staffed almost entirely by clerical climbers: protégés and chaplains of Sheldon such as Thomas Tomkins (the licensor of the first ten-book edition of *Paradise Lost*) and Samuel Parker; or prebendaries and archdeacons such as Richard Perrinchiefe, Herbert Thorndike, and Simon Patrick, a class of ecclesiastical administrators whose professional advancement was tied to their contribution to a succession of hot-tempered print campaigns.[12] Walton's *Lives* are most politically resonant when they measure their distance from this careerist company. Their author is a member of the laity, an amateur writing without a university education and without any presumption of theological opinion or controversial expertise. He is not alienated from the world of power and privilege — in fact, he is a habitual guest at its welcoming table — but he consistently presents himself as one standing apart from the professional class of clergy striving to rise within it. Walton's loyalties, as expressed in the *Lives,* are attached to men and moral values, not to doctrine and theological ideas.

The readership Walton addresses is assumed to share these same prepolitical traits. It is composed of plain-speaking and unexceptionable men whose public-mindedness is reflexive rather than deliberative, removed from the fashionable venues of critical discussion, disagreement, and debate. In the social world the lives imagine, arguers are always "restless" and invariably large town or city based. The *Life of Hooker* offers a salient example of this negative construction, put into the mouth of an "ingenious" Italian observer, who on a visit to London during the 1590s "scoffingly" exclaims, "That the common people of *England* were wiser than the wisest of his wiser Nation; for here the very Women and Shopkeepers, were able to judge of Predestination, and determine what Laws were fit to be made concerning Church-Government."[13] In this sarcastic scene of democratic citizenship, London is transformed into a city of theologians, with opinions about church discipline and Calvinist soteriology being handed down in every home and street. Class orientation is part of the scene's framing, as gender is part of its drama: the Italian is "ingenious," an adjective that may simply mean "discerning" but is able to carry additional meanings, such as "high-minded," "of noble disposition," "noble-born." What matters, however, is how this elite mentality is able to speak for a less privileged readership. Writing about the 1590s in the 1660s, Walton protests the expansive public culture of the intervening decades: the changing nature of print culture and communicative practice that early modern scholars have explored by adapting Habermas's concept of the public sphere. As we saw with the *Eikon Basilike* in chapter 1, the evocation of an outspoken and argumentative populace represents an attempt to foreground *popular* ambivalence about the rapidly changing conditions of national public life.

Walton's lives offer an answer and tell a story to those people who felt locked out of or left behind by new forms of political engagement and public judgment. It is a story promulgated on behalf of a governing class, and for refractory and illiberal ends, but it appeals to segments of the population beyond the elite, soliciting their support by offering an alternative model of public selfhood, based not on the exercise of reason but on the defense of traditional loyalties and passionate attachments. The remainder of this chapter will be devoted to exploring this alternative model, which, it should be stressed, was as much an expression of the altered conditions of public discussion as it was a reaction to their emergence. It builds on the insights of recent scholars regarding the local causes of Anglican conformity and triumphalism to which Walton's lives were unquestionably put, but it diverges from them in seeking a more capacious account of the lives' popularity and political intelligibility beyond these immediate aims. By addressing—and mobilizing—a nonpolitical community of readers, members of what I am calling the "silent public sphere," the lives perform, I believe, their most deeply resonant and unobtrusive political work. To show how this work is achieved, I will focus on a figure by no means marginal to the literary and political imagination of the *Lives*: the lowborn servant who outlives his lord and master.

Walton's servant characters constitute an eclectic cast, adapted from a range of models including Plutarch's *Lives* and the New Testament Gospel narratives as well as from Walton's own highly colored renderings of recent national history. At their most straightforward, they operate as surrogates for their author-biographer, a role that would appear to concede a great deal to the practical realities of Walton's position after the Restoration: the loyal server as the dissembled double of the remunerated time-server; the appointed fiction-maker's most urgent and necessary fiction. Yet while Walton's servants play a part in the *Lives*'s complex apprehension and occlusion of their own story of politicization, what most unites them is a simpler, more dramatic, imperative: their refusal to abandon the bodies of the dead. Out of this refusal, Walton creates a sequence of charged set pieces, scenes of confrontation, insurrection, alienation, and defiance that stoke fears of a rapidly changing world and celebrate the virtue of those who refuse to change with it. Impelled by tragic decency, Walton's servant characters become the bearers of a value system that is out of step with the new social and political order in which they find themselves. Their refusals, I will argue, mount a populist defense of hierarchies and traditions against the democratizing initiatives of later Stuart culture.

1

When the Puritan minister Samuel Clarke sat in his study in Threadneedle Street, London, on October 10, 1661, to write the epistle that would introduce his latest biographical compilation, *A collection of the lives of ten eminent divines, Famous in their Generations for Learning, Prudence, Piety, and painfulness in the work of the Ministry* (1662), he had reason to feel cautiously optimistic about the progress being made toward a national church settlement. The return of the monarchy in May 1660 had brought with it hope for a comprehensive church in which a broad spectrum of Protestant believers, moderate Puritans and Presbyterians, as well as Episcopal Anglicans, might be accommodated. Negotiations among religious leaders had been ongoing and would not be definitively foreclosed until the Cavalier Parliament (so-called because of the Anglican royalism of the majority of its members) enacted a strict legal code, beginning with the Corporation Act in December 1661, against Nonconformist worship. The act was swiftly followed by other legislation that ruled out the inclusion, or "comprehension," within the Church of England of the Presbyterians and moderate Puritans that Clarke was working to bring into the national church. In October 1661, this political defeat was still several months in the future, however, and so Clarke gathered together a spectrum of respectable Protestant opinion, from John Cotton, minister of the Massachusetts Bay Colony at the one end to the Archbishop of Ireland, James Ussher (the only "life" in the collection that Clarke wrote himself), a moderate Episcopalian at the other. "He was then so far from a *Prelatical* spirit, that on the contrary he was an Advocate for, and Patrone of godly and conscientious *Non-conformists*," remarked Clarke of Ussher, creating a portrait of a bishop working against the inherited prejudices of his office.[14] Ranged between Cotton and Ussher were the men closest to Clarke's own convictions and career path: representatives of the Jacobean mainstream that had run into trouble during the Laudian ascendency of the 1630s, and of the Presbyterian party that congregated in London during the 1640s, where Clarke himself arrived to take up a living in 1643.[15] In his introductory epistle, Clarke distinguishes these Puritan divines from the radical religious activities of the sects: "I am not ignorant," he writes, "how some of late have endeavoured to besplatter, and to bring an Odium upon the Names of some of our former Worthies (whose Lives I have formerly published), as though they were *Fanaticks, Anabaptists,* ... enemies to the State, Traytors, &c." His letter reassures the reader that this miscategorizing of persons will be corrected and its injustices redressed: "A Resurrection there shall be of Names as well as of Bodies, at the farthest at the last day."[16] By substituting for the theological category of "souls" the nontheological and discursive category of "names," Clarke writes over the sectarian heresy of mortalism, the belief held by the Leveller Richard Overton, and by the poet John Milton, that the soul dies along with the body and is resurrected with it. His alternative pairing of names and bodies takes scriptural warrant from Revelation 20:12, which prophesizes the opening of the Book of Life, the registry of names of the faithful predestined to salvation, on the Day of Judgment. In his epistle, Clarke claims for himself a forerunning version of this nominating power, anticipating the moment at which the contents of his book of lives and those of the heavenly Book of Life will be found to be identical, name for name. This deferred scene of biographical vindication, of names and bodies joyously reborn into publicly secure identities, ends the epistle on an outwardly triumphant but tacitly defeatist note. The following year Clarke would be one of the Nonconformist ministers ejected from his parish under the terms of the Act of Uniformity, "the black Act for Conformity" as he would afterward refer to it, which excluded non-Anglicans from preaching or from teaching in the grammar schools and universities.[17]

As Peter Lake argues, Clarke's 1661 collection is delicately situated: still hopeful that the restoration of the monarchy would bring with it a comprehensive church settlement that might incorporate Puritan and Presbyterian believers, but preparing also for the possibility of defeat by an Anglican party seeking a return to prayerbook conformity and an unmodified episcopal government.[18] Its selection of just ten eminent divines may have been influenced by another biographical collection published just a few months earlier, Clement Barksdale's *Memorials of worthy persons,* which organized its brief lives into Pythagorean "decads," or groups of ten. In a prefatory letter dated April 23, 1661, Barksdale dedicates the first edition of the *Memorials* to George Montagu, an incoming member of the Cavalier Parliament that was to convene just two weeks later, on May 8. "Some *Gentlemen* are here mixed with the *Church-men,*" he writes, "And I heartily pray, they may be alwaies conjoyned, and lovingly united, for their mutual, both temporal and eternal, happiness."[19] Promoting a companionate marriage of cloth and robe, Barksdale's collection stands a little to the side of Clarke's, pitched more directly to the legislative occasion of Parliament's meeting. Still, their aims are close enough for Clarke to submit his own team of ten for consideration in Barksdale's ongoing biographical series, petitioning for incorporation within its Pythagorean decads — "a perfect number," according to Thomas Stanley in his *History of Philosophy,* "comprehending in it all difference of numbers, all reasons, species, and proportions" — an apt symbol of their mutual hopes for an inclusive national church.[20]

The attempts by Barksdale and Clarke to use their biographical collections to broker a religious consensus were joined in January 1662 by an altogether more prestigious and highly anticipated publication: John Gauden's complete edition of Richard Hooker's *Of the Lawes of Ecclesiastical Politie,* a philosophical defense of the practices, duties, and governance of the Elizabethan Church of England. As the ghostwriter of the *Eikon Basilike,* Gauden had been rewarded at the Restoration with the bishopric of Exeter, but he remained eager for further preferment. Now with this latest literary venture, the wealthier bishopric of Winchester appeared to be within his sights. His edition draws a parallel between the restoration of the Stuart monarchy and the restoration of Hooker's ecclesiastical masterpiece, celebrating the publication of all eight books of the *Polity,* only five of which had been printed during Hooker's lifetime. Its title page alerts the reader to this new and unseen material, proclaiming the *Polity* "Now compleated…out of his own Manuscripts, never before Published."[21]

Gauden opens his biographical preface by acknowledging the support of the Anglican hierarchy, singling out Gilbert Sheldon for particular praise. It is, he declares, only "by the care of some Learned men, especially of the Right Reverend Father in God, *Gilbert,* now Lord Bishop of *London,*" that "those genuine additions are now made of the *three last Books,* promised and performed by him [Hooker], but long concealed from publique view, not without great injury to the publique good."[22] From this evidence it would appear that the high church community gave their backing to Gauden, supplying him with Hooker's extant manuscripts. These included a manuscript version of book 7 (since lost), the only book of the *Polity* yet to appear in some form in print, which took up the question of the origins and authority of episcopal office. The irregular pagination of Gauden's edition supports the theory that book 7 was a last-minute, perhaps hasty and inadequately vetted, insertion, set once the volume was already at the printing house.[23] It made public for the first time Hooker's belief that episcopal government was divinely approved but not divinely commanded, and that, despite its apostolic foundation, the office stood upon no surer privilege than "the custome of the Church, choosing to continue in it."[24]

This was hardly the full-throated, unequivocal endorsement of *de jure divino* episcopacy that religious hard-liners were looking to Hooker to supply. And if Hooker's views were unforeseen, so, too, was the use that Gauden chose to make of them, presenting the *Polity* as a blueprint for a moderate and ecumenical, not, as he puts it, "super-ceremonial" or "solely-ceremonial," religious settlement.[25] Still worse, his prefatory life of Hooker proved an uneven and unenthusiastic piece of hagiography. Based loosely on the biographical sketch in Thomas Fuller's *Church-History of Britain* (1656), it portrays Hooker as a reclusive bachelor, burying himself first at Oxford University and then in the "living sepulchres" of a succession of country livings, "out of the crowd, noise, and tintamar" of other men. In Gauden's telling, Hooker is crippled by shyness, unable to stand in the pulpit and meet the gaze of his congregants: "so far from *any life* in his looks, gestures or pronunciations, that he preached like a *living*, but scarce *moving statue*: His eyes *stedfastly* fixed on the same place from the beginning to the end of his *Sermons*; his *body* unmoved, his tone much to an *Unisone*, and very *unemphatick.*" Later he falls victim to a trick known in coney-catching pamphlets as the "cross-bite," in which the provincial visitor to London is first ensnared by a prostitute and then blackmailed into paying for her silence. In a compensatory gesture for these humiliating ordeals and repressed desires, Gauden depicts Hooker as a stylistic strongman, a "Samson" or "mighty Hercules" whose prose is endowed with all of the masculine virility and heroic energy his life so conspicuously lacks. It is, writes Gauden, "at once *liberal* and *elegant,* copious and comely, with a majestick kind of *ampleness,* and stately luxuriancy, as the ancient Roman Buildings: or as bodies that are *fair* and *full, sinewy* and *beautiful,* handsome and yet *athletick,* having no flat redundancy *in his stile or matter,* nothing *defective* or *impertinent*: so *unaffected, impartial, profound, solid, conspicuous* and *conscientious,* that as was said of *Pindars Odes,* he is both *full, fluent and sublime,* yet *serene* as the firmament: a Torrent indeed, but untroubled, carrying all before him with weighty and convincing *reasonings.*"[26] Gauden's own torrent continues to mix metaphors for many more lines.

The embarrassment to Sheldon, whose name was publicly affixed to Gauden's edition, must have been acute. In an attempt to limit the damage, he commissioned Walton to write a replacement life, affirming Hooker's commitment to episcopal rule and correcting Gauden's unsavory account of his solitary lifestyle. Walton drew upon Fuller's revised character sketch of Hooker, published in his *Worthies of England* (1662), which, among several substantive changes, corrected the crucial error that had led Gauden astray:

"For, whereas I reported him to die a Bachilour, he had Wife and children, although indeed such as were neither to his comfort, when living, nor credit when Dead ."[27] Capitalizing on Fuller's retraction, Walton replaces the urban scam of the blackmailing prostitute with the altogether more respectable one of a scheming mother and her nubile daughter. His Hooker is equally as guillible as Gauden's, but now he is tricked into renouncing the Edenic conviviality of the male collegium — "that Garden of Piety, of Pleasure, of Peace, and a sweet Conversation" — for the "corroding cares" and drudgery of marriage. At the heart of Walton's *Life* lies a single, telling, and almost certainly spurious, anecdote. Hooker's former Oxford pupils Edwin Sandys and George Cranmer pay a visit to their beloved teacher, now also a husband and father, in his modest Lincolnshire parish. There they find him reading a book — "it was the *Odes* of *Horace*," remarks the narrator offhandedly — while tending his sheep on the village commons. Afterward, he is herded home "to rock the Cradle."[28] This pastoral tale quickly passed into Hookerian lore: the *Polity* was written to escape the clutches of a shrill and shrewish wife, helping the church to escape the clutches of those shrill and shrewish Presbyterians.

Hooker's unhappy marriage served a further need, assisting Walton in what is still the most remarkable, and reprehensible, achievement of the *Life*: its discrediting of the final three books of the *Polity*. In a lengthy appendix, Walton spins a lurid tale of widowly malfeasance, comparing Hooker's manuscript drafts to victims of infanticide by explaining how they were abandoned cruelly after his death.[29] As a result, the views they articulate cannot be attributed to Hooker with any measure of certainty, a convenient conclusion given their conflict with the official views of the Restoration church. Walton's *Life* went on sale in late 1664 or early 1665, its Anglican credentials on prominent display. The volume carries the imprimatur of George Stradling, chaplain to Sheldon, who had since been promoted to Canterbury, and a dedication to Morley, thanking him for his hospitality and friendship during its period of composition. (Morley, too, had received a promotion. He was now the Bishop of Winchester, the position that Gauden had hoped would be his.) On its title page, the *Life* introduces Hooker as "the Author of those learned books of the Laws of *Ecclesiastical Polity*." The exact number of books is left unspecified. In 1666, a second edition of Hooker's collected works was printed. It still included all eight books of the *Polity* but was now prefaced, preemptively, with Walton's life of its wronged and misused author.

With the *Life of Hooker,* Walton resumed his biographical practice after more than a decade — the life of John Donne had first been published in 1640; that of Henry Wotton in 1651 — harnessing the resources of a form he had set aside in favor of the literary dialogue of *The Compleat Angler.* The immediate impetus for his emended portrait came from Sheldon and Morley, who leaned on his literary credentials to separate Hooker not just from the false fanfare of Gauden's edition but from Hooker's own writings, canonizing the man while amputating his text. That the one achievement now demanded and, to an extent, depended upon the other tells us how quickly and completely the political situation had changed in the three years since Clarke sat in his study in the heart of London and assembled his cast of ministers to serve in a national church. But the *Life of Hooker* is not merely fulfilling this narrow goal and exclusionary remit: it is also dramatizing the religious conviction that comes from ordinary and everyday practices of worship. In describing these practices, the *Life* appoints itself the custodian of a popular religious memory it is itself largely responsible for creating. One character, in particular, bears the melodramatic burden of this common memory — the "poor parish clerk" of Bishopsbourne in Kent, Hooker's last ministerial posting and burial place.

2

The clerk enters the narrative as a comic foil, doffing his cap as a mark of respect to Hooker before discovering to his consternation that Hooker has performed the same deferential gesture toward him. Their deeper acquaintance takes place only after Hooker's death when the clerk, now himself an old man, appoints himself the custodian of a monument to Hooker erected by a local Laudian landowner, Sir William Cowper, on the church's chancel wall.[30] The monument brings visitors to Bishopsbourne and the clerk appoints himself their guide, accompanying them to the altar, standing with them at Hooker's graveside, and sharing stories of the man he remembered and served. These rites of memory continue uninterrupted until the religious crises and upheavals of the 1640s. "It so fell out," writes Walton, "that about the said third of fourth year of the long Parliament, the present Parson of *Borne* was Sequestered (you may guess why) and a *Genevian* Minister put into his good living."[31] The new incumbent easily persuades the parishioners to adopt his reformist ways of worship, nominating the day when they are to begin receiving the sacrament by sitting up rather than by kneeling at the Communion rail.

The question of whether a congregant should kneel to receive the sacrament had long been a source of contention between Conformists, who grouped it under those ceremonial observances that were indifferent and so governed by ecclesiastical authority, and Puritans, who objected that the practice was a vestige of popery, an act not of good order and obedience but of adoration and idolatry.[32] The Puritan opposition to kneeling during Communion resurfaced during the prayerbook negotiations of 1661, in which Walton's patron, George Morley, assumed such a prominent role. When the *Book of Common Prayer* was reinstated the following year, it directed the laity to receive Communion all "meekly kneeling," although a rubric was inserted to insist on the proper interpretation of the gesture, expressive only "of our humble and grateful acknowledgment...and for the avoiding of such profanation and disorder in the holy Communion, as might otherwise ensue."[33] Writing in the years immediately following the Restoration religious settlement, Walton relocates this ongoing dispute to what might be considered the *sanctum sanctorum* of ceremonial Anglicanism: the altar at which Hooker had officiated and before which his monument now stood. The clerk watches as the parishioners approach the Communion rail:

> When the Clark saw them begin to sit down, he began to wonder, but the Minister bad him *cease wondering, and lock the Church door*; to whom he replied, *pray take you the Keys, and lock me out, I will never come more into this Church, for all men will say my Master* Hooker *was a good Man and a good Scholar, and I am sure it was not used to be thus in his days;* and report says, the old man went presently home and died; I do not say died immediately, but within a few days after.[34]

Endowed with all of the stature and dignity of a latter-day John of Gaunt, Walton's superannuated parish clerk may be extraneous to the plot of the biography, but he articulates the rationale behind the writing of it: "All men will say...it was not used to be thus." His lamentation carries authoritative force not simply because it invokes the legendary figure of Hooker but because it derives from his own memory and experience. The clerk becomes the readers' witness to the past, he authenticates the past for us, and he delivers its death knell before exiting in order to die himself. Read in this way, and despite Walton's apologetic addendum, his death makes good symbolic sense. A relic of a better age whose loss he articulates, the speaker cannot long survive his elegiac utterance.

For early modern readers, the altercation at the altar would have registered as a textbook example of classical *parrhesia*: the vehement and censorious speech of a commoner to a person of power. In her account of seventeenth century life-writing, Debora Shuger argues that this type of free speech, in which the speaker is emboldened to cast rebuke although at considerable risk to his or her own person, is held up as the truest performance of selfhood. Shuger considers the frank and bold speech of the *parrhesiastes* to have become by the end of the sixteenth century a "specifically Puritan trait," and she instances Walton's *Lives,* and Walton's representation of Hooker in particular, as an example of an alternative value system, presenting men conspicuous for their expressive reserve rather than for their outspoken and angry zeal.[35] Further confirmation of Shuger's reading is provided by the title page to the 1666 edition of the *Polity,* which excises two of the four applauding adjectives — "learned, godly, judicious, and eloquent" — with which Gauden had garnished its author's name on the 1662 title page. "Godly" is a predictable omission, "eloquent" a more telling one, presumably unsuited to the milder and less strident Hooker that Walton had fashioned.[36] The clerk's outburst is all the more striking, then, for its appropriation of an outspokeness that had come culturally to be identified with his Puritan opponent. In this parallel universe, it is he who is the victim of religious exclusion and dispossession, a parochial Saint Peter driven to surrender the keys to his master's church.

Composed a little more than a decade later, Walton's *Life of Sanderson* (1678) was also to feature a civil war tale of a rapacious minister — on this occasion a Scottish "Covenanter," a signatory to the 1643 Solemn League and Covenant that allied the Scots to the English Parliament both militarily and in matters of religious discipline. The tale is narrated to the reader in real time, on the return journey from London to Lincolnshire, a route undertaken multiple times over the course of the biography, always reluctantly and in haste. Here it is not just the journey but also the tale that the narrator feels obliged to trace:

> And in the way thither I must tell him, That a very Covenanter and a Scot too, that came into *England* with this unhappy Covenant, was got into a good seques-tred Living by the help of a Presbyterian Parish, which had got the true Owner out. And this Scotch Presbyterian being well settled in this good Living, began to reform the Church-yard, by cutting down a large Ewe Tree, and some other Trees that were an ornament to the place, and very often a shelter to the Parishioners; who excepting against him for so doing, were answered, *That the Trees were his, and 'twas lawful for every man to use his own as he, and not as they thought fit.*

No one comes forward to dispute the minister's assertion of his property rights. Instead, the narrator makes the following observation: "I have hear'd (but do not affirm it) That no Action lies against him that is so wicked as to steal the winding sheet of a dead body after 'tis buried; and have heard the reason to be, because none were supposed to be so void of humanity, and that such a Law would vilifie that Nation that would but suppose so vile a man to be born in it: nor would one suppose any man to do what this Covenanter did. And whether there was any Law against him I know not; but pity the Parish the less for turning out their legal Minister."[37] Initially, the narrator addresses a different criminal action: the theft of the winding sheet from a buried corpse. Such a case had in fact come before the Leicester assizes in 1613 when one William Haynes was tried for exhuming four bodies in order to steal the shrouds in which they were wrapped. The case acquired a grisly celebrity. Walton could have found it in Edward Coke's *Institutes,* where the judge's verdict of larceny is explained. For the dead, writes Coke, "being but a lump of earth, hath no capacity" and can therefore possess no property, not even their own bodily remains. It is therefore the case that the thief's crime is committed against the owner of the linen from which the shroud was made, not against the corpse from which it is stripped.[38]

Not being a jurist, Walton's narrator rules differently. There can be no specified punishment for the act of stealing a winding sheet, he reasons, because it would be a far worse crime to admit this crime's possibility, calling into question not merely the rule of law but the morality of the nation. The narrator identifies the Covenanter with the grave robber on the basis that, he, too, has committed an act for which the law appears to have made no penal sanction. Ultimately, however, it is not the law's inadequacy but its abrogation upon which his judgment turns. By expelling their "legal Minister," the parishioners have already acted to suspend the rule of secular law and with it the higher spiritual law of faith and conscience.

By comparing the destruction of the churchyard and its ancient yew tree to the hypothetical crime of stealing a winding sheet, Walton's narrator performs an argumentative move familiar from early modern case literature. Casuistry, the putting forth of a situation or dilemma that requires ethical negotiation or the exercise of moral judgment, remained a popular practice throughout the seventeenth century, despite the charges of sophistry and disingenuousness routinely leveled against it.[39] It is through his casuistical expertise that Walton's Sanderson first claims the attention of Charles I, this "conscientious King," as Walton labels him, who appoints him his chaplain in 1631. "I carry my ears to hear other Preachers, but I carry my conscience to hear Mr. Sanderson," Walton reports the king to have quipped, creating a profile of Sanderson as the spiritual counselor to the highest and the humblest in the land.[40] The showcase demonstration of Sanderson's court of conscience comes just a few pages earlier when he intervenes in a neighborly dispute between a litigious landlord and a destitute tenant, the father of seven children, who cannot pay his rent. Invoking the Gospel's parables of the unforgiving servant (Matt. 18:21–35) and unjust steward (Luke 16:1–13), Sanderson draws a distinction between the necessity of charity and the rule of law: "This he told him.... That the Law of this Nation (by which Law he claims his Rent) does not undertake to make men *honest* or *merciful*; but does what it can to restrain men from being *dishonest* or *unmerciful*, and yet was defective in both."[41] The deficiency of the laws of England, their negative purpose of deterrence, dictating only what is forbidden and what permitted as opposed to making an attempt to elevate the criminal conscience, and their failure even on these narrow grounds, is the lesson that Sanderson preaches. Its application to the case of the churchyard, where the Presbyterian minister invokes a purely legalistic definition of right and wrong, is deliberate and clear.

Among Sanderson's casuistic endeavors is his 1652 study, "The Case of using or forbearing the Established Liturgy stated and resolved," which circulated widely in manuscript, achieving a degree of notoriety among the Interregnum Anglican community, both those who remained in England

and those who entered European exile.[42] Addressed to ministers, the study makes the case for political and religious conformity, squaring the doctrinal obligation to preach from the now prohibited Anglican prayerbook with the pastoral obligation to protect the spiritual well-being of one's flock. Counseling ministers to forgo their use of ceremonies and outwardly adhere to the policies of the Cromwellian church in order to avoid expulsion by the parliamentary authorities, Sanderson describes what he takes to be the only alternative action: "the delivering over the sheep of Christ, that lately were under then hands of faithful shepherds, into the custody of ravening wolves" who "will be sure to misteach them one way or other, viz. either by instilling into them Puritanical and Superstitious Principles, that they may the more securely exercise their Presbyterian tyranny over their judgements, consciences, persons, and estates; or else, by setting up new lights before them, to lead them into a maze of Anabaptistical confusion and frenzy."[43] Brian Duppa, the ejected Bishop of Salisbury, described Sanderson's conciliatory counsel as "partly apologetical for himself, and partly instructive to others," almost, although not quite, accusing him of acting as a casuist in his own extenuating cause. He "could wish, if it were possible, the printing of it might be prevented," citing fears that "the secrets of it" might compromise the show of Anglican unity.[44] In fact, the case study did not make its first complete appearance in print until 1678, when it formed part of the materials adjoined to Walton's *Life,* as *Bishop Sanderson's Judgment concerning submission to usurpers* and carrying its own title page.[45] Walton's longtime bookseller, Richard Marriot, sold *Bishop Sanderson's Judgment* separately as well as bound in with Walton's *Life,* and it remains unclear how much creative control Walton exercised over its inclusion. What is clear is that Walton adopts the alarmist language of Sanderson's tract, spinning its dark prediction of "Presbyterian tyranny" into his own parabolic tale of sheep and wolves.

The tale of the churchyard was an especially pointed one in the spring of 1678 when the *Life of Sanderson* went to press, "hastned" from Walton so that he had no opportunity to make editorial emendations. It appeared at the end of a decade in which Walton's ecclesiastical patron, George Morley, had once more assumed a prominent role in national politics, rejoining the Privy Council in 1674 as part of a broader alliance between the crown and the bishops coordinated by the Lord Treasurer Thomas Osborne, the Earl of Danby. These were also years in which the bishops' temporal powers — their influence over royal policy, their weight as a voting bloc in the House of Lords, and their obdurate defense of the 1662 religious settlement against calls for broader inclusion or limited toleration — were becoming increasingly unpopular, making the bishops themselves a recurrent target of attack. Public hostility toward the Anglican hierarchy further intensified when Parliament turned to debating the royal succession, the question of whether and under what conditions the openly Catholic heir, James Duke of York, should be permitted to accede to the throne of England. These debates, which in their later stages would come to be known as the Exclusion Crisis, took place against a background of persistent and virulent anti-Catholicism, stoked by a pamphlet press that took delight in detailing the crimes and conspiracies of the church of Rome. In March 1677, the government introduced a bill in the House of Lords dedicated to the "further securing the Protestant religion." Seeking to place constitutional limitations on the future powers of a Catholic monarch, the bill proposed, among other measures, to transfer the right to appoint bishops to the bishops themselves and away from the crown, where it had been vested since the 1534 Act of Supremacy. The so-called "Bishops' bill" was decried in the House of Commons as an assault on the royal — and hence civil — supremacy in matters of church government. Somerset MP John Malet accused it of setting "nine Mitres above the Crown — *Monstrum horrendum!*," while Andrew Marvell declared it to be "a great invasion on Prerogative," for "here Bishops make Bishops (as inherent a right to the Crown as any thing possible)." Marvell proceeded to publish the bill's proposals in their entirety in his famous redaction of the 1677 parliamentary session, *An account of the growth of popery and arbitrary government.*[46] There, as elsewhere in the oppositional literature, the power-hungry bishops were held up as a reason for excluding James from the line of succession altogether. Any limitations imposed upon the royal prerogative, so this argument maintained, would only increase the powers of the priesthood. Divine right bishops were no more attractive a prospect than a Catholic prince.[47]

Yet if it made sense for Walton to write the life of a bishop, mounting a defense of the episcopal office, then Sanderson was not an obvious candidate to have chosen for this task. Despite holding the Regius Chair in Divinity at Oxford from 1642, Sanderson spent the civil war years in his

Lincolnshire parish of Boothby Pagnell, showing a lack of interest in royalist politics and avoiding national affairs whenever he could. Walton plays on this isolationist stance, aligning his own ostensible reluctance to write history with Sanderson's reluctance to participate in it. "I cannot lead my Reader to *Dr. Hammond* and *Dr. Sanderson* where we left them at *Boothby Pannel*," explains the narrator, "'till I have look'd back to the long Parliament, the Society of Covenanters in *Sion Colledge,* and those others scattered up and down in *London,* and given some account of their proceedings and usage of the late learned *Dr. Laud,* then Archbishop of *Canterbury.*"[48] When the narrator does finally return to Boothby Pagnell, he discovers that the life — as opposed to the *Life* — of Sanderson has been proceeding in his absence. Abducted by parliamentary soldiers and imprisoned at their garrison in Lincoln, Sanderson has been carried out of his own biography. Orchestrated for dramatic effect, Sanderson's captivity relocates the village parish with its quiet churchyard, the centerpiece of Walton's imperiled Anglican geography of inn and field and riverside, to the frontline of the fighting, its politicization unwelcome and always coming from elsewhere. In 1678, the immediate polemical objective was to remind readers of the criminal record of the Nonconformist community, their unrestrained rapaciousness and lack of conscience. In a further twist, Walton's Scottish Covenanter boasts that he is acting within the requirements of the law, exposing the limitation of the civil magistrate in governing conduct and demonstrating the need for strong spiritual authority and judgment. Newly schooled by the parable of the greedy presbyter and the foolish parish, the reader is primed to greet Sanderson, still the benevolent master of his own churchyard, with gratitude and with relief.

But if the tale of the churchyard makes its own sense of the politics of the later 1670s, its urgency and argumentative ingenuity are by no means exhausted by that interpretative framework. It was surely a deliberate choice by Walton to imitate the case literature identified with his biographical subject, a literature that would later make its way, on the one hand, to the letter pages of the *Spectator* and *Athenian Mercury* and, on the other, to the early novel.[49] At the same time, the scenario recognizably belongs to the broader scheme of Walton's biographical writings, recurring to, and forming a pair with, the civil war tale from the *Life of Hooker,* in which the parish clerk stoutly defends the cause of ceremonial worship. In both of these episodes, the subject of the biography is notably missing: Sanderson because he is busy attending to his own parish; Hooker because he has been dead for over 40 years. Of the two, Sanderson's absence is the more striking, occasioning a casuistical repudiation that comes not from a biographical character but from the Waltonian narrator who intervenes within his own tale-telling enterprise. If, in the *Life of Hooker,* the parish clerk is a surrogate for the biographer, then, in the *Life of Sanderson,* Walton is emboldened to dispense with the need for surrogates altogether. The boldness of his intervention may itself be sufficient explanation for the analogy of the Presbyterian minister and the grave robber, the extravagance of which appears opportunistic and entirely politically driven. But there is, I believe, a further reason why Walton presses this particular analogy, one that has less to do with political circumstance than it does with the representation of his own biographical practice. To appreciate the analogy's importance, and to bring into view the full scope of its author's ambition, we need to turn back to the first life that Walton wrote, to 1640, to Donne, and to Plutarch.

3

The *Life of Donne* opens with a narrative describing a makeshift funeral:

> And, if I shall now be demanded as once *Pompey's* poor bondman was, "(The grateful wretch had been left alone on the Sea-shore, with the forsaken dead body of his once glorious lord and master: and, was then gathering the scatter'd pieces of an old broken boat to make a funeral pile to burn it (which was the custom of the Romans;)" *who art thou that alone hast the honour to bury the body of* Pompey *the great?* So, who I am that do thus officiously set the Authors memorie on fire?[50]

Situating himself in relation to Plutarch, Walton modestly identifies with Pompey's slave, the "poor bondman," who has the honor, out of all proportion to his station, of burying the famous general he has served. In the *Life of Pompey,* Plutarch opposes the fidelity of this bondsman, named Philippus, with the treachery of another Roman soldier, the deserter Septimius, who, having entered the employ of Pompey's Egyptian assassins, strikes the first blow from behind against his former master. After the assassins have dispersed, a third servant arrives, an army veteran who recalls serving under Pompey during his first campaign. The veteran approaches Philippus and inquires, "O frend, what art thou that preparest the funeralls of *Pompey* the great?" Their colloquy concludes with the veteran joining the bondsman in performing the makeshift funeral rites, repatriating himself— "that I may not altogether repent me to have dwelt so long in a straunge contrie" — by washing and dressing Pompey's headless body.[51]

The veteran's question to the slave is the one that Walton poses to himself: "So, who I am that do thus officiously set the Authors memorie on fire?" Its answer is deferred until the end of the preface when Walton pictures Donne in heaven: "And if the Authors glorious spirit…can have the leasure to look down and see me, the poorest, the meanest of all his friends, in the midst of this officious dutie, confident I am that he will not disdain this well-meant sacrifice to his memory."[52] The shared term across these framing moments — the shoreline burial at the start of the preface and the communion of saints at its close — is "officious" or its cognate, "officiously." Derived from the Latin *officium,* a compound of *opus* and *facio* and so signifying a duty or task that one does for another, to act officiously is to act obligingly and with an eagerness to serve, although the modern, and now dominant, sense of officious as uninvited, obtrusive, and self-forwarding action was also available by the start of the seventeenth century. Milton deploys the adverb in just this pejorative sense in his radical prose pamphlet, *Areopagitica* (1644), describing the licensing laws of the Catholic Church as a "rare morsell so officiously snatcht up, and so ilfavourdly imitated by our inquisiturient Bishops, and the attendant minorities their Chaplains."[53] In this example of usage, "officiously" not only characterizes the bishops' meddling in state affairs but also carries a further pun on "offices," authorized forms of divine service, including the liturgy. For Milton, the haste with which the greedy English bishops have laid hold of and sought to replicate the mechanisms of papal censorship is characteristic of their more general "officiousness," or appetite for offices, all of the popish rites and rituals stripped away by Protestant reformers. Walton's glossing of his biographical labors as being "officiously" undertaken risks the same danger of semantic drift from duty to undulyness. Like Milton, he, too, plays upon the connection to priestly offices and to one specific office in particular: the *Officium pro defunctis,* or office for the burial of the dead.

The elaborate medieval office of burial had been excised from the 1553 and 1559 versions of the *Book of Common Prayer* on the grounds that the souls of the Protestant dead, no longer trapped in purgatory, had little need for the petitions of the living. Even this reformed order of burial proved theologically controversial, however, as Puritan opponents took issue with what they saw as the persistence of superstitious practices: the chaperoning of the corpse to the gravesite and the promise of eternal life at the moment of its committal, which they claimed to be a proxy form of intercessionary prayer. The Westminster *Directory for the publique worship of God,* the official replacement for the *Book of Common Prayer* between 1645 and 1660, explicitly forbade "the customes of kneeling down, and praying by, or towards the dead Corps, and other such usages in the place where it lies" as well as all "praying, reading, and singing both in going to, and at the Grave." Such rites, it declared, were "no way beneficiall to the dead, and have proved many wayes hurtfull to the living." At the 1649 burial of Charles I in the chapel at Windsor Palace, the officiating minister, William Juxon, was forbidden to read from the prayerbook burial service.[54] The Donne preface was written before these sterner prohibitions took effect, although it may respond to an earlier phase of the same controversy when a number of prominent Caroline churchmen, including Lancelot Andrewes, John Cosin, and the Laudian bishops Richard Montagu and William Forbes, broke publicly with the Calvinist orthodoxy of early Stuart England by announcing their wish to resume praying for the souls of the departed. For this group of "avant-garde" divines, praying for the dead was not a popish affectation but an established practice of the early church that sought to hasten the day of resurrection for all believers.[55] It is in the context of this Laudian movement to secure the prayers' revival that we might read the "officiously" performed rituals of the Donne preface. Walton offers his biography not simply as a service of commemoration for the departed but also as a rite of burial, a substitute religious office "well-meant" by the living and which the dead "will not disdain."

Of course, the most famous of all stories about Donne *is* the story of his death, obsessively rehearsed first by Donne himself and then by Walton, who kept amplifying his narrative account — initially for the 1658 edition of the *Life* and later for the collected *Lives* of 1670, the version from which I am quoting here. As death approaches, Donne poses for his funeral monument, impersonating the corpse he is soon to be. The preparations for this sitting are described as a series of deliberate actions, each one a mortification of his living flesh: "Several Charcole-fires being first made in his large Study, he brought with him into that place his winding-sheet in his hand;

and, having put off all his cloaths, had this sheet put on him, and so tyed
with knots at his head and feet, and his hands so placed, as dead bodies are
usually fitted to be shrowded and put into the grave." The tolling of the verb
with its changing prepositions — put off, put on, put into — marks the order
and stations of Donne's passion. These same ritual actions are repeated at
Donne's actual death when, Walton tells us, "he closed his own eyes; and
then, disposed his hands and body into such a posture as required not the
least alteration by those that came to shroud him."[56] The dramatic power of
this performance comes from the care and deliberateness with which Donne
soothes his body to its fate. Are we to imagine him reaching up to close his
eyes with his hands, as a mourner would do, rather than letting them fall shut
of their own accord? The contrast between Donne's well-disposed body and
the abandoned body of Pompey in Walton's Plutarchan preface could hardly
be more striking. Yet in each case, Walton takes us to the moment at which
the dying man loses control over what happens to his body, even — or especially — if, like Donne, he exerts that control to the very end, the "minute's
last point" of his earthly life.[57]

Donne's death shroud was to have its own celebrity afterlife. Memorialized
in Donne's funerary monument, which stood in St. Paul's Cathedral until
the great fire of 1666, and in the engraved frontispiece to Donne's final sermon, *Deaths Duell* (1632), the winding sheet is also the structuring conceit
of John Marriot's commendatory verse, "Hexastichon Bibliopolae," part
of the front matter to the 1633 posthumous edition of Donne's collected
poems, to which Walton contributed an elegy:

> I See in his last preach'd, and printed booke,
> His picture in a sheete; in *Pauls* I looke,
> And see his Statue in a sheete of stone,
> And sure his body in the grave hath one:
> Those sheetes present him dead, these if you buy,
> You have him living to Eternity.[58]

Patterning the long closed vowel sounds of "see" and "sheet" — also
"preached" and "these" — the speaker refers first to the frontispiece to *Deaths
Duell* ("his picture in a sheete"), then to the monument in St. Paul's ("a sheete
of stone"), and finally to the linen shroud after which portrait and sculpture

are modeled. Donne's statue was carved out of marble, but the verse intends a pun on the name of its famous sculptor, Nicholas Stone, whose work inspired a short-lived trend for shrouded funeral monuments, with their bravura displays of enfolding, falling cloth.[59] None of these memorial forms — of linen, of marble, and of the engraver's line — are able to compete with the printed book, however. Only its paper sheets prove death-denying, although the closing couplet makes poetic immortality contingent upon consumerism, an afterlife for a price.

John Marriot, or "Jo. Mar." as he is here initialed, was a bookseller who lived in Donne's parish of Saint Dunstan's West. His shop was on Fleet Street, inside the churchyard that, after Saint Paul's, was the most important center of the burgeoning London book trade. Also on Fleet Street stood the linen draper shop of Izaak Walton, who became a resident of the parish in 1624, the same year that Donne accepted the living and started preaching there. In 1635, Marriot put out a second, posthumous edition of Donne's poetry, an octavo volume now notorious for grouping Donne's secular poetry together as juvenile works distinguished from and superseded by the religious verses of his mature years. The new arrangement is justified by an epigraph under the frontispiece portrait of a youthful Donne. Reversing the conventions of the prodigy volume, which proclaim the boyish appearance and precocious gifts of the rising poet, the epigraph celebrates the late works as the truest expression of the poet's achievement. "Witness this Booke, (thy Embleme)," it instructs Donne the ingenue who looks out at the reader from his portrait: it "begins / With Love; but endes, with Sighes, & Teares for Sinnes."[60] Beneath this closing couple are the initials "IZ: WA:" or Izaak Walton. In its narrative movement from erotic declarations to penitential tears, Walton's epigraph previews the conversion story of his *Life of Donne,* the poet's protracted resistance to and final embrace of the vocation of preacher. The *Life* appeared five years later, prefacing the first folio edition of Donne's collected sermons. It was published by Richard Marriot, who had by then taken over his father's bookselling trade. Focused on the parish of Saint Dunstan's West, these local connections offer an explanatory framework within which the beginnings of Walton's biographical career, its origins in the effort to assemble, promote, and impose narrative order upon the first printed editions of Donne's poems, are to be understood.

Leaping now from the beginning of that career to its end, we can see how the narrator's strange and seemingly gratuitous analogy between the Covenanter's destruction of the churchyard and the grave robber's theft of a winding sheet in the *Life of Sanderson* is charged with the memory of Donne's iconic relationship to his burial shroud. A "lively artifact" — to borrow Joseph Roach's term for objects "that seem to want to speak for themselves" — the shroud fixed the afterimage of the famous poet and preacher in the public's imagination, its folds wrapped tightly to hold the dead body intact, its knots fastened loosely to allow the resurrected body to break free.[61] Walton had knowingly collaborated in the construction of this legendary Donne, offering the definitive, and still irresistible, backstory to his final self-portrait, taken from life, as his own awaiting corpse. In his narrative rendering of this stage-lit scene, Donne's winding sheet assumes a function analogous to the saint's attribute, a physical object that identifies its owner by referring to the trial and spectacle of his death.

In one sense, however, Donne's burial shroud and the saint's attribute are importantly different. Unlike the saint's attribute, which is unique to its martyred or beatified possessor, grave clothing is a common property, worn by all the bodies, whether coffined or uncoffined, interred in all the churchyards of England. If the comparison of the Presbyterian minister to the grave robber mobilizes the memory of Donne's singular death, then it does so in the service of a universalizing vision of the departed. I have suggested that the analogy serves the political times, setting Anglican continuity and commemoration and inclusion against Puritan interruption and expropriation and erasure. Yet the figure of the stolen winding sheet — stolen from the unnamed corpse but also, and more importantly, from the bookseller's epigraph to the 1633 *Poems* and Walton's *Life of Donne* — does more than construct their tendentious opposition. It is, we remember, the Waltonian biographer who draws the imperfect parallel between the grave robber and the Presbyterian minister ostensibly to mount a moral argument against the minister's lawful action. Yet the parallel delivers more than it promises, producing the grave robber as a powerful foil to the biographer, whose primary duty, as Walton defines it, is to care for and protect the dead. By recurring to and ransacking his own literary past, Walton represents the biographer as the antithesis of the grave robber. Given the symbolic significance of the winding sheet to the story of his own biographical career, it is difficult not to read the parallel as Walton's most overdetermined, and narratively gratuitous, articulation of what he takes to be the saving powers of biography within a volatile political world.

The grave robber reverses the pattern established by the servant figures of earlier lives — Pompey's bondsman and Hooker's parish clerk — who positively exemplify the duties of the biographer. Coming between them in the chronology of the lives's composition is another servant character who is introduced in the preface to the *Life of Herbert*. Drawn from the Gospel narratives, Walton uses the example of this servant to conjoin his Anglican lives within a Christian historiography reaching back to the Incarnation, and to the life of Jesus.

The *Life of Herbert* first appeared in 1670, both separately and in a volume that collected Walton's four lives and published them together for the first time. Separately, it constituted a slim octavo volume that included a selection of letters written by Donne and Herbert to Magdalen Herbert, née Newport, the poet's mother.[62] Much of the early narrative of the *Life* is dedicated to describing Donne's friendship with Magdalen Herbert, a personal relationship from which, by paralleling and patterning episodes, Walton is able to infer a literary one, presenting Herbert as Donne's poetic son. As the *Life of Donne* pivots on the fulcrum of "Jack" Donne's religious conversion to "Doctor" Donne, so the *Life of Herbert* also divides in two: its first half describes Herbert's brilliant career as a university orator at Cambridge; its second (covering only the last three years of Herbert's life), his holy calling to the ministry of the tiny parish of Bemerton, a short distance from Salisbury. Having taken up this humble residence, Herbert sets about teaching his rude and unlettered parishioners the daily offices, collects and responses, vigils and feast days that make up the liturgy of the Church of England. Walton drew much of this material from *A Priest to the Temple; or, The Country Parson*, a character of the habits and qualities of a "true pastor" scripted in the style of a rhetorical manual or courtesy book, which Herbert wrote during his tenure at Bemerton in the early 1630s and which was printed by the ejected Anglican minister Barnabus Oley in 1652.[63] Sharon Achinstein has rightly argued that such heavy emphasis on ceremonial practice cannot be abstracted from the ongoing attempts by the Restoration church to promote and enforce conformity of worship. She joins others scholars in describing how Walton's *Life* sought to consolidate Herbert's standing within an Anglican devotional tradition, putting itself in competition with dissenting interpretations of Herbert's Calvinist theology and plain style by Richard Baxter, Oliver Heywood, Faithful Teat, and John Bryan. Herbert's collection of religious lyrics, *The Temple* (1633), was already an established bestseller by the time Walton's *Life* appeared in 1670, but its three subsequent reprintings, in 1674, 1678, and 1679, came shackled to his hagiographical narrative.[64]

These two ways of understanding the *Life of Herbert* — as a text that conscripts Herbert into a particular version of literary history and as one that conscripts him into a particular version of ecclesiological history — come together in the introduction to the *Life,* which interprets an episode recounted in all four of the Gospel narratives: the anointing of Jesus in the house of Simon the leper by Magdalen Herbert's biblical namesake, Mary Magdalene.

> In a late Retreat from the business of this World, and those many little Cares with which I have too often incumbred myself, I fell into a Contemplation of some of those Historical passages that are Recorded in Sacred Story; and, more particularly, of what had past betwixt our Blessed Saviour, and that wonder of Women, and Sinners, and Mourners, Saint Mary Magdalen.... I do now consider, that because she lov'd much, not only much was forgiven her, but that, beside that blessed blessing of having her sins pardoned, she also had from him a testimony, that her Alabaster box of precious oyntment poured on his head and feet, and that Spikenard, and those Spices that were by her dedicated to embalm and preserve his sacred body from putrefaction, should so far preserve her own memory, that these demonstrations of her sanctified love, and of her officious, and generous gratitude, should be recorded and mentioned wheresoever his Gospell should be read; intending thereby, that as his, so her name should also live to succeeding Generations, even till time shall be no more.[65]

Walton's narrative expands upon Jesus's rebuke to the complaining disciples in Matthew 26:13, rendered in the King James Bible as: "Verily I say unto you, Wheresoever this gospel shall be preached in the whole world, there shall also this, that this woman hath done, be told for a memorial of her." The disciples' complaint is a financial one: spikenard, gathered high in the Himalayas, and other rare spices imported from the East are too costly to waste in this impulsive manner; the ointment might have been sold instead and the proceeds donated to the poor.[66] Only Mary understands that the body of the incarnate Christ is too precious to be made an object of economic calculation, however charitable its purpose. Her expenditure of the luxurious oils is made in anticipation of the far greater expenditure of Christ's sacrifice. Both are absolute gifts, transcending the world of financial dealings and inaugurating an alternative economy of service and reward. As Mary has vowed to preserve the earthly body of Jesus from corruption, so he will perpetuate her earthly name until the Last Judgment, the day when commemoration ceases and all the bodies of the dead are raised up.

Walton's glossing of Mary's unsolicited actions as "these demonstrations of her sanctified love, and of her officious, and generous gratitude" echoes the language he had previously used to describe Pompey's slave, the "grateful wretch" who prepared his master's body for its makeshift shoreline pyre, in the preface to the *Life of Donne*.[67] Just as the slave's conduct risked being judged "officious" in the negative sense of untimely and unwelcome, so Mary's anointing must endure the disciples' preliminary censure before the true value of its office is revealed. Indeed, the dispute over the lost sale price of her ointment, as it is told in the Gospel narratives, is rather like a tough-minded Herbert poem (of the kind that Walton is generally presumed to have been less interested in), in which the disciples' charitable protest, seemingly the right response to Mary's impulsive action, is brusquely countermanded by Jesus, who is thinking not of the needs of the poor but of the coming ordeal of his death. Mary's service is needful because no man, not even the son of God, can prepare his own body for the grave. Through her example, Walton again claims for the biographer this sacred responsibility and role.

The preface continues, after its account of Mary's anointing of Jesus, to create a genealogy for Christian biography, extending backward from Herbert to Walton's previous biographical subjects, Donne and Henry Wotton, to the incarnate Jesus. In contrast to this genealogy, which incorporates Walton's *Lives* into the chronological span of Christian history, stands Mary's "Alabaster box of precious oyntment," a lyric object with the power to prevent time's damages. The box calls attention not just to the task of biography but to its status as a poetic construct, proposing an expressive equivalence between Herbert's poetry and Walton's *Life*.

Throughout his lyric collection, *The Temple*, Herbert makes significant use of olfactory effects, presenting the sensory perceptions of taste and smell as ways, outside of the agency or control of the speaker, of knowing and being known by God. This affective, as opposed to analytic or rhetorical, impulse of Herbert's poetic imagination accords well with the tenets and practices of Anglican ceremonialism. Walton treats it as basic to Herbert's conversion experience. During his first days at Bemerton, after his retreat from the world and when all thought of secular advancement has been renounced, Herbert is imagined enacting the scenario of his poem, "The Odour": "he seems to rejoyce in his thoughts of that word Jesus, and to say the adding these words, *my Master* to it, and the often repetition of them, seem'd to perfume his mind, and leave an oriental fragrancy in his very breath."[68] Here is no articulate act of introspection, only a kind of self-inflicted surrender as the words fill Herbert's mind and mouth and he gives himself over to their smell.

The lyric that the Magdalene preface recalls most nearly, however, is not one that Walton appropriates as part of the biographical record. Instead, it traces its influence back to *The Compleat Angler,* where it is quoted in its entirety, after a rainstorm has freshened the meadows, diffusing their natural perfume.[69] The poem is "Vertue," and the Magdalene preface picks up the metaphor of the perfume box in its third stanza:

> Sweet spring, full of sweet dayes and roses,
> A box where sweets compacted lie;
> My musick shows ye have your closes,
>   And all must die.

As readers have noted, the perfume box is also a music box, a metaphor not just for the apostrophized season, but for the stanza — and the lyric poem — that compresses all of nature's riches into its coffined form. In this somber exercise, the epithet "sweet" is itself prophetic: only things that "must die" possess a scent or smell. It is possible Herbert was thinking of Gertrude's parting words, "sweets to the sweet," over Ophelia's flower-strewn grave.[70] More immediate and resonant echoes come from other of Herbert's poems. There is the "chest of sweets" from which the swaddling clothes, prematurely elegized as "little winding sheets," are taken in "Mortification." Or there is the body of the incarnate Christ, that "rare cabinet" in which, the speaker reminds God, "all thy sweets are packt up," in "Ungratefulnesse." In another poem, it will be the piercing of this fleshy body which causes it, like a perforated pomander ball, to release its richest and most fragrant perfume. Here, though, the cabinet allures not because it is rare or exotic but because it is intimately familiar: "this box we know; / For we have all of us just such another."[71] Typically, although not universally, in Herbert's poetry, petals and bodies (and minds) yield perfume only through violence: they are crushed and constricted, excruciated, torn, and pierced. In the dramatic monologue "The Sacrifice," Herbert's Jesus compares Mary Magdalene's ointment to the rarer perfume released by his efflorescent body, denying their parity: "Not half so sweet as my sweet sacrifice: / Was ever grief like mine."

It is impossible, of course, to reconstruct Walton's reading of Herbert's poetry, or to do anything more than speculate about the range of references he might have discovered "compacted" into the box of perfumed things in "Vertue," the poem we can be sure that he knew. But it is possible to see how the Magdalene preface and, especially, the iconographic object at its center, the "Alabaster box of precious oyntment," makes a selective homage to Herbert's poetry and its affective or sense-based expressions of devotional experience. At the same time, the preface enables Walton to pattern his own biographical practice after the Gospel writers. On multiple occasions, he presents Herbert as a Christ figure, drawing parallels with events in the life of Jesus. One episode shows him, at the age of 12, astonishing his teachers at Westminster School by disputing with the fiery Scottish Presbyterian Andrew Melville, as Jesus had astonished his parents by disputing with the priests in the temple in Jerusalem (Luke 2:46–52). Another finds him, on his regular walks from Bemerton to Salisbury to hear the cathedral choir, pausing to expound the Bible's teachings to whomever he meets, "as our blessed Saviour after his Resurrection, did take occasion to interpret the Scripture to *Cleopas,* and that other Disciple…in their journey to *Emmaus*" (Luke 24:13–27).[72] Yet the "box" biography, unlike the "box" poems of *The Temple,* does not emblematize violent suffering, the intoxicating scents of a body smashed and broken. Nor does it press the paradox of the Incarnation, the confining of divinity within vulnerable flesh. Rather, by enclosing Herbert in a box, Walton undertakes to keep his earthly remains imperishable, sealed off from the corrupting air of religious controversy. Its sweet smells are not the odors of sacrifice but the preserving—and conserving—powers of biography itself.

The political, as opposed to the purely aesthetic, implications of this distinction can more easily be appreciated by considering another figure of containment, Milton's representation of the book as a "violl" in his prose work *Areopagitica* (1644): "For Books," declares Milton in these memorable lines, "are not absolutely dead things, but doe containe a potencie of life in them to be as active as that soule was whose progeny they are; nay they do preserve as in a violl the purest efficacie and extraction of that living intellect that bred them" (YP 2:492). As with Walton's "Alabaster box," so Milton's "violl" is presented as a repository or a receptacle of uncommon preservative power. But it is, rather, the differences between the box and the vial that bespeak the radically different contents and conceptualizations of public knowledge that each imagines. Milton's "violl" powerfully elides the distinction between the discursive agency of the living and the dead, endowing books with a superlative, even a liberated, form of the potency and personality of their parent author. Books can still act in all the ways that humans do in this Miltonic world of continuing heroic possibility: "I know," he continues, "they are as lively, and as vigorously productive, as those fabulous Dragons teeth; and being sown up and down, may chance to spring up armed men." (YP 2: 492). By invoking the story of Cadmus, who watches as the dragon's teeth he has planted become fighting warriors, Milton emphasizes the militant power, as well as the political and revolutionary violence, that books are able to incite.

Walton's alabaster box, by contrast, derives its creative intensity from the very distinction that Milton's vial strives to overcome. Its powers represent not a life-giving exemption but an irrevocable confirmation, deadening the dead by salving and decorating them, preserving them exquisitely for their postmortem lives as Anglican saints. These powers encode a biographical poetics at the summons of political occasion. And yet they offer a more expansive understanding of the political than the conformity and toleration debates of the Restoration allow us to see. Through their evocation of a quieter, simpler, and more traditional way of life, their depiction of unsung servants, disengaged from the divisive politics of the day but prepared to stand in resistance to radical change, Walton's lives reach out to and strive to cultivate what we might call the "silent public sphere." Here, we might say, the dead are enshrined so as to reappear in public not as political *agents* capable of advancing their own polemical urgency but as *patients* of a depoliticizing, and so repoliticizing, biographical discourse.

CHAPTER THREE

THE LIFE IN MINIATURE

JOHN AUBREY AND
THE ART OF ABBREVIATION

HAVING DESCRIBED THE splendor of Philip Sidney's funeral procession through the London streets to Saint Paul's in 1587, John Aubrey concludes his life of the Elizabethan courtier, poet, and military hero with a personal memory of the procession's reenactment, dating from his own childhood in 1635:

> When I was a boy 9 yeares old, I was with my father at one Mr. Singletons an Alderman and Wollen-draper in Glocester, who had in his parlour over the Chimney, the whole description of the Funerall engraved and printed on papers pasted together, which at length was I beleeve the length of the roome at least. but he had contrived it to be turned up on two pinnes that turning one of them made the figures march all in order. It did make such a strong impression on my young tender phantasy, that I remember it as if it were but yesterday. I could never see it elswhere. The house is in the great long street over against the high steeple. and 'tis likely it remaines there still: 'tis pitty 'tis not re-donne.[1]

The nine-year-old Aubrey was looking at what might best be described as a souvenir program for Sidney's funeral — a 38-foot roll made up of 30 engraved plates, depicting 344 figures walking two by two, some identified by name, others summed by number, some with heads covered and bowed like the stone mourners of medieval tomb sculptures, others with heads raised and turned around to speak with those following on in the cortege behind (fig. 3).[2] Thanks to Mr. Singleton's mechanical contrivance, the child

Fig. 3. Thomas Lant, *Sequitur celebritas & pompa funeris* (1588), plates 6, 7, and 16, engraved by Theodor de Brii. By permisson of the Folger Shakespeare Library.

Aubrey was able to imagine himself among the Elizabethan crowd that lined the streets to watch the procession pass by on a February day in 1587, a fixed viewpoint across which the mourners would have paraded as though across time itself.

Sidney's funeral procession is staged multiple times in this fabled scene: in the London streets, within the pages of the printed roll, and on the walls of a Gloucestershire parlor room. In this last and latest staging, the engraved figures parade within an interior space the geographical coordinates of which are not imperial or metropolitan but, rather, parochial and domestic: adjectives of scale — "great," "long," "high" — apply to the everyday world of street and steeple rather than to the magical properties of sword and shield. Aubrey's nostalgia is all for the lost simulacrum, not for the original event, a heroic age replicable through mechanical design. His sense of dispossession appears the keener not simply for a clarity of recollection ("I remember it as if it were but yesterday") but for his wishful conjecture that the decoration may yet exist intact in the sanctum of the parlor interior. "'Tis likely it remains there still," he writes, where "still" captures the idea of the parade as unmoved but also unmoving, waiting for another hand to turn the pin and set its figures on the march once more.

This brief episode, annexed to Aubrey's longer, but still comparatively short, life of Sidney, lends itself to a number of interpretations. It is, perhaps foremost, a memory of boyhood, that age of "young tender phantasy," distanced and of diminutive scale but also preserved against change, existing just as it always had. Personal memory broadens readily into historical allegory. The funeral parade is not merely a mechanical toy but a metonym for the English nation in the decade before the civil wars, a social and political elite numbered, united, and marching in one direction. Aubrey was fond of dating all kinds of lost worlds, including those of oral memory, folktale, and fireside storytelling, to a sepia 1630s.[3] This perfect picture of England offers itself as an exercise in miniaturization. Its presiding artist figure is not the great national hero, the soldier-poet Sidney, nor even the child Aubrey, the future biographer, but Mr. Singleton, an alderman and, like Izaak Walton, a linen draper, who by dint of his manual craftsmanship is able to fit the legendary parade of Elizabethan heroes inside the modest dimensions of his parlor room. His home production offers itself as a paradigm for Aubrey's biographical project in the making, for Aubrey, too, is crafting human subjects on small scales and as component parts of some larger, comprehensible whole. "'Tis pitty 'tis not re-donne" regrets the narrator Aubrey of Mr. Singleton's parlor parade, and the reader is surely meant to understand that it *is* being "re-donne": that, collectively, the "Brief Lives" are proposing themselves as just such a historical reenactment and feat of obsessive engineering, a world in miniature, but a world separated from its high political occasion and repurposed for the living space of the home.

Throughout this study, I have been arguing that it is in their apparent avoidance of politics that late seventeenth century lives are at their most actively political. Replacing arguments with human interest stories that prove more emotionally satisfying and easier to follow, biographical narratives perform their work of persuasion at a remove from the controversies they seek to influence. With Izaak Walton's lives as its focus, chapter 2 showed how the use of personal histories to launder political opinions might be understood both as a development simultaneous with the rise of a culture of public reason and as a populist reaction to it. In Walton's "silent public sphere," I suggested, it is the older, habitable — also imaginary — geographies of the parish and the riverbank that conserve the promise of a collective and quieter way of life. In this chapter, which examines Aubrey's book of lives, commonly known as his *Brief Lives,* I will again be concerned with the modest and more familiar knowledge that the biography holds in reserve, protecting it from rational examination or critical scrutiny. For Aubrey, however, the curation of this kind of knowledge, a knowledge that claims no public relevance and seeks no argument, does not propose a foundation for common living but celebrates dispersal, rather, of idiosyncratic and singular traits of character.

1

Aubrey worked up his *Brief Lives,* the majority no more than three or four paragraphs and the shortest just two words in length, between 1680 and 1692, after decades of lawsuits had forced him finally to sell his family estates in Wiltshire and Herefordshire and adopt a peripatetic lifestyle, evading creditors and staying with one friend after another in a succession of house visits that frequently involved humiliating errands and secretarial duties. By this time, too, he had already spent more than a decade as a fact finder and fact checker for his friend and fellow antiquarian Anthony Wood, a sometimes uneasy collaboration that began with their meeting in Oxford in 1667 and would end only with Wood's death in 1695. Aubrey's biographical researches contributed to Wood's history of Oxford colleges and buildings, the *Historia, et antiquitates universitatis Oxoniensis* (1674), and, much later, to his encyclopediac registry of Oxford-educated writers, clerics, and statesmen, the *Athenæ Oxonienses,* which filled two thick folio volumes when it was finally published in 1691–92. But starting in 1680, Aubrey felt moved to write up his biographical findings himself, a decision he describes to Wood in a series of cheerful, chatty letters running from late February to May of that year. Having arranged his notes on Thomas Hobbes into a narrative that "will be at least 8 sheetes," Aubrey reports how "it came into my mind Sunday last taking a pipe of tobacco in my chamber (my hand now being-in) to write my hon[oure]d friend Sir W. Petty's life."[4] What Aubrey sketches here are the rudiments of a practice we would now call authorized biography, writing the lives of men to whom he had close personal ties and upon whose cooperation he could depend. Almost immediately he began to enlarge his plans for a permanent repository of biographical information about public figures, akin to the repositories of objects and instruments for scientific study housed at Gresham College in London, host to the Royal Society, and, in Oxford, the recently erected Ashmolean Museum. By the end of February, Aubrey had embarked upon lives of Christopher Wren, Robert Hooke, John Pell, and Francis Bacon; by the end of March he had "made a Kalendar of 55 persons" about whom he planned to write, and toward which he had already contributed lives of Walter Raleigh, Edward Davenant, John Suckling, Edmund Waller, Thomas Randolph, William Camden, William Oughtred, and Lucius Carey, Lord Falkland; by the end of May he reports the completion of 66 lives, "a book of 2 q[uire]s close written," proud of, if not also a little taken aback by, his uncharacteristic productivity.[5]

These epistolary progress reports to Wood offer the best account of the rapidly expanding scope of Aubrey's scheme, from its initial focus on a small group of experimentalists — contemporaries and intimates of Aubrey from his undergraduate days at Oxford University in the early 1640s, from the London Interregnum circle of Samuel Hartlib in the 1650s, and from the

meetings of the Restoration Royal Society in the 1660s — to just about anyone he thought of public significance among his contemporaries and from the
century past. His approach opened biography to new professions and classes
of people: laborers, surveyors, merchants, mechanics, mathematicians, astrologer, instrument-makers, and craftsmen, who joined the ranks of the school-
men, poets, soldiers, and courtiers familiar from humanist lives and of the
saints, martyrs, and churchmen canonized in ecclesiastical ones. Subsequent
letters to Wood report new projects occurring within this broadened
remit. A tip-off from the actor John Lacy about William Beeston — theater
impresario and son of Christopher Beeston, Shakespeare's colleague in the
Lord Chamberlain's company and owner of the Phoenix playhouse in Drury
Lane — in September 1681 spurred plans to write the lives of the English
poets as a separate, stand-alone collection. "After the opiating quality of the
mince-pies is exhaled," writes Aubrey to Wood a few days before Christmas,
"I will begin with old Mr Beeston about the Lives of the Poets." Beeston's
death a few months later put this idea to rest, although he is cited as a source
in Aubrey's lives of Jonson, Shakespeare, Spenser, and John Suckling.[6] Of
Spenser, reports Aubrey, "Mr. Beeston says, he was a little man, wore short
haire. little band and little cuffs" (*Brief Lives,* 1:605). In his recent biography of the poet, Andrew Hadfield refers to this description as "not especially vivid or helpful," suggesting only that Spenser was "a man of modest
attire…not a flamboyant courtier."[7] Nonetheless, it is characteristic of the
kind of detail Aubrey was drawn to and that demands a particular kind of
attention from the reader, who must reach behind the disclaimer of reported
quotation — "Mr. Beeston says" — to encounter its wit and dramatic
instinct. Aubrey catches Spenser in a sort of sartorial self-sequestration,
a body confined at the wrist and throat. Furthermore, and by a kind of irresistible logic, the poet who boxes himself in also writes in boxes: "little band
and little cuffs" might equally be taken as describing the bounded form of the
Spenserian stanza, self-contained and syntactically shut up, ending invariably with a period. On the same slip of paper, Aubrey records an anecdote
from John Dryden of when the wainscoting was taken down in Spenser's
former bedchamber in Pembroke College, Cambridge, and an "abundance
of Cards" discovered behind it "with stanza's of the Faerie-Queen written on
them" (*Brief Lives,* 1:604–05). The hidden notecards offer further proof of

Spenser's secretive and self-denying personality: a metaphor for the closeted ego from which an entire epic would come.

Marked by laurel wreaths, some of which encircle a familial coat of arms, the English poets are grouped together at the end of the first manuscript volume of the *Lives*. A decade later, Aubrey embarked upon another project of group biography, an "Apparatus for the Lives of our English Mathematical Writers," modeled after Diogenes Laertius's *Lives of the Eminent Philosophers*, and influenced by Thomas Stanley's multivolume *History of Philosophy*, which came out serially in 1655, 1656, 1660, and 1662 before being reprinted in its entirety in 1687. "An Apparatus" was evidently conceived as a separate work, written on sixteen leaves of foolscap folio, paged and stitched together, its contents planned out in a list of names on the opening page (*Brief Lives*, 1:722–23).[8] It begins with another of Aubrey's chance encounters, this time not with a promising source like Beeston, but with an early printed book. "I did see many yeares since in a countrey-man's house a little booke in octavo in English, called *Arsmetrie*, or the art of Numbring, printed in an old black letter, about [the reign of] Henry 8. The authors name I doe not remember." An asterisk leads to a note in the margin, "quaere in Duck-lane" (*Brief Lives*, 1:725). There is no record of whether Aubrey's visit to the secondhand booksellers in Duck Lane turned up the missing name; certainly, he never went back, as he sometimes did, and emended the note.[9] The irrecoverable author, irrecoverable from history but also from the crannies and crevices of his own memory, is one of many losses that Aubrey records and which come to assume their own conjectural life within his manuscripts. Here the predicament seems at least partly playful: no "life" can begin without a name.

Aubrey's career is notorious for such unrealizable schemes, mislaid persons, and abortive projects. His inability to publish anything under his own name or bring anything to a finished state within his lifetime placed him under the exigency of scripting an editorial afterlife for his manuscripts, which he repeatedly and anxiously entrusted to Wood's keeping, sometimes without being entirely certain whose hands they were presently in.[10] The three bound volumes of lives that Aubrey did assemble are replete with gestures of draftiness: their pages an expressive confusion of blank spaces, rows of points, rules, Latin legalese, and shorthand notations — *vide, quaere, q., quot, inter nos* — abbreviations, interlineations, and crossings out. Wide margins play host to pointing hands, while coats of arms, family trees, horoscope charts, and line drawings divert the flow of words around them. Interleaved notes, written on pocketbook-sized slips of paper, might also be pinned or pasted in.

Biographical details are disposed in close proximity, but not generally in ways that spell out their logical connection. Take, for example, these preliminary particulars about the seventeenth century poet, parliamentary historian, and translator of Lucan, Thomas May (1599–1650): "a grand acq: of Tom. Chaloner. could when inter pocula) speake slightly of the Trinity. shammed. amicus. Sr Rich: Fenshawe. clap" (fig. 4).[11] Friendships, alehouse antitrinitarianism, a gulling (or disturbed gravesite), and a case of gonorrhoea. It is hard to imagine an assemblage more unexpected in its contents or more economical in its telling. The miscreant single words "shammed" and "clap" are held in a kind of paratactic quarantine, although the repeated sounds of *sham*med, *am*icus, and Fen*sh*awe suggests a continuous train of thought on the part of their transcriber, running, where by accident or by plan, straight through the period. A different leap of association can be made by consulting Aubrey's separate notes on Thomas Chaloner, which report his fondness for spreading false stories or "shams" around the law courts of Westminster Hall, returning at noon to discover how they had been distorted and embellished in his absence.[12] In the entry's running order, such credulousness follows immediately upon religious skepticism, a more dangerous error to which the freethinking — and free-speaking — May was evidently prone. Aubrey's handwriting is hard to decipher: "shammed" may instead be "shamed," a veiled reference to the public humiliation of May's corpse, dug up, along with those of 20 other people, from Westminster Abbey in January 1661 and thrown into a pit in a churchyard nearby.[13] Other details, too, presuppose a knowledge of recent history to which they don't directly refer. The two friends, the regicide Chaloner and the royalist Fanshawe stand separate, their proper names encapsulating the conflict of loyalties that May experienced on the eve of the civil war when he chose to join the parliamentary side.[14] A forward slash functions as a terminal punctuation mark, marking a short pause that consolidates these fragmentary details into a provisional grouping. Their words and phrases are not disposed entirely at random, but without an explicit narrative they remain intractable, each exercising a kind of sovereignty that extends no further than itself.

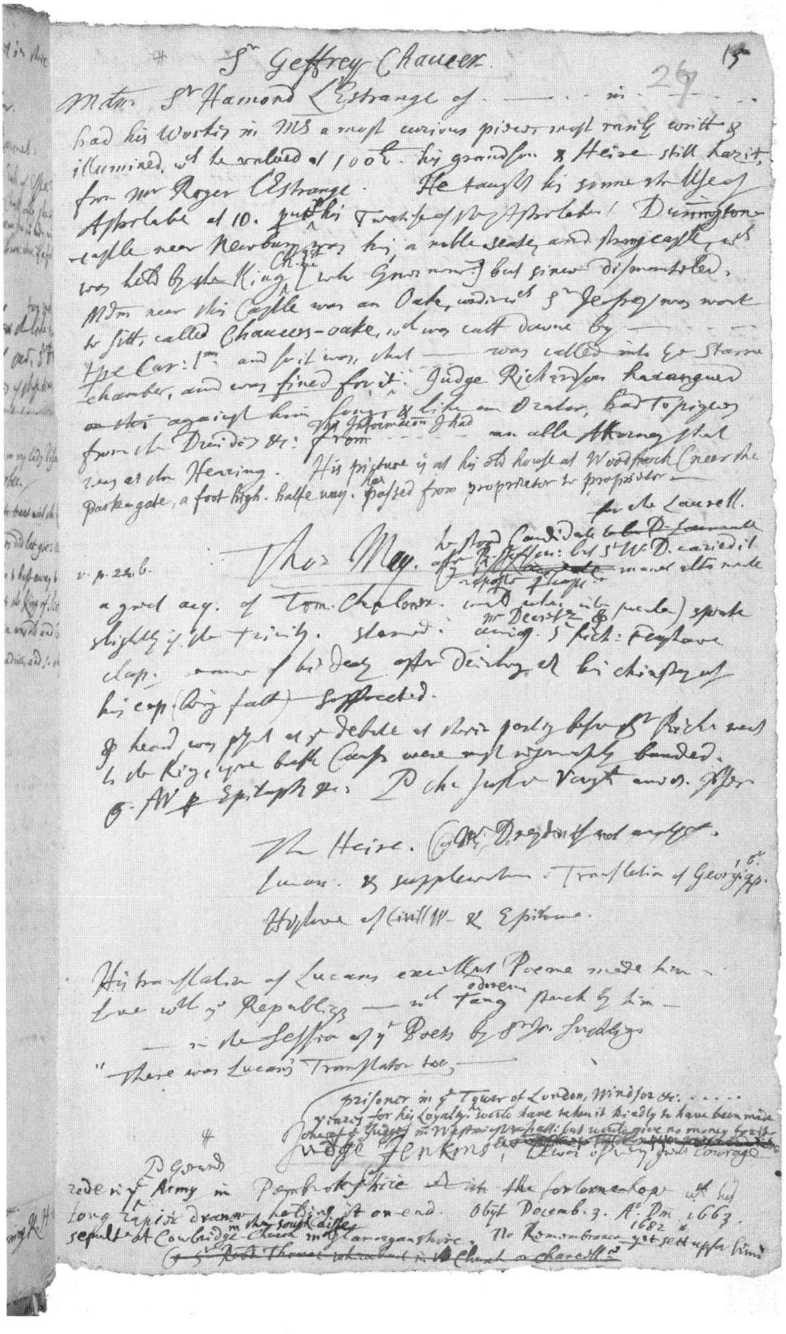

Fig. 4. MS. Aubrey 8, fol. 27r. Lives of Geoffrey Chaucer and Thomas May.
By permission of The Bodleian Libraries, The University of Oxford.

With this evidence, it is easy to see why scholars, even as they have mined Aubrey's biographical notes for their serviceable contents, have not been inclined to think of him as an especially careful or considered writer, only as a somewhat unreliable conduit between themselves and other early modern figures of prominence. Christopher Ricks, one of the few critics to have taken seriously the lives' stylistic effects, remarks that "Aubrey thrusts upon us the choice between apprehending his prose as genius or as ingeniousness," keeping the reader in a state of unsteady wonder, always prey to the suspicion that "he is imagining things."[15] The dilemma Ricks poses is preempted, although in no way removed, by Aubrey's characterization of the *Lives* as a miscellaneous production, their contents thrown together at different times according to the vagaries of their occasion. The first volume originally carried the Greek title (since worn away), Σχεδιάσματα, or "Schediasmata," meaning things made extempore, brought together hastily, suddenly, or on the spur of the moment (*Brief Lives,* 1:3).[16] Contingencies and emergencies, the unpredictability of encounter, the absence of premeditated design: these are all claimed by Aubrey here.

But in fact, and as Kate Bennett, Aubrey's most recent editor, has scrupulously shown, many of the lives in his manuscripts do possess a recognizable shape (fig. 5). It is clear that Aubrey was in the habit of planning out the organization of a life in advance, dividing up the page into fields or boxes to be filled in later: the name of the subject top and center; the manuscript foliation to its right; down the left, a wide margin for running notes. At the head of the margin, the outline of an escutcheon would be drawn; facing it on the right, or sometimes in the center, a blank horoscope diagram. Other spaces are left empty for epitaphs, memorial inscriptions, and lists of works to be transcribed. Bennett notes how these graphic arrangements constitute the earliest stage in Aubrey's process of composition, "a marking out, in terms of textual space, of the knowledge to be desired."[17] This method of specifying, by allocating space to, requisite information is replicated at the sentence level, where lacunae or rows of points reserve room for relevant details, typically a name or date, to be searched out and added later when found. Midway down the first page of the life of Milton, one of these skeleton sentences appears: "He was borne A.D.... the... day of... about... a clock in the..." (*Brief Lives,* 1:660). By giving prominence to certain kinds of information and assigning

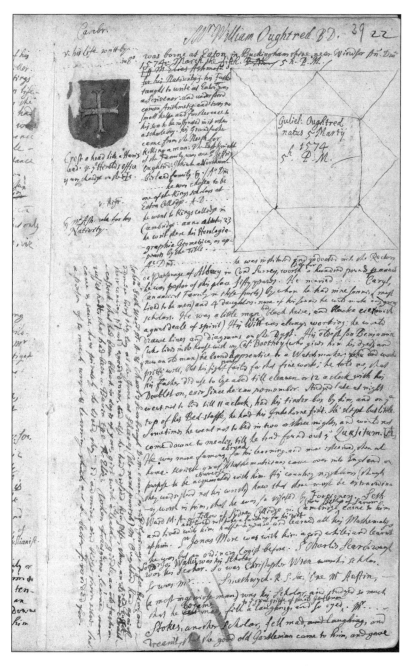

Fig. 5. MS. Aubrey 6, fol. 39r. The Life of William Oughtred. By permission of
The Bodleian Libraries, The University of Oxford.

a fixed place for them, Aubrey stabilizes (and, to an extent, standardizes) his biographical notes.

These aspects of Aubrey's preparation inform our understanding of his writing practice. They reveal how graphic features, such as the coat of arms and the horoscope chart, have taken over the role of connective grammar, building relations of hierarchy and subordination into the visible scaffolding of the manuscript page. They also make visible the ongoing tension between the page's articulated structure with its preset fields and classifications and the material to be fitted within it. Spillage is everywhere evident in Aubrey's manuscripts, making the organizational outline of a life most noticeable at the points at which it breaks down or is abandoned altogether. Reading them, one discovers how the ordering of information stimulates its increase, and not solely because empty spaces initiate a search for the facts to fill them. By spatializing the life, Aubrey escapes chronology but reifies wholeness, the total coverage toward which his incremental research aims.

Throughout his writings, Aubrey deploys a varied vocabulary for referring to his lives — "remarques," "observables," "memoranda," and "adversariis" (literally, things turned toward one; at hand) — but a term he uses consistently is "minutes," as in "these minutes," or "these minutes of lives." Related etymologically to the smallest denominations of creature or coinage ("mite"); related also to the partition of sound ("minim"), a "minute" is a rough copy of a document, typically delivered in a summary or abbreviated form. Its closest relation would be the memorandum or, further abbreviated, the memo, a note of something that needs to be remembered. Generically, the written form of the "minute" descends from the medieval *scriptura minuta,* or "small writing," a preliminary record of a legal document taken down by a scribe in tiny script, and from which a fair copy would later be engrossed, written up in a larger and more legible hand.[18] By the early modern period, minuting was predominantly an administrative practice, an economical way to bundle information, record transacted business, or issue a set of instructions. In this bureaucratic environment, considerations of size were superseded by those of number: the "minute" compressed information by using fewer words rather than writing those words out within a minimum of space, and with the aim of saving time as much as paper or cost. Yet despite these changing efficiencies, the function of the minute remained essentially the same: to store knowledge that was to be written up more expansively elsewhere. Its purpose was to preserve content in a form that made it available to other users, and it housed this content on a basis that was only ever temporary, no matter how far into the future this basis might extend. Minutes weren't authored because their contents weren't necessarily proprietary to their transcriber, who was often a servant or secretary, taking down notes by dictation.

The labor of minuting tended to be anonymous and perfunctory, but it might have also required judgment. Aubrey describes how Bacon would, when walking in the woods around Gorhambury Manor, have "his servant Mr Bushell attending him with his pen and inke horne to sett down his present Notions." His ambulatory cogitations proved more successful, however, when his secretary Thomas Hobbes accompanied him: "his Lordship would employ him often in this service whilest he was there, and was better pleased with his <u>Minutes</u>, or notes sett downe by him, then by others who did not well understand" (*Brief Lives*, 1:218). The underlining and capitalized "M" are Aubrey's, bestowing upon Hobbes's minutes the esteem that Bacon had declared them to deserve.

Both as a working method and as a technique for storing and transmitting information, minuting can be considered a practical choice for Aubrey, a form of writing that was occasional, haphazard, and cumulative, a building onto but also and just as often a crisscrossing back. Minuting enabled Aubrey to gather information piecemeal in discrete, small-sized notes that could be taken down in haste and transcribed later, a writing of shreds and snatches, but also a writing undertaken in real time and of empirical intensity. The temporality of the "minute," its ease and speed of composition, is also bound up with other economizing advantages. Designed to be written quickly, a "minute" can also be read quickly, scanned for information already pared down to its essentials. This made it easily extractable, a carrier of contents that had already been parceled out. This last advantage seems especially important for Aubrey who, as regularly as he entered biographical information into his folio manuscripts, retrieved it upon request, copying queries and answers into letters, hundreds of them for Wood.

Yet Aubrey's preference for the shorthand form of the minute was not solely practical, even if he adopted it for practical reasons. Rather, it enabled Aubrey to develop something like an experimental poetics, and a poetics

founded on a remarkable idea: that lives should not be told in epic proportions but in incremental bits and pieces. This turn to the small makes sense,
as many of the men Aubrey most admired were miniaturists, inventors and
practitioners of modes of working in little, including the experimental micro-
biologist Robert Hooke and the fashionable Restoration miniaturist Samuel
Cooper. Their observational craft and experiments with scale inform the
radical shrinkages and engrossments that Aubrey performs, often with satirical glee, upon his biographical subjects. A productive tension runs through
the lives between the low status of the minute, its transitory existence and
provisional completeness, and the high status of the miniature art form, its
refined technique and polished finish. These conflicting significations help to
account not only for the compositional method but for the bold premise of
Aubrey's lives: that it is information of modest dimension, information associated with intimacy and privacy and belonging to the ordinary and everyday
that is at once most minutable and, in time, most valuable.

We have seen how Aubrey uses the manuscript page to impose spatial
order upon the manifold events of a life, allotting room and opening searches
not for what actually happened but for particular bits of information he
has selected in advance to record. But we have seen, too, how minuting, as
a bureaucrat's way of gathering and storing information, is as much a technique for managing time as it is for managing space. The broader temporal
imperative of Aubrey's biographical labors is written into their common title,
"Brief Lives," where the adjective qualifies both senses of the noun — the life
as it is written and, more poignantly, the life as it is lived. It is the business
of the "minute" to take up as little time as possible because there is a limit
to the time we all have. In a time-bound world, the scribe cannot linger. In
order to capture, one is obliged to abbreviate. Yet the temporal discipline of
the "minute" has as much to do with its projected longevity as it does with
the fleeting moment of its composition. As a form of writing, the "minute" is
future oriented, preparing knowledge for its later consultation and use. For
Aubrey it is important that the afterlife of the "minute" not be one of fixed
or only retentive but of changing value. His minutes age, and their aging process is integral to his estimation of their worth. Aubrey planned carefully for
the maturation of his short-lived minutes, as we can see by considering the

way he speaks about them to his friend, antiquarian ally, and co-conspirator, Anthony Wood.

2

Aubrey was actively resistant to the idea that his lives might be printed during his own lifetime, fearing that he would be charged with seditious libel and, in particular, with partaking in *scandalum magnatum,* or the defamation of peers. Writing in late October 1688, just days before the landing of William's Anglo-Dutch fleet at Torbay and with anti-Catholic violence breaking out across England, Aubrey pleaded with Wood to deposit his manuscripts in the safety of the Ashmolean Museum, scared that they might be seized and destroyed or, potentially worse, seized and read: "you are lookt upon as a Papist, and in these tumultuous Times your papers will be searcht,...and so in leaving any thing in your hands, it would be a means to have them lost....And you knowe, that in my Memoranda of Lives there are some things that may make me obnoxious to Scandalum Magnatum, and have heretofore written a letter or two which I wish were turnd to ashes."[19] Even outside of these emergency conditions, Aubrey regarded his manuscript lives as part of a collecting culture, material objects to be examined under the closed conditions of friendship and mutual interest, rather than as part of a publicly circulating discourse. Sharing with Wood his intention to compose a life of William Petty — "which will be a fine thing, & which he shall peruse himselfe, & then it shall be left among your Papers, for Posterity to read (published)" — Aubrey invokes two different audiences: the indefinite audience of the future and the immediate audience whose extension is limited to just one person, the subject of the life.[20] What differentiates these two audiences is not simply their size, however, but the nature of their interaction with Aubrey's text. Posterity is invited to "read" a printed life; Petty to "peruse" its manuscript contents.

A founding member of the Royal Society, Aubrey was intimately familiar with its protocols for managing the process by which proper credit for an invention or discovery was adjudicated. Presentations of books and manuscripts took place almost every week and the Society responded by nominating members to conduct a more thorough examination of their contents and report back to a subsequent meeting. The term of choice for such acts of delegated reading was "perusal," a recurring word in the records collected by Thomas Birch for his *History of the Royal Society of London* (1756–57). The following entries are typical of its general usage:

> Mr. Boyle brought in some printed copies of a part of his *Experimental History of Cold*, with a desire, that they might be recommended to the perusal of some of the society, to collect from thence such experiments, as are there proposed and wished to be made, or such as were by him made but imperfectly. The president took one of them, and delivered the rest to Dr. Goddard, Dr. Merret, Dr. Whistler, Dr. Balle, and Mr. Hooke, upon condition to answer the end, for which they were presented by the author.

> Mr. Howard produced some observations on the second comet, as they were sent to him by his brother from Vienna; which were recommended to the perusal of Mr. Hooke.

> Mr. Hooke produced a Latin letter sent him from a Bohemian with a little book in the German tongue. The letter was ordered to be read at the next meeting, and the book to be delivered to Mr. Oldenburg, that he might peruse it, and give an account of it at the next meeting.[21]

As a verbal action, "to peruse" derives from the Anglo-Norman word *peruser,* to examine a person before a trial. The Royal Society's adoption of the term preserves a good deal of the original connotations of its use: the experimental scene of perusal is a form of trial in which evidence is submitted for examination in the expectation of a verdict. Perusal provided an opportunity for contributors to solicit practical support and funding for works-in-progress, such as the experiments Robert Boyle desired to see performed, or performed under better conditions, in order to test the conclusions of his *Experimental History of Cold,* already in print at the time of its presentation to the Society. For those whose credentials were less institutionally secure, it offered a peer review process that might lead to professional opportunities and endorsement; for the Society itself, it was a way of generating conversation and experimental activity as well as of establishing, regulating, and securing the production of new knowledge.[22] It is this specialized understanding of perusal as a reading practice kept private but directed to a public purpose that Aubrey imagines for his biographical manuscripts during his own lifetime.

The convention of perusal, or of a registered first reading, is invoked by Aubrey in a letter to Wood dated June 15, 1680, and accompanying the three folio manuscripts of lives that Aubrey was then ready to deliver into his keeping. Other letters address Wood on familiar, exclamatory, and even apostrophizing terms — "Dear Friend!," "My Singular good Friend!," "Kind Friend!," "Deare AW!," "Deare Anthony," "O Anthony!" — suggesting that Aubrey intended this one to assume the more formal function of a prefatory statement, telling the official story of his text.[23]

> To my worthy friend Mr. Anthonie à Wood Antiquarie of Oxford.
>
> Sir!
>
> I have according to your desire, putt in writing these Minutes of Lives, tumultuar-ily, as they occurr'd to my thoughts: or as occasionally I had information of them: they may easily be reduced into order at your lesiure by numbring them with red figures, according to time and place etc. 'Tis a Taske that I never thought to have undertaken, till you imposed it on me: sayeing that I was fitt for it, by reason of my generall acquaintance, having now not only lived above halfe a Centurie of yeares in the world, but have also been much tumbled up and downe in it; which hath made me much knowne: besides, the moderne advantage of Coffee-howses in this great Citie; before which, men knew not how to be acquainted, but with their owne Relations, or Societies. (*Brief Lives,* 1:37)

Richocheting off the adverb "tumultuarily," the opening of Aubrey's letter characterizes the compositional moment as one of alternate contingencies: the outcome of an unplanned encounter either with one's own thoughts or with those gleaned from other people.[24] In establishing his credentials for this sort of ad hoc collecting of intelligence, Aubrey praises the London coffeehouses for having taught men how to meet and mingle with people outside of their immediate social circle. This praise follows immediately upon his characterization of the "coffee-house" conditions of his own life, provid-ing an equivalent, if involuntary and more violent, version of these same pedagogical opportunities. The world was already Aubrey's coffeehouse, so he tells us, and he a veteran operator, if not also a tutelary spirit, of its haphazard social space. Here, as elsewhere in his manuscripts, Aubrey refers to his writings as "these Minutes of Lives," small forms that are now to be made smaller, "reduced into order," at the regulatory leisure of Wood's "red

figures," an invitation to ruthlessness that would be enthusiastically taken
up by Aubrey's Victorian editors. By imagining these editorial attentions,
Aubrey transforms Wood into a miniaturist, and in the strictest etymological sense. His rubrications have their roots in the Latin word *minium,* the red
pigment used to emphasize initial letters in a manuscript in order to catch the
eye and organize the reader's experience.[25] In the original division of labor
that the letter proposes, Aubrey's "tumbling" and Wood's "numbring" are
seen as separate, yet complementary activities.

Further into the letter, Aubrey imposes an additional editorial obligation
upon Wood, declaring a need not just for the abridgment but also for a more
drastic expurgation of his unruly biographical notes. The change of duty
produces a change of setting as the action moves from the coffeehouse to the
confessional:

> I here lay-downe to you (out of the conjunct friendship between us) the Trueth,
> the naked and plaine trueth (and as neer as I can, and that religiously as a Poenitent
> to his Confessor) nothing but the trueth: which is here exposed so bare, that the
> very <u>pudenda</u> are not h̶i̶d̶ covered, and affords many passages that would raise a
> Blush in a young G̶i̶r̶l̶e̶s̶ Virgins cheeke. So that after your perusall, I must desire
> you to make a Castration (as Raderus to Martial) and to sowe-on some Figge-
> leaves i.e. to be my Index expurgatorius. / (*Brief Lives* 1:38)

Aubrey's fondness for clarifying and dilatory parentheses ratchets up the
drama of these deposing sentences, interrupting the speech act of complete
surrender performed by the first and cutting into the punitive operation
enjoined by the second. He invokes the naked pudenda, (a term derived
from the Latin gerundive "pudendum" — that of which one ought to be
ashamed — and referring to the genitalia of either sex) as evidence of his full
and sincere confession, although it is the imagined reaction of an unseasoned
reader, not that of his confessor, that ends up claiming his attention.[26] Caught
unaware, the young virgin blushes, a body exposed by the exposure of bodies
not her own. Ostensibly, it is in order to prevent this blush that Aubrey calls
preemptively for his manuscript's dismemberment, demanding the cutting
off of what he admits to being a vicariously exhibitionist text. The last, and
appropriately the shortest, of Aubrey's parenthetical asides refers to the expur-
gated edition of Martial's epigrams prepared by the Jesuit Mathieu Rader
for use in grammar schools.[27] By invoking Martial as his literary precursor,
Aubrey likens his "Minutes of Lives" to an epigrammatic miscellany. Like the

epigram, the "Minute" can be of varying length and shape. Like the epigram, too, its permissive form raises questions of permissible content, holding in tension the causal, populist, and the throwaway, on the one hand, and the selective, scandalous, and thrillingly salacious on the other. After subjecting the lives to his own "perusal" or detailed examination, Wood is to serve as Aubrey's "Index expurgatorius," a list of passages to be removed from printed books promulgated by the post-Tridentine, Counter-Reformation papacy, and which, as Aubrey and Wood would both have known, the curators of the Bodleian Library had long been repurposing as acquisition guides for the theological holdings in their collection.[28] Schoolboyishly boastful, the series of mock solicitations with their prurient air of crypto-Catholic intrigue consolidate the closed coterie of two that constitutes the letter's governing fiction. Aubrey has crafted a confessional in which to disclose not his own but other people's secrets.

In closing, Aubrey's letter returns to the theme of hidden mysteries: "These arcana are not fitt to lett flie abroad now, till about 30 yeares hence: for the author and the Persons (like Medlars) ought to be first rotten" (*Brief Lives,* 1:39). The comparison of decomposing corpses to medlars, brown-skinned apples that have to be left to rot before they are ready to be eaten, occurred later to Aubrey and is marked by a caret in the manuscript. His simile might equally be applied to the information he has gathered, for the timing of its release is complicated by how time has acted upon it, an action measured dramatically by the breadth of time his letter takes to read. Facts, too, become tastier when they are put aside for a while. The letter's overarching comparison is between what Aubrey now refers to as "these arcana," secrets too volatile to permit their release from the coffined container of his manuscripts, and what he had earlier referred to as "these Minutes," contents instantly apprehended, plucked "tumultuarily" out of the air of a promiscuous public discourse. Information so received is, by the letter's end, unsuitable to be released. What were "Minutes" are now "arcana," both by virtue of their concealment and by virtue of their remaining exactly what they are, were, and had always been. Put another way, Aubrey's instinct is not to discover information but to cover it. The letter performs a sort of reverse striptease whose excitement has all to do with what is first available and then taken out of view. To be sure, Aubrey's manuscript notes did contain what had to have been publicly sensitive and unsanctioned information:

allegations, accusations, affiliations, and assignations of various kinds, and of political, religious, sexual, scientific, and financial significance. But in the vast majority of instances, the assembled "arcana" that make up these lives are comprised of something in addition to the hidden mysteries whose revelation makes apparent a sacramental or mystically charged truth. Much more radically, the arcana of Aubrey's lives consist, rather, in the overlooked and the commonplace, the objects of a kind of knowledge that had never before been recognizable *as* knowledge, unless the facts were gathered as the subject of secretive interest. That it is the things we don't think to conceal that incriminate, and so individuate, us is the organizing principle of Aubrey's esoterica of the everyday. This bold celebration of the quotidian facts about the men and occasionally women whose stories Aubrey relates is fully in evidence in one of the most ambitious of his lives, an abbreviated biography instructive less for its influence on what scholars know than for its influence on what scholars have powerfully desired to know about its notorious subject, the poet John Milton.

3

In 1932, Helen Darbishire published her influential scholarly edition of *The Early Lives of Milton*.[29] Darbishire gathered together six lives, two in manuscript and four in print. All were written by contemporaries of Milton who either knew him or had access to people who knew him: his nephew Edward Phillips, his pupil Cyriack Skinner (identified by Darbishire as John Phillips, brother of Edward), the Whig propagandist John Toland, the early eighteenth century editor of *Paradise Lost* Jonathan Richardson, and the two friends, antiquarians, and biographers, Aubrey and Wood. Darbishire broke new ground in her meticulous transcription of many of the typographical features of Aubrey's manuscript pages, reproducing them as faithfully as she could on the printed page. She also attempted to recreate the sequence in which Aubrey originally composed his notes, explaining how he filled up all four sides of one folio sheet before moving onto a second and then a third, which were later folded and bound into the first. This respect for the local idiosyncrasies of Aubrey's research runs athwart the overarching aim of her edition, however, which was to bring the early lives of Milton to greater critical notice by assembling and presenting them together as a canonical grouping. To that end, she emphasized the clear filiations among the lives, the topics they shared, and the ways in which they borrowed from and reinforced one another. Thus homogenized, the early lives came to constitute a set of common biographical "truths," familiar to Miltonists, but seldom parsed out to the particular life in which they first appeared. The Milton that emerges from their conflation is predominantly political and polemical, responsive, as Thomas Corns has shown, to earlier hostile representations of Milton, and, perhaps more powerfully still, to Milton's own vaunting and combative self-representations.[30] Yet there is little ground of commensuration between this public political Milton, a product of the ideological clashes of the English civil wars and, later, of the Glorious Revolution, and the more private Milton whose daily habits, household inmates, unwelcome visitors, and familial relations are laid before us in Aubrey's manuscript notes.

Aubrey had probably been introduced to Milton at the Pall Mall house of Lady Katherine Ranelagh, the favorite sister of Robert Boyle, whose son Richard became a pupil of Milton's in 1652. Certainly, Milton and Aubrey frequented the same intellectual circles during the 1650s and were on friendly terms with many of the same people, including the Boyles, but also Samuel Hartlib, William Petty, and Seth Ward. Aubrey was also acquainted with Cyriack Skinner, another of Milton's early biographers, from the meetings of the Rota Club, the republican debating society convened by James Harrington in 1659–60.[31] "He was scarce so tall as I am," writes Aubrey of Milton, adding in the space above a pointing manicule: "Q[uaere] quot feet I am high," and in the space above that, "Resp[onsum] of middle stature" (*Brief Lives,* 1:661).[32] This description offers the likeliest proof that Aubrey had, in fact, met Milton and taken the opportunity to size him up directly. It makes manifest Aubrey's extraordinary personalization of the biographical fact, here accentuated by the tense shift from Milton's past life to his own, fact-checkable present one. Forwarding a view of biography as an observational art, Aubrey inserts himself as the observer, but an observer who, and here in a literal sense, becomes the measure of the man he is observing. We have never seen the poet Milton in quite this way before because we have never seen him through Aubrey's perspective, eye to eye.

In reporting Milton's life, Aubrey leaned heavily upon the testimony of family members: the poet's brother, Christopher Milton; his nephew Edward Phillips (in whose hand appears a list of Milton's writings and a curriculum of study for his pupils, of which he himself was one); and, in particular, Milton's third wife and young widow, Elizabeth Minshull. Aubrey was adept at squeezing information out of widows, and his indefatigable tracking down of mothers, servants, wives, and daughters suggests that he moved comfortably within a world of female sociability, perhaps because he, too, came to live the life, and perform the unrecognized and subsidized labor, of a poor relation or household dependent. An interlineation identifies Minshull by name (elsewhere she is referred to generally as "his widowe" or the Latinate "vidua"), characterizing her as "a gent. person a peacefull and agreeable humour," strong evidence of her ready compliance with Aubrey's requests for information (*Brief Lives,* 1:662, 664). Aubrey's relations with widows could be a lot more fraught than this. For although he sought imaginatively to occupy the widow's subject position, he often did so competitively and with the intention of supplanting her domestic prerogatives, including her customary right to dispose of the household moveables after her husband's death. The rivalrous resemblance between biographer and widow is illustrated by the unfortunate fate of Charles Cavendish's prized collection of mathematical manuscripts. Aubrey estimates their value by their bulk, "as many…bookes, as filled a Hoggeshead," reporting with indignation how they were sold "by weight to the past-board makers for Wast-paper" by the widow of Cavendish's legal executor, who himself died soon after (*Brief Lives,* 1:90). It is Aubrey, however, who first makes the manuscript books vulnerable to economic calculation, converting them into a household commodity, the equivalent of the wine or oil or of the corn, tobacco, or sugar that would more typically be stored in a large cask or "Hoggeshead," and sold at a bulk rate. His housekeeping imitates even as it indicts the widow's own.

In the inventory of domestic goods that "the late Mrs. Elizabeth Milton" left at her death in 1727 appear at least two items that she had shown to Aubrey close to half a century before: "Mr Miltons Pictures & Coat of Arms" (£10 10s) and "1 Large Bible" (8s).[33] Aubrey makes mention of the pictures in his manuscript notes, using the first to date the poetic calling of the child Milton, "A. D. 1619, he was ten yeares old, as by his picture: & was then a Poet"; the second to urge its superior likeness over the engraved portrait frontispiece of the 1645 *Poems,* "His widowe haz his picture drawne very well and like when a Cambridge-schollar, which ought to be engraven; for the

Pictures before his bookes are not <u>at</u> <u>all</u> like him" (*Brief Lives,* 1:660, 662). But it is the large family Bible that truly stimulates his biographical imagination. Here he found the crucial information of the poet's date, day, and hour of birth: "John Milton was born the 9th of december 1608 die veneris half an howr after six the morning" (1:670) The entry, copied verbatim from the bible's flyleaf in an unknown hand, identified by Darbishire as Minshull's, cost Aubrey considerable effort and its achievement constitutes its own minor plotline running through his notes. We saw earlier how he used ellipses to write a skeleton sentence, announcing the information he still needed. Later and in a different place he drew a manicule, writing alongside it, "quære Mr Christopher Milton to see the date of his Brothers Birth" (1:668).

For Aubrey, the date of birth mattered so badly because a horoscope could not accurately be cast without one. He had begun collecting the horoscopes or "genitures" of famous men in the early 1670s, and he continued the practice with his lives, many of which are written around horoscope charts, a miniature, and diagrammatic, form of biography in their own right. Elias Ashmole was a close friend of Aubrey's and one of the foremost copiers and collectors of genitures. Among those in his collection is one cast of "M^r. John Milton. Authour of Iconoclasses" by the astrologer John Gadbury, a specialist producer of the celebrity horoscopes that enthusiasts like Ashmole and Aubrey would exchange, collect, and copy into their notebooks.[34] Astrological fact-finding, the binding of a life history to heavenly cycles, motions, and alignment, is no longer a preoccupation of biographical studies. Still, the astral drama that Aubrey took seriously as an object of study is theoretically resituated and recurrent in William Kerrigan's seminal psychobiographical study, *The Sacred Complex: On the Psychogenesis of Paradise Lost,* in which sidereal determinations are replaced by psychic ones departing from the same evidentiary basis — a record of the poet's nativity. Reading the births and deaths inscribed in the Milton family Bible, Kerrigan notes how "the creations proceed down the page under the influence of a prior history — an unmentioned mother and a father who need not be mentioned, since to name the son is to name him."[35] The "unmentioned mother" returns in Kerrigan's later excursus on the "lethal gift," which, Milton was to learn, had also "been inserted into his beginning." Kerrigan quotes Aubrey: "His father read without spectacles at 84. His mother had very weak eyes, and used spectacles presently after she was thirty years old."[36] Here Kerrigan, too, proceeds under the influence of a prior history; his study of psychogenesis reinterpreting at its moment of inception the investigative rubric of Aubrey's manuscript notes.

A fruitful life to juxtapose to Milton's is that of Sir Thomas Morgan (1604–79), a mercenary soldier of fortune whose public profile made him an ideal subject for exactly the genre of biography — that of the statesman or military general — that Aubrey can generally be seen to disrupt or disintegrate. As a young man, Morgan had fought in the various European theaters of the Thirty Years' War before returning to England and rising through the ranks of the parliamentary army under the patronage of Lord Fairfax. Appointed second-in-command to George Monck, Morgan took part in the commonwealth invasion of Scotland under Cromwell in 1651, once again rising under his new military patron to the rank of major-general. In 1659, after a further interval of fighting in Europe, Morgan marched north to rejoin Monck, holding Scotland for him when Monck marched south to London early in 1660. Morgan was rewarded with a baronetcy for his part in securing the restoration of the Stuart monarchy; at his death he held land in four counties, including a considerable estate in Herefordshire.

Very little of this biographical history is related in Aubrey's cursory life, however, which is mostly taken up with the report of an encounter some two years prior to the Restoration after Morgan had taken part in the successful seizure of Dunkirk from the Spanish by a combined Anglo-French expeditionary force:

> Sir John Lenthall told me, that at the Taking of Dunkyrke Marshall Turenne, and (I thinke Cardinall Mezarine too) had a great mind to see this famous Warrior; they gave him a visitt, and wheras they thought to have found an Achillean or gigantique person, they sawe a little man, not many degrees above a dwarfe, sitting in a hutt of Turves, with his fellowe soldiers, smoaking in a pipe about 3 inches, or neer so long. with a green hatt-case on. he spake with a very exile tone, and out cry-out to the soldiers, when angry with them, Sirrah, I'le cleave your Skull. as if the wordes had been prolated by an Eunuch. (*Brief Lives,* 1:543–44)

Aubrey's retelling displays an exaggerated concern for accurate measurement: Morgan is "not many degrees above a dwarfe"; his pipe is "about 3 inches, or neer so long." This reduction in scale corresponds in turn to the deflation of the French dignitaries: it is their "great mind" that is set in pointed contrast to the "little man" whom they in fact encounter; their imaginative enlargement that is cut dismayingly down to size. The adjective "Achillean" adds a literary dimension to the Frenchmen's act of erroneous aggrandizement, situating the encounter within the field of epic and of mock-epic whose denigrations often depend upon such moments of literal belittlement. Read within these conventions, Morgan's off-duty pipe and "green hatt-case" propose themselves as homely and nonsensical substitutions for the arms of the epic hero — the ash spear "weighty, long, and tough," and "great helm" of Achilles whose divine properties and provenance are meticulously inventoried in the arming scene of *Iliad* 19.[37]

Aubrey's overt dwelling on the little and the low achieves the opposite effect from Milton's description of Satan's spear in book 1 of *Paradise Lost*: "His spear, to equal which the tallest pine / Hewn on Norwegian hills, to be the mast / Of some great ammiral, were but a wand, / He walked with to support uneasy steps" (1.292–95). These lines, too, depend for their satirical effect upon the thwarted expectations and exertions of the perceiver, yoking objects together in mismatched comparison. In what is still the best reading of them, Stanley Fish points out how the reader cannot help but be fooled by the principle of equivalence established at the outset and appearing to govern the set of correspondences that follow, so that spear and mast are taken to be first of the same monumental and then of the same diminutive size.[38] Something of the deconstructive quality of this passage, although not its complex operations upon the reader, is present in Aubrey's overscrupulous measurement of Morgan's pipe, a pipe that really is "but a" pipe even upon a second reading. Milton's simile plays with the possibility of belittling Satan before allowing him to become unimaginably large once more in the reader's overstretched imagination. Aubrey, by contrast, does not shrink or enlarge Morgan, whose littleness is simply and irredeemably life-sized.

The Frenchmen's visit to Morgan's turf hut rewrites the visit of the Achaean heralds to Achilles, also seated outside his hut, in the first book of the *Iliad* (1.380–404). Like Achilles, like Thersites, too, his other Homeric double, Morgan is angry, displaying an irascibility that becomes the last redoubt of the heroic personality the French commanders had hoped to meet in their epic sightseeing. His reported brag (each word underlined separately as though for greater emphasis), "<u>Sirrah</u>, <u>I'le</u> <u>cleave</u> <u>your</u> <u>skull</u>," combines heroic grandeur and colloquial impatience, offering a comic mishmash of high and low. The verb "cleave" evokes the actions of Malory's Arthurian knights slaughtering their foes or, indeed, those of Gabriel smiting Moloch during the feudal war in heaven in *Paradise Lost* who "anon / Down clov'n to the waste, with shattered arms / And uncouth pain fled bellowing" (6:360–62), while "Sirrah" recalls the coarse language of the Tudor tavern, a contemptuous address to inferiors as the renowned warrior threatens to start murdering members of his own side. With all this, the closing detail is almost too much to take. Emasculating Morgan in one final rhetorical sweep, Aubrey reaches for the Latinate verb "prolate," to lengthen or elongate a word or syllable, at the very moment he is about to cut Morgan off. Aubrey's devastating comparison operates on the opposite end of the body to Morgan's completing his performance of the demise of the military man of fortune, first into smallness and then into sterility. Here, writ small and made smaller, is a history of the English civil wars and Restoration.

Aubrey's satirical belittlement of Morgan shows him playing self-consciously with epic and mock-epic and missed-epic effects. Such experiments with scale are recurrent through his biographical writings, overcharging and enlarging, on the one hand, reducing and diminishing, on the other. The changes of perspective further accentuate the incommensurability of the lives themselves, which, despite Aubrey's gestures toward a totalizing system, remain a loose assemblage and reward distracted reading. By moving in and out of focus, the lives also bespeak their situatedness in a culture given to sustained reflection on questions of optics and visual perspective. Aubrey was himself convivial with many of the figures in Restoration London most central to these aspects of the scientific revolution and to the artistic world that intersected with it. He was an acquaintance of the King's Limner, Samuel Cooper; an admirer since boyhood of the philosopher Thomas Hobbes; and a friend to the greatest and most illustrious lens man of the century, Robert Hooke.

4

The rapturous reception of Robert Hooke's *Micrographia; or, Some physiological descriptions of minute bodies made by magnifying glasses* (1665) turned its cast of insects into overnight celebrities, captured in a series of engraved, fold-out plates that opened to two or four times the size of the regular folio page. In the classical epic tradition, insects are social creatures, members of a hive or swarm or heap whose natural order offers a model for cooperative human relations. Hooke's insects, by contrast, are solitary specimens set against a blank background, the possessive individuals of the liberal-democratic state. In the prose descriptions that accompany his drawings, Hooke playfully humanizes his insects, introducing each one as though it were an entry in a volume of "characters," one of the most popular literary forms of the seventeenth century.[39] The louse, for example, conforms to the character type of the career politician: "This is a Creature so officious, that 'twill be known to every one at one time or other, so busie, and so impudent, that it will be intruding it self in every ones company, and so proud and aspiring withall, that it fears not to trample on the best, and affects nothing so much as a Crown." With the pun on crown, referring both to sovereign authority and to the human scalp, the insect's preferred feeding ground, Hooke portrays the louse as a political pretender, a tireless assailant who "will never be quiet till it has drawn blood."[40]

The most striking feature of Hooke's engraving of the louse is the single strand of hair clasped in the curled claws of its forelegs, a reminder of its absent human host (fig. 5). The strand cuts diagonally in front of the exposed underside of the insect, establishing the drawing's scale. Behind it, we are offered a view of the inside of the louse's transparent body freighted with its cargo of human blood. In his verse satire, *The Last Instructions to a Painter* (1667), Marvell transforms this magnified hair into the statesman's staff of office, a prop or accessory item intended for show but paraded as though for combat. "With Hooke then, through the microscope, take aim," he instructs, weaponizing the experimenter's instrument so as to bring his political enemy Thomas Clifford into focus under its lens. In the aperture's bright circle, Clifford is isolated and delivered up to derision: "all men laugh / To see a tall louse brandish the white staff" (16–18). As in the world of men, so in the world of insects, being the tallest of the smallest remains a matter of distinction.[41] In Hooke's drawing, the louse is shown vertically, as though standing upright. No longer a creeping thing, but a figure of self-importance, he looks the same as any other aspiring public official who pays to sit for his portrait.

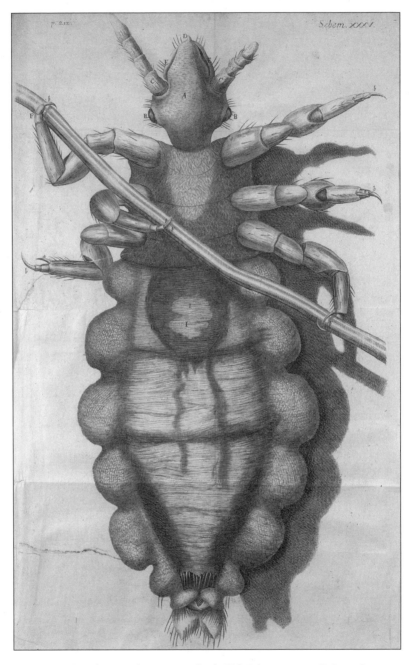

Fig. 6. Robert Hooke, *Micrographia* (1667), Schematic xxxv, "A Louse."
By permisson of the Folger Shakespeare Library.

In his inventorying of the features of his insect specimens in *Micrographia,* Hooke devotes considerable attention to describing their eyes, marked on his drawings by the letter *B.* Describing the louse, Hooke notes its "two black shining goggle eyes BB," observing not just their protuberance but their unusual placement, "where other Creatures ears stand," on the side of the head. Describing the shepherd spider, he observes "the curious contrivance of his eyes, of which (differing from most other Spiders) he has onely two, and those plac'd upon the top of a small pillar or hillock...BB, placed back to back." Most spectacularly, Hooke reports cutting off the head of a gray drone fly and positioning it face upward so as to observe its "clusters of eyes." In the representation of this view, the fly stares out at the reader, surrounded by an aureole of hatched shadows that approximate the microscope's circular aperture.[42] Aubrey, too, is drawn to describing the eyes of his subjects, which are typically referred to in the singular, as though disembodied and fixed on the microscope's object plate. Of Francis Bacon, he reports two competing observations: "He had a delicate, lively hazel Eie" is the assessment of Thomas Hobbes, while "Dr. Harvey told me it was like the Eie of a Viper" (*Brief Lives,* 1:210). James Harrington has a "quick-hott-fiery hazell-Eie" (1:322), the hyphenation replicating the switches of the eye's rapid movement. Of Hobbes, "He a good Eie, and that of a hazell colour...when he was earnest in discourse, there shone (as it were) a bright live-coale within it."[43] Of the Cavalier poet, John Denham: "His Eie was of a kind of light goose-gray; not big: but it had a strange piercingness, not as to shining and glory, but like a Momus) when he conversed with you, he lookt into your very thoughts" (1:351). Aubrey proceeds cautiously, by qualification and elaboration, as though anticipating the moment when Denham's keen eye will be turned back on him. He likens the poet to the Olympian God of scandal and censure, a Momus-scope as opposed to a microscope. Denham's perspicacity may be especially intimidating, but all the eyes that Aubrey describes are unnervingly active, performing the drama of intellection in a kind of uncomfortable close-up.

Aubrey's friendship with Hooke was close and enduring. After the loss of his estates, he frequently stayed with Hooke in London, and he used Hooke's rooms in Gresham College as a forwarding address for his letters. The *Brief Lives* include an affectionate life of Hooke, which, as William Poole has pointed out, seems intended to function at least in part as an endorsement of Hooke's claim in intellectual property disputes involving other experimentalists, most notably in his long-running quarrel with Isaac Newton over the mathematical laws of gravitation.[44] The narrative thread of Aubrey's notes begins with Hooke's boyhood meeting of the portrait miniaturist, John Hoskins:

> At…yeares old John Hoskyns the Painter being at Freshwater to drawe pictures for…Esq, Mr Hooke observed what he did and thought he, why cannot I doe so too? so he getts him Chalke, and Ruddle, and coale, and grinds them, and putts them on a Trencher, gott a pencill and to worke he went, and made a picture; then he copied (as they hung up in the parlour) the Pictures there, which he made like. Also he being a boy there at Freshwater, he made an…..Diall on a round trencher: never having had any instruction. His father was not Mathematicall at all. (*Brief Lives,* 1:96–97; ellipses are Aubrey's)

By close observation, and through a kind of innate resourcefulness, the child Hooke is able to manufacture the painter's colors and pigments and copy his techniques, mastering with naïve facility the art of portraiture. A second anecdote sees him fashion a timepiece out of a trencher, the same domestic utensil that had served him as a makeshift artist's palate.[45] Aubrey's notes follow Hooke to London where his vagrant existence as an autodidact continues. Apprenticed both to the fashionable portraitist Peter Lely and to the miniaturist Samuel Cooper, he soon recognizes that he needs no masters, only more introductions and opportunities. The next episode in this intellectual picaresque finds him lodging with Mr. Busby, the master of Westminster school, where "he learnd to play 20 lessons on the Organ" and "invented thirty severall wayes of Flying." Also, "in one weekes time ~~was master~~ made him selfe master of the first VI Bookes of Euclid" (1:97).

Aubrey's correction to this last of Hooke's achievements is telling, insisting as it does on the reflexive, self-assertive nature of his mathematical learning. Equally telling, perhaps, is the shift from narrating to quantifying — 20 lessons, 30 ways, 6 books — Hooke's hyperbolic, maniacal accomplishments. But it is the connections that Aubrey draws between Hooke's restless experimentalism and his apprenticeships in the portrait studios of Lely and, especially, of Cooper that are of most interest here. Aubrey gives Cooper the title of "Prince of Limners of this Age" (*Brief Lives,* 1:97), an epithet attached to his name whenever it appears in his biographical notes.

Cooper does not receive a life of his own, although he makes guest appearances in those of Petty, Samuel Butler, and Thomas Hobbes, an itinerant artist figure and, in a sense, a stand-in for Aubrey himself.[46]

Richard Wendorf has pursued the comparison between Aubrey and Cooper, noting how the "naturalist effects" of Aubrey's unfinished lives have much in common with those produced by Cooper's unfinished studio sketches.[47] Unlike his finished miniatures, which might require as many as eight separate sittings, Cooper's sketches were drawn from life in a single session. They tended to be larger than the miniature's standard oval, which, by the middle of the seventeenth century had already increased in size to nearly three and a half inches and focused more closely around the subject's face. After his death in 1672, Cooper's sketches sold for considerably more than the worked-up miniatures derived from them, evidence, according to John Murdoch, that "Cooper and seventeenth-century connoisseurship were elevating the sketch to a special status…attributing to it a kind of authenticity that came from its qualities of speed, instinctive comprehension, and lack of labor or afterthought."[48] Wendorf calls attention to the way in which Aubrey's jottings might similarly be thought of as written in a "sketch style," a performance of expressive mastery of and in the moment. By this account, Aubrey's compositions are at their most stylized wherever they appear most careless, participating in a broader cultural shift in representational markets and tastes.

Aubrey's commitment to direct experience and the kinds of stylistic accommodations that might be made to it receives a different kind of confirmation in the fate of an anecdote about Hobbes's passion for birding while he was an undergraduate at Oxford. The anecdote reads as follows:

> At Oxford Mr Thomas Hobbes used in the summertime especially to rise very early in the morning, and would tye the Leaden Counters (which they used in those dayes at Christmas, at Post and Payre) with packthreds, which he did besmere with birdlime, and bayte them with parings of cheese and the Jack dawes would spye them a vast distance up in the aire,* and as far as Osney-abbey, and strike at the bayte, and so be harled in string which the wayte of the Counter would make cling about ther wings.
>
>   * This story he happened to tell me, discoursing of the Optiques, to instance such sharpnes of Sight in so little an Eie. (*Hobbes*, 425)

Marked with an asterisk, Aubrey's marginal addendum reframes the blood sport as an intellectual exercise, a lesson in optics in which keenness of vision is shown not to correlate to the size of the physical eye. Despite their tiny frame, the jackdaws are able to "spye" the cheese pairings that the hunter-virtuoso uses to bait his birdlimed counters, repurposed from the gambling card game "Post and Pair." Aubrey's narrative does not invert the viewpoint: it is the sharpness of the birds' vision that remains the focus of scrutiny despite the fact that the birds themselves, made diminutive by distance, are equally the object of Hobbes's human vision, picked out in the high, wide and geographically specified ("as far as Osney-abbey") sky. He had a curious sharp Sight, as he had a sharpe Witt," writes Aubrey of Hobbes later in the life (443). Ultimately, however, Hobbes is shown to possess an intelligence that the birds lack, marking a species distinction between mere visual capacity and the ability to penetrate its operations and causes. The jackdaws descend from heaven not as celestial messengers but as inferior creatures to be dissected and eaten.[49]

This birding scene never made it into the official, posthumous life of Hobbes, a composite volume in Latin containing Hobbes's prose autobiography and a commentary by Richard Blackburne, which appeared under the imposing title *Thomae Hobbes Angli Malmesburienses philosophi vita* in 1681, with a second edition in 1682. This was a project that Aubrey had initiated with William Crooke, Hobbes's longtime publisher, enlisting Blackburne to work up and translate into Latin his biographical research notes. Aubrey's letters to Wood from the first half of 1680 present a growing litany of complaints against Blackburne, who is described as being "magisterial" and "much against Minutiae."[50] Aubrey was particularly exercised by Blackburne's decision, on the advice of John Dryden and of Dryden's friend and patron John Vaughan, Third Earl of Carbery, to omit any reference to Hobbes's early years of service as a page in the Cavendish household, and he lost patience with his reluctance to include other details, including Hobbes's summers spent birding in Oxford. A letter written to Wood from London on March 27 captures Aubrey's sense of injury and beleaguerment:

> Dr Blackbourne haz more than half donne, and will doe you right, and for his style, Mr Dryden (the Poet Laureat) and my Lord Jo Vaughan much approves it! but for the compiling, they two agree to leave out all minute things there will be the

trueth, but not the whole. / ... Tis writt in a high style. Now I say the Offices of a Panegyrist, and Historian, are much different. A Life, is a short Historie: and there minutenes of a famous person is gratefull. I never yet knew a Witt (unles he were a piece of an Antiquary) write a proper Epitaph, but leave the reader ignorant, what countryman etc[.] only tickles his eares with Elogies.[51]

Two months later, Aubrey would expostulate: "Pox take your Orators and poets, they spoile lives and histories. The Dr sayes that I am too Minute; but a hundred yeare hence that minutenesse will be gratefull."[52] Aubrey's defense of minutiae — the small and seemingly inconsequential details that are typically omitted from the public record — rests on a distinction among literary offices and genres: the Panegyrist and the Witt (also the Orator and Poet), who only applaud and praise, are ranged against the Antiquary and Historian, who inform and instruct. This generic distinction is also a matter of style and content. Blackburne and his literary backers prefer a grand or "high style," the achievement of which usurps the priority of accumulating detail.

The manuscript life of Hobbes that Aubrey prepared separately, and in a state of protest, is by far the longest that he wrote, comprising eight quarto gatherings or some 64 pages. Its full title, *Supplementum vitæ Thomæ Hobbes,* specifies its relation and incited opposition to Blackburne's printed Latin life even before its prefatory remarks to a reader Aubrey imagines to be prepossessed against details and their worth: "For that I am so Minute, I declare I never intended it; but setting downe in my rude draughte every particular (with purpose, upon review, to cutt-off what was superfluous and triviall) I shewed it to some Friends of mine (who also were of Mr Hobbes's acquaintance) whose judgements I much value; who gave their opinion and 'twas clearly their sense to let *all* stand" (*Hobbes,* 418). Somewhat disingenuously, Aubrey here accepts "minuteness" as an attribute of his authorial self, but he ascribes it to his compositional practice, a matter of getting everything down before deciding what should be stripped out. Minuting here is not a method of abbreviation but of accumulation: writing small means writing countless things. It is only at his friends' insistence and initiative, Aubrey declares, that he has ended up keeping everything in.

Wood believed that Aubrey's choice of title "Supplementum" was too self-effacing, demanding querulously in the margin of the manuscript copy, "What need you say Supplimentum [*sic*]? pray say 'The Life of Thomas

Hobbs.'"[53] But Aubrey stuck with it, insisting on the status of his life as an addendum, a surplus of materials that the printed life had discharged. His complaints to Wood about the "minute things" that Blackburne had omitted run from March to May 1680, months that he announced his resolution to begin writing up his biographical research into a freestanding collection of lives. It is hard not to believe that his increasing frustrations over the one drove his determination to embark upon the other. His commitment to detail is articulated more boldly, without the supporting narrative of supportive friends, in a declarative statement that stands alone at the end of the preface's first paragraph: "The Recrementa of so learned a person are valueable." A marginal interpolation half withdraws the declaration: "Meliorate this word," it instructs of the asterisked "Recrementa," derived from the Latin *recrementum,* and referring to various types of refuse, organic, excremental, and metallurgical (*Hobbes,* 417). In the debate between page and margin, the debate between the Wit and the Antiquary is reenacted: the verbal imperative exhorts betterment, correction, politeness, refinement, while the lowering noun encompasses the very rawest of raw materials. With some misgiving, Aubrey declares himself on the side of refuse, not rapturous praise.

In 1923, Lytton Strachey wrote a short essay defending Aubrey from the censorious judgment of Richard Garnett, keeper of printed books at the British Museum library and author of the entry on Aubrey for the first *Dictionary of National Biography* (1885–1900). Of Aubrey, Garnett had written, "He certainly is devoid of literary talent, except as a retailer of anecdotes; his head teems with particulars which he lacks the facility to reduce to order or combine into a whole. As a gossip, however, he is a kind of immature Boswell."[54] In his answer, first printed in the weekly newspaper, the *Nation and Athenaeum* in 1923 and later gathered into the essay collection *Portraits in Miniature* (1931), Strachey positions Aubrey not as a disappointing forerunner to Boswell, but as his methodological foil and alternative, declaring, "A biography should either be as long as Boswell's or as short as Aubrey's. The method of enormous and elaborate accretion which produced the *Life of Johnson* is excellent, no doubt; but, failing that, let us have no half-measures; let us have the pure essentials — a vivid image, on a page or two, without explanations, transitions, commentaries, or padding. This is what Aubrey gives us; this, and one thing more — a sense of the pleasing, anxious being who, with his odd old alchemy, has transmuted a few handfuls of orts and relics into golden life."[55] Two Shakespeare allusions are stitched into Strachey's "one thing more": the first from *Richard III,* when Richard speaks of gulling his victims with his scriptural thievery: "And thus I clothe my naked villainy / With odd old ends, stol'n forth from Holy Writ" (1.3.334–35); the second from *Troilus and Cressida,* when Troilus inveighs against Cressida for her sexual betrayal: "The fractions of her faith, orts of her love, / The fragments, scraps, the bits and greasy relics / Of her o'er-eaten faith, are bound to Diomed" (5.2.158–60).[56] Combining these with his own prose, Strachey patterns plosives, creating a run of *d* sounds that culminate in the rhyming of "old with "gold," an enactment of the alchemical transformation that his sentence describes. Through these purloined parts, parts that already in their dramatic context have been derogated to the status of bits and pieces, Strachey canonizes Aubrey as an unlikely but likeable artist figure, the practitioner of an occult art of leftovers and leavings, small things brought to life in forms that epitomize but seldom elaborate. Here refuse is the very stuff of praise.

Strachey's biographical portrait is, to be sure, heavily self-interested, claiming Aubrey as an ally in his own postwar assault on Victorian hero worship in the expansive Boswellian mode. His reclamation of the brief life as a modernist artwork inscribes hostility and provocative intention within Aubrey's minutes, reengaging and overtly politicizing their miniature form.[57] As this study has shown, the life in the seventeenth century works hard *not* to politicize itself in such an open manner, declining to acknowledge or give credence to its expertise in argument. In his cultivation of the "minute," Aubrey adopts his period's biographical reticence without adopting the ideological energies behind it. His documentation of details eliminates the need for any adjudication on the part of the biographer whose task is simply to gather and store them in a usable form. We might think of his minutes as subliterary or nonliterary or perhaps even antiliterary, poised in between and holding apart the two meanings of the word "life": the life that is on the way to being written and the life that has already been lived.

CHAPTER FOUR

Parallel Lives

Crusoe, Clarendon, and Defoe's Cavalier

THE FIRST SENTENCE of *The Life and Strange Surprizing Adventures of Robinson Crusoe* (1719), now known simply as *Robinson Crusoe,* may deserve more attention than it has traditionally received:

> I was born in the year 1632, in the city of *York,* of a good family, tho' not of that country, my father being a foreigner of *Bremen,* who settled first at *Hull*: He got a good estate by merchandise, and leaving off his trade, lived afterward at *York,* from whence he had married my mother, whose relations were named *Robinson,* a very good family in that country, and from whom I was call'd *Robinson Kreutznaer*; but by the usual corruption of words in *England,* we are now call'd, nay we call our selves, and write our name *Crusoe,* and so my companions always call'd me.[1]

Here in miniature is the life of Crusoe senior: his emigration from Germany to England, his successful career in trade, and his socially advantageous marriage to a Yorkshire gentlewoman. The Anglicization of the family surname from Kreutznaer to Crusoe marks the final stage of incorporation into the middle state of bourgeois English life, a state whose blessings Crusoe the father will attempt to inculcate into his youngest son.[2] With this brief paternal backstory Daniel Defoe shows how Crusoe inherits the mercantile instincts of his father even as he spurns his father's advice. His decision to leave home and his voyage from England to the Caribbean continue the westward movement that Crusoe senior, now confined by gout, had already begun.

By choosing Bremen as the birthplace of Crusoe's father, Defoe connects Crusoe's family history to the larger outlines of European history and to the controversial foreign policy of George I, Elector of Hanover, in particular. In 1712, Hanover had seized the German duchies of Bremen and Verden from Sweden, and in 1715, less than a year after his coronation, George was urging the British fleet, originally sent to the Baltic to protect merchant shipping, to block Swedish supply lines to their military bases in Germany. This was illegal under the 1700 Act of Settlement, which stipulated that a monarch who held territories independently of the British crown could not use British resources to defend or maintain them.[3] The resulting debate split the ruling Whig party: one side lobbying Parliament to supply money for George's anti-Swedish policy, the other protesting that British money should not be used to support Hanoverian expansion.[4] Bremen and Verden were only formally ceded to Hanover in the summer of 1719, a few months after the publication of *Robinson Crusoe,* and Defoe could reliably have expected his first audience to spot the political allusion. Buried within the family history of its eponymous hero, the reference to Bremen engages, if only momentarily, a contemporary debate over British foreign policy and mainland Europe. More importantly, it supplies a European context for its own story, making Crusoe and "the whole Anglo-Saxon spirit" (James Joyce's words) embodied within him the product of European migration, one of Defoe's many ripostes to the nationalist fiction of the "True-Born Englishman."[5]

The alacrity with which *Robinson Crusoe* abandons these European relations, both familial and geopolitical, and sets sail for North Africa, South America, and the Caribbean has long been interpreted as a marker of its narrative ambition as well as a cause of its enduring success.[6] In a chronological foreshortening that puts the death of his eldest son at Dunkirk in 1658 prior to the first sea voyage of his youngest son in 1651, Crusoe's father cautions Crusoe against the dangers of leaving home too soon, reminding him of the fate of his brother, "to whom he had used the same earnest perswasions to keep him from going into the Low Country wars, but could not prevail, his young desires prompting him to run into the army where he was kill'd."[7] Of course, from a literary historical, as opposed to a paternal, standpoint, the resemblance between the two prodigal brothers would appear to matter less than their motivated opposition. Compressed and killed off within a single sentence, Crusoe's brother pursues the career that Crusoe avoids by leaving the old world behind; to this dead brother belongs the story that Defoe conspicuously chooses not to tell in *Robinson Crusoe.* To the extent that the one represents the emerging culture of economic capitalism and bourgeois accomplishment, the other the declining culture of feudalism and aristocratic honor, the choice of protagonist and the choice of first casualty in his plot seem satisfyingly appropriate for a work routinely associated with the beginning of the English novel.[8] As a character type, Crusoe's brother is already dead when Crusoe sets sail on the open sea.

It remains the case, however, that Defoe kills off Crusoe's older brother, the superannuated soldier fighting in the confessional conflicts of seventeenth century Europe — "an heap of Conspiracies, Rebellions, Murders, Massacres, Revolutions, [and] Banishments," according to the king of Brobdingnag in conversation with another sailor and younger son — only to revive him less than a year later in his *Memoirs of a Cavalier*.[9] Written consecutively during 1719 and 1720, the life stories of Crusoe and the Cavalier juxtapose mercantile and military adventurism, two ways of seeing the world that Defoe places in deliberate historical relation. As they turn back to war-torn Britain and Europe, the *Memoirs* supplies a context that modifies a reading of *Robinson Crusoe;* it traces the years preceding and embracing the English civil wars and their impact upon its narrator-protagonist, the war-mongering Cavalier. That this context is already implicit in the domestic preliminaries to Crusoe's narrative further suggests its explanatory — and imaginative — force.

In this final chapter, I propose to trace the development of the fractious history of the written life into the eighteenth century through Defoe's recuperation of the fraternal counterexample to Crusoe and the telling of his story in the *Memoirs of a Cavalier*. Previous chapters have shown how biography triumphed in popular political discourse because it was able to resist, despite its often radically conservative leanings, the form or appearance of argument. The historical conditions of this triumph, it has been further suggested, belong to a postwar era that had lived through two turbulent decades of war and revolution — decades that had seen not only the rapid expansion of public political activity but also, and as a corollary to this expansion, a popular dislike and mistrust of its open and adversarial nature. From its inception, therefore, the English civil wars have played a determining role in this study's account of how the biography, through its routing of political beliefs through personal life stories, was able to exert a regressive influence over public culture. In this chapter, I move the civil wars to the thematic foreground, showing how Defoe threads seventeenth century history through his fictionalized biography of the royalist Cavalier, undertaking a joint interrogation of the literary form and of the historical events that had occasioned its rise to prominence.

The work that invented the civil war as a subject of interest for the eighteenth century was Edward Hyde's (the Earl of Clarendon's) *History of the Rebellion and Civil Wars in England,* brought forth with great fanfare in 1702–04 to mark the beginning of a new Stuart reign.[10] While the work's initial celebrity was bolstered by Hyde's family connection to his granddaughter, Queen Anne, its political notoriety was secured by its Tory handlers, who immediately put it to use in their hot-blooded campaign against religious dissent. Yet if a majority of eighteenth century readers got their history from Clarendon, they did so as much for literary reasons as for political ones, marveling at its aristocratic poise and, especially, its biographical portraits of historical persons, each as finely worked as a prose poem, and as aloof from argument.

In an editorial note to *Memoirs of a Cavalier* that has never, to my knowledge, been discussed, Defoe signals his intention to take on this Clarendonian consensus, a consensus formed around the *History's* literary sensibility and immanent ideology, but whose potential political effects had been rendered explicit by the Tory platform rolled out under its name. The editors who composed the note form part of the *Memoirs'* fictional apparatus, and they prove comically reluctant to commit to their adversarial position, backing away from their initial sweeping statement, which calls out Clarendon by name: "In a Word, this Work is a Confutation of many Errors in all the Writers upon the Subject of our Wars in *England,* and even in that extraordinary History written by the Earl of *Clarendon*."[11] We shall have occasion to return to this bold declaration, and, especially, to what I take to be its key word, "Confutation," with its announcement of the *Memoirs* as a type of biographical counterargument to Clarendon's multivolume masterpiece. For now, though, I want to submit the editors' note as an interpretative tip-off, the weight and significance of which remain to be determined as we turn first to Defoe's *Memoirs* and then, taking one last look at the biographical culture of the early Restoration, to Clarendon's *History.*

1

Defoe's *Memoirs* introduces itself as the autobiographical account of a Shropshire gentleman who, desirous to postpone "a very advantageous Match…with a young Lady of very extraordinary Fortune and Merit," sets out on a grand tour of Europe in the company of a university acquaintance, one Captain Fielding, in the spring of 1630 (*MC,* 9). By turning his back on domestic commitment, the Cavalier enlists in a distinguished company of antimarital adventurers that includes Pantagruel and his sidekick Panurge from François Rabelais's *Le quart livre* (1552) and Bertram and his sidekick Parolles from Shakespeare's *All's Well That Ends Well* (1602–03). Uniting this bachelor tradition with the biblical tradition of the prodigal son, Defoe describes the Cavalier's wanderings among the Catholic nations of Europe, France, Italy, and imperial Austria, which culminate in his desire to see the army of the famous Spanish general Count Tilly, currently besieging the Protestant city of Magdeburg. The sack and torching of that city marks a turning point in the Cavalier's European education — "a sad Welcome into the Army for me, and gave me a Horror and Aversion to the Emperor's People, as well as to his Cause" (*MC,* 47). Before the fires are out, he abandons the city and his previous notions of war as a spectator sport and joins the Protestant forces mustering to defend the nearby city of Leipzig from the imperial advance.

The remainder of part 1 of the *Memoirs* describes the Cavalier's military service in Germany. Spurred on by his companion Captain Fielding and by the acquaintance of a Scottish officer, Sir John Hepburn, the Cavalier enters the Swedish army as a volunteer, sharing in their victory at the Battle of Breitenfeld (1631). From this point onward, his fortunes rise with those of the Swedish king, the swashbuckling Gustavus Adolphus, who quickly establishes de facto dominion over southern Germany. Adolphus's unexpected death at the Battle of Lützen (1632), together with the rout of the Swedish-Protestant army at Nördlingen (1634), marks the second turning point in the Cavalier's adventures. Disillusioned by defeat, he crosses from Germany into the United Provinces intending to observe the fighting between the Dutch Republic and Spain. But the tactical war of attrition, so different from the open battlefields and dashing gallantry of the German theater, soon wearies him and he resolves to return to England.

Back in his native Shropshire, the Cavalier becomes an avid consumer of European news, following the movements and meeting of armies across the continent: "I could not but be peeping in all the foreign Accounts from *Germany*, to see who and who was together" (*MC*, 121). His reading represents a metafictional move on Defoe's part since the foreign news books, or *corantos*, upon which his hero seizes constitute the main source for the *Memoirs'* battle scenes. Defoe drew in particular upon *The Swedish Intelligencer*, compiled by the Anglican clergyman William Watts, which celebrated the progress of Gustavus Adolphus, "that *Caesar* and *Alexander* of our times," in seven parts and numerous issues between 1632 and 1634.[12] The Cavalier's addiction to the newsbooks serves a further purpose, foregrounding his inability to return to the routines and concerns of civilian life. Hunting, traditionally the pastime of the warring classes, provides some distraction, but the Cavalier admits to hankering "after a warmer Sport" (*MC*, 121). His wish is answered by the deteriorating relation between Charles I and his Scottish subjects, who, refusing to accept the Anglican prayerbook, move into open rebellion in 1639. The Cavalier waits eagerly for the action to begin: "I confess I did not much trouble my Head with the Cause; but all my Fear was, they would not fall out, and we should have no Fighting" (*MC*, 121). Part 1 of the *Memoirs* ends with the uneasy détente between the English army and the Scottish rebels — many of whom the Cavalier recognizes as his former comrades-in-arms — setting the stage for part 2, which follows the Cavalier's fortunes in the royalist army from the Second Bishops' War of 1640 to the decisive defeat at Marston Moor in 1644, and his final surrender of arms in 1646.

At the beginning of part 2 of the *Memoirs,* the Cavalier renounces his former eagerness to fight for fighting's sake and subjects himself to interpretative pressure for the first time in his narrative:

> I confess, when I went into Arms at the Beginning of this War, I never troubled my self to examine Sides: I was glad to hear the Drums beat for Soldiers; as if I had been a meer *Swiss,* that had not car'd which Side went up or down, so I had my Pay. I went as eagerly and blindly about my Business, as the meanest Wretch that listed in the Army; nor had I the least compassionate Thought for the Miseries of my native Country.... I had seen the most flourishing Provinces of *Germany* reduced to perfect Desarts, and the voracious *Crabats,* with inhuman Barbarity, quenching the Fires of the plundered Villages with the Blood of the Inhabitants. Whether

this had hardened me against the natural Tenderness which I afterwards found return upon me, or not, I cannot tell; but I reflected upon my self afterwards with a great deal of Trouble, for the Unconcernedness of my Temper at the approaching Ruin of my native Country. (*MC,* 125)

This passage establishes the interplay between heedless action and retrospective atonement, familiar from the structure of spiritual autobiography, to which the Cavalier has frequent recourse during the second half of his *Memoirs.* Anxious to demonstrate repentance, he abases himself with two comparisons: the first to the professional mercenary ("a meer *Swiss*"); the second to his servile inferior ("the meanest Wretch"). A third comparison follows between domestic and foreign bloodshed, but here the Cavalier is quick to distance himself from wartime butchery, positioning himself as a bystander and naming "the voracious *Crabats,*" or Croatians, as its perpetrators. By conceding their temporary influence, the Cavalier is able to reassert his essential difference. The "inhuman Barbarity" of the Crabats forestalls but cannot prevent the recovery of his "natural Tenderness," the moral birthright of his English blood.

In vilifying the Croatian cavalry regiments, the Cavalier follows the example of seventeenth century news sheets and pamphlet propaganda, which persistently linked them to civilian atrocities, and, in particular, to cannibalism. "Among the Imperiallists is a base sort of rascally horse-men which serve them, and are called Croats," informs one 1638 tract, *The Lamentations of Germany:* "The tenth part of them are not of that Countrey: for they are a miscellany of all strange Nations, without God, without Religion, and have only the outsides of men, and scarce that too. They make no conscience of murthering men or women, old or young, yea, the very innocent babes; and like the beasts among whom they are bred, doe sometimes eate them, when other food might be found."[13] An outpost of the Habsburg Empire, the Croat lands (now part of modern day Hungary and Croatia) lay along the military frontier between Christian Europe and the Muslim Ottoman Empire. The Croats were at once the defenders and pariahs of Europe — stigmatized as godless, brutish, multiethnic, and indescribably alien. The *Lamentations of Germany* depicts them as cannibals not by need but by natural compulsion. A companion woodcut shows a man dangling a naked baby from its one remaining leg, the gnawed stump of the other hangs from his mouth. Its heading: "Croats eate Children."[14]

With the outbreak of hostilities in Britain, the ethnic stereotype of the Croatian cavalry man was imported wholesale from Europe. "I care not for your Cause, I come to fight for your halfe-crown, & y^r handsome woemen," the Croatian soldier of fortune, serial rapist, and celebrated horseman, Carlo Fantom, is reported to have declared. In his biographical researches on Fantom, Aubrey describes how bullets would pass right through his body as if by magic, making soldiers afraid to shoot at him.[15] Initially, Fantom served in the parliamentary army, only later defecting to the king, but it was the royalists who were widely perceived to be welcoming mercenary fighters trained up in the bloody land wars of Europe. Parliamentary news sheets kept up a constant stream of atrocity stories featuring a foreign-born soldiery, "outlandish papists" from Ireland, France, and Spain, led by a French queen, Henrietta Maria, and the foreign-born nephews of Charles I, the Princes Maurice and Rupert.[16] One 1644 pamphlet, *A Copie of the Kings Message sent by the Duke of Lenox,* repurposes the violent iconography of the *Lamentations of Germany* in its frontispiece illustration of French troopers cheerfully impaling and slaughtering English children.[17]

Defoe shows the Cavalier at once protesting and reproducing these comparative assessments of European and British warfare. Excusing the brutal royalist assault on Leicester, for example, he pleads the relative difference of degree rather than the absolute one of kind: "What was our taking of *Leicester* by Storm, where they cried out of our Barbarities, to the sacking of *New Brandenburgh,* or the taking of *Magdeburgh?* In *Leicester,* of 7 or 8000 People in the Town, 300 were killed; in *Magdeburgh,* of 25000 scarce 2700 were left, and the whole Town burnt to Ashes" (*MC, 168*). To insist upon these numerical differences, the Cavalier must perforce entertain a more general similarity, aligning English royalists with Spanish imperialists, whose tactics he once abhorred. The choice of Magdeburg is particularly inauspicious since it was the carnage the Cavalier saw there that first moved him to join his Protestant brothers in arms. Now, without knowing it, he appears to have changed sides.

The wartime behavior with which the *Memoirs* is most fascinated, however, is plunder, much of it opportunistic but always structured by social hierarchy and status. Coined either from the German verb *plündern* or from the Dutch *plunderen,* the English seventeenth century verb "to plunder"

entered from outside, arriving around the same time as the foreign mercenaries from Europe. According to the *Oxford English Dictionary,* an early, if
not the earliest, instance of its use comes from the *coranto* or foreign newsbook, *The Swedish Intelligencer* — Defoe's source, as we remember, for the
European portion of the *Memoirs* — which speaks of how the "*Swedish*
Dragooners...plundered the Townes of *Wurtbach* and *Waldsee,* neere unto
Weingarten."[18] Over the next decade, the word became a favorite of parliamentary propagandists who used it to describe the conduct of royalist troops
under their Bohemian commander, Prince Rupert. In his 1647 *History of
the Parliament,* Thomas May emphasizes the connection between the lexi-
cal origin of the word "plunder" and the barbaric wartime practices it picks
out; both word and action, he suggests, are European imports of recent date:
"Many Townes and Villages he [Prince Rupert] plundered, which is to say
robb'd (for at that time first was the word plunder used in *England,* being
borne in *Germany,* when that stately Country was so miserably wasted and
pillaged by forraigne Armies)."[19] A 1644 mock elegy puns opportunistically
on Rupert's recent elevation to the English peerage, addressing him not as the
Duke of Cumberland but as the "Duke of *Plunderland*."[20]

Defoe pairs scenes of plunder across the two parts of the *Memoirs:* the
first centers upon the Cavalier's servant George, disguised as a gentleman,
and a company of Swedish dragoons; the second upon the Cavalier himself, disguised as a country ploughman, and a cast of rustic Englishmen. The
one is a parodic mirror of the other: George's gift of fortune and upward
social mobility are paralleled by the Cavalier's fall down the ladder of social
rank, losing all claim to aristocratic status. But the Cavalier's story is also
part of a more elaborate scheme, I will argue, offering a satirical retelling of
Charles II's narrow escape from the Battle of Worcester, one of the most
cherished myths of Stuart historiography. Repudiating this story's traffic in
cliché, but also, and more importantly, its turn to biography to give narrative
form to the theory of sacral kingship, Defoe performs his own act of plunder,
running away with the Tory spoils and burying them in pastoral obscurity.

In the first half of the *Memoirs,* the Cavalier, his servant George, and the
multinational volunteers serving in the Swedish army enrich themselves by
plundering the towns and villages of southern Germany.[21] After the Swedish
victory at the Battle of Breitenfeld, the Cavalier's servant spends three days

looting the surrounding countryside while his master is busy attending to his wounded companion Captain Fielding. Before embarking upon this plundering spree, the servant prudently disguises himself in the clothing of a gentleman from among the dead lying on the field. His strategy pays off when he falls in with a party of Swedish dragoons who mistake him for an officer and place themselves under his command. The newly formed company takes a village, hurriedly abandoned by a regiment of the enemy's horse, the plunder of which they promptly appropriate. Returning to his master, the servant proudly displays his share of the take: "60 or 70 Pieces of Gold, 5 or 6 Watches, 13 or 14 Rings, whereof 2 were diamond Rings...Silver as much as his Pockets would hold...three Horses, two of which were laden with Baggage," and a small fardel or bundle which, on further examination, is found to contain linen, plate, rings, a pearl necklace, and more silver (*MC,* 66–67). The following day, as though to emphasize the limitless possibilities of wartime acquisition, they discover a silk purse full of gold ducats secreted inside the saddle of one of the three captured horses. "Thou art born to be rich, *George,*" declares the Cavalier (*MC,* 69).

The upwardly mobile disguise of the Cavalier's servant after the victory at Breitenfeld is paralleled by the Cavalier's downwardly mobile disguise after the royalist defeat at Marston Moor (1644). Attempting to rejoin the remnants of Prince Rupert's scattered cavalry, the Cavalier disguises himself as a country ploughman, his two comrades as a farmer's wife and a cripple, and enters Leeds to gather news of the parliamentary army. Unlike his companions, who quickly assimilate themselves to their new surroundings and station, the Cavalier remains at a loss: "I walked up and down the Town, but fancied my self so ill disguised, and so easy to be known, that I cared not to talk with any Body" (*MC,* 208). Events quickly catch up with this self-assessment. On the road out of the city, the Cavalier encounters "three Country Fellows on Horseback" (*MC,* 209), one of whom stops to address him. Unable to understand the question being put to him and finding himself incapable of answering in the local idiom, the Cavalier pretends not to hear and attempts to ride on. Confronted for a second time, he loses patience: "*Na, but ye's not gang soa,* says the Boor, and comes up to me, and takes hold of the Horse's Bridle to stop me; at which, vexed at Heart that I could not tell how to talk to him, I reached him a great Knock on the Pate with my Fork, and fetched him off of his Horse" (*MC*, 209). The Cavalier quickly makes off, but, finding himself pursued, is obliged to stab one of the men with his farmer's fork and shoot the other with his pistol. Reunited with his two companions, he learns that the fellow was inquiring about the horse which he recognized as belonging to his brother: "They said the Cavaliers stole him," one of the injured men tells the soldier disguised as a farmer's wife, "but 'twas like such Rogues; no Mischief could be done in the Country, but 'twas the poor Cavaliers must bear the Blame" (*MC*, 210–11). Arriving at the next village, the three royalist outlaws are warmly welcomed by the inhabitants who offer them shelter. The Cavalier tries to sleep but is disturbed by the groans of his host lying in the bed next to him, who, he shortly discovers, is none other than his unfortunate victim from the day before. The host does not recognize his assailant and is duped into taking back his brother's horse, but this act of restitution, and the comic plot it completes, is almost beside the point. The Cavalier's irascibility and propensity to violence reveal the unsavory side of aristocratic privilege, but his travels incognito among the rural peasantry develop a more pointed satire of the political fiction of sacral kingship.[22]

In a move that takes the *Memoirs* beyond its more realistic historical engagements, Defoe's narrative sequence — the Cavalier's flight from the battlefield, his days spent in disguise hiding in country towns or in the woods and mountains, and his interactions with the loyal yet credulous and ruthlessly exploited villagers — supplies a revisionist and deflationary rewriting of the most memorable episode in Stuart historiography, Charles II's escape from the Battle of Worcester in 1651. The stuff of popular legend, featured prominently in coronation poems, printed in numerous versions during the Restoration, and endlessly retold by Charles himself, who dictated an official version to Samuel Pepys at Newmarket in October 1680 (at the height of the Exclusion Crisis when the idea of sacral majesty held considerable and expedient appeal), the narrative outlines of the escape plot would have been immediately recognizable to Defoe's first readership.[23] Disguised first as a country man, then as a serving man, and finally as a woodcutter, and aided by a supporting cast of plucky English subjects, Charles successfully eluded the parliamentary forces for six weeks by taking refuge in country houses, barns, and, most famously, in the branches of an oak tree before his safe transport to the Continent could be arranged. Restoration retellings linger over the cosmetic details of Charles disguise — his shorn hair, his face and hands "made of a reechy complexion, by the help of the Walnut-tree leaves" — so as to emphasize in turn the impossibility of ever disguising the authority and aura of kingship.[24] As Elliott Visconsi observes, Aphra Behn incorporates this romance ideal of inalienable majesty into her account of the royal slave, *Oroonoko* (1688).[25] Like Charles, Oroonoko dresses down in order to avoid discovery; like Charles, he finds that his natural nobility admits of no disguise: "He shone through all, and his osenbrigs (a sort of brown Holland suit he had on) could not conceal the graces of his looks and mien; and he had no less admirers than when he had his dazzling habit on; the royal youth appeared in spite of the slave."[26]

The romance of Charles at Worcester, together with the political reading of sovereignty it supported, developed into a flexible apology for Stuart kingship. The majority of retellings emphasize the paradox of the disguised yet unmistakable sovereign, but some also play upon the contractual nature of Charles's descent from king to country fellow, treating his disguise as a form of reverse coronation by the people. In *An exact narrative and relation of His Most Sacred Majesties escape* (1660), Charles's change of dress is carefully itemized as a series of separate donations: Richard Pendrill contributes "a Jump and Breeches of Green course Cloth and a Doe skin Leather Doublet"; his brother, Humphrey, a hat, "an old Gray one that turned up its Brims"; Edward Martin "the Shirt (which in that Countrey Language they call'd an Hurden or Noggen Shirt, of Cloath that is made up of the coursest of the Hemp)"; and William Creswell his shoes.[27] As with Behn's account of Oroonoko's osenbrigs, the author displays a self-conscious mastery of sartorial parlance, retaining the "Countrey Language" of his peasant characters for the edification, and entertainment, of his more sophisticated London audience. In Isaac Fuller's sequence of paintings of the escape (c. 1662), the first, *Charles II Changing into Richard Penderel's Best Suit of Clothes,* depicts this ritual moment of investiture, showing Pendrill helping Charles into his brown doublet, while the second, *Charles II Discovered by Colonel Careless and William Penderel Seated on a Tree-Stump in Boscobel Wood,* depicts the adoration of the peasantry, as the colonel bends to kneel before Charles who sits, legs akimbo with his flies undone.[28] Once Charles looks the part, he is taught to act the part: "They had much adoe all that day to teach and fashion his Majesty to their Country guise, and to order his steps and straight body to a hobbing, jobsons gate, and were forced every foot to mind him of it; for the Language, his Majesties most gracious converse with his People in his Journey to, and at *Worcester,* had rendered it very easie and very tunable to him."[29] Charles's failure to conceal his upright posture is countered by the facility with which he speaks to his subjects. Like Shakespeare's Prince Hal, linguistic dexterity makes Charles the "king of courtesy," the model prince.[30]

In pointed contrast, Defoe's Cavalier displays none of the magnanimity so prominent in these royal escape narratives, or in the romance topos of the aristocrat-as-peasant upon which they are based.[31] His disguise is not the voluntary gift of the people, having been obtained by force "at a Farmer's house, which for that particular Occasion we plundered; and I cannot say no Blood was shed in a Manner too rash…but our Case was desperate, and the People too surly, and shot at us out the Window" (*MC,* 207). The Cavalier's hostile investment offers a version of kingship in which status is wrested from the people without their consent. An opponent of indefeasible hereditary right, Defoe here reduces the grounds of royal privilege to an original act of thuggery. His conquest accomplished, the Cavalier next proves contemptuous of the common tongue, which Charles, the romance hero, imitates so readily. His failure to communicate with the country fellows whom he meets on the road is less a function of incapacity, however, than of an exalted and inexpugnable sense of his own superior station. The idea of moving unrecognized around the kingdom is inconceivable to the Cavalier, and he waits for the moment when his true nature will show itself, differentiating him from his boorish disguise. That moment of recognition, and the naturalized aristocratic status confirmed by it, is never forthcoming. Defoe frustrates the expected plot progression from disguise to revelation, presenting instead an aristocrat who is unidentifiable as such because he does not measure up to the status expectations of the English people.

The progressive implications of Defoe's parody are particularly clear in its final episode when the Cavalier and his renegade companions take refuge in the forest of Swale. In contrast to Boscobel wood with its hospitable oak tree, Swale is an uninhabited wilderness, framed by "vast Mountains" (*MC,* 217) that loom large in the Cavalier's proto-romantic imagination. History recedes, "for no Soldier had ever been here all the War, nor perhaps would not, if it had lasted 7 Years" (*MC*, 217), as the locale of the quest reasserts itself. Corresponding, on the one hand, to Crusoe's Caribbean island and, on the other, to the forest of Epping where the group of exiled Londoners quarantine themselves in *A Journal of the Plague Year* (1722), Swale becomes a testing ground for self-sufficiency and individual endeavor. But in a landscape so barbaric that it cannot support acts of barbarism, the Cavalier and his retinue of aristocratic warriors have nothing and nobody to live on, and they depart after only four days of pastoral retirement, rejoining Prince Rupert and the war at Kendall. Unlike Crusoe or the enterprising band of London artisans — middle class heroes all — the Cavalier proves incapable of sustaining himself on the land. Instead, Defoe shows him and his class to be parasitical on the people they oppress, and on the warfare that licenses their predatory aggression.

Readings of the *Memoirs* have tended by and large to cancel out its internal contradictions, investing either in its romance plot of heroism and honor or in its realist story of violent aggression and increasing disillusionment. Maximillian Novak advances the former view, styling its first-person protagonist as "Defoe's version of the ideal Cavalier — brave, idealistic, fair — the model created by Clarendon in the character of Falkland in his *History of the Rebellion*."[32] Apparent in his aristocratization of the family name and in the coat of arms he displayed on the frontispiece to his epic poem *Jure divino*, Defoe's social aspirations, so Novak reminds us, were bound up with fantasies of battlefield heroism: in 1685 he joined the Duke of Monmouth's disastrous uprising against James II, and in 1703 he proposed military service as suitable atonement for his political satire, *The Shortest Way with the Dissenters*.[33] Taking the opposing position, Paula R. Backscheider and Sharon Alker contend that the *Memoirs* anticipates the "antiwar" project of the Enlightenment, casting the Cavalier in the role of the terrorizing yet traumatized soldier, no less modern in his own way than Crusoe himself.[34] As Backscheider puts it, "the lasting power and appeal of *Memoirs of a Cavalier* come[s] from its utterly unexceptional hero, its pessimism, and its philosophically nihilistic conclusion rather than from its evocation of the seventeenth or eighteenth century."[35]

While I concur with Novak's characterization of the Cavalier as a specifically Clarendonian fiction, I am not persuaded that the *Memoirs*, with all of its comic misfires and uncomfortable shifts of tone, provides a plausible vehicle for chivalric nostalgia, not even in the disguised form of authorial fantasy. Nor do I believe that it grapples with questions of trauma, psychological damage, and mental breakdown in quite the ethical way that Backscheider and Alker want to propose. As we have seen, the *Memoirs* deploys the tropes of status identity unevenly and at times with heavy-handed irony, signaling its awareness that these are scripted and not natural roles. And as we have also seen, the *Memoirs*'s historical sweep ends not with the human tragedy of war but with the political comedy of the Cavalier's escape narrative — challenging the place of storytelling and, especially, of biographical storytelling in a royalist imaginary that hovers around history but disclaims responsibility for arguing its terms. We can see now why the *Memoirs*'s concluding action must be left incomplete, denied the restoration (and so denying the Restoration) that would bring it to a definitive ending. Instead, Defoe suspends the narrative at the Cavalier's surrender of his arms, appending to it a list of providential judgments. To readers, the inclusion of these judgments has long posed an interpretive problem: the editors of the 1766 Edinburgh edition pronounced them spurious, "added and interpolated after the MS. was out of the possession of the author," although by author they meant the Cavalier himself and not Defoe. Backscheider terms the list "hasty and artless"; James Boulton, "unsatisfactory and discrepant." Only Alker considers it to be a successful addition, symptomatic of the Cavalier's psychological breakdown under the pressures of his wartime experience.[36] Open ended and unexplained, the Cavalier's turn to a controlling providence might variously be considered a correction, cancellation, subordination, or supplementation of the personal history that precedes it. Certainly its motive is not one of self-appraisal, not even of the kind that Crusoe achieves by internalizing a providential order and applying it to his own life on the island, but a radical form of self-avoidance. It takes the example of a third party — "a *Roman Catholick Gentleman of Lancashire*" (*MC,* 272) — for the Cavalier to begin parsing human history in divine terms, but the ethical convenience of this method, and hence the psychological plausibility of its adoption, is surely in part what Defoe wants us to see. By privileging a theology of divine agency over personal accountability, the Cavalier does not so much edit history as edit himself out of history, a tactic that can only be perceived ironically given the pains Defoe has taken to edit him in.

2

Having ended by abdicating from his own narrative, the Cavalier leaves it vulnerable to other owners, a situation Defoe promptly literalizes by having his manuscript seized as battlefield plunder by a Parliamentarian. This seizure supplies the occasion for the framing story of the *Memoirs* when, in a move customary of his historical fictions, Defoe begins the text with an editorial statement, relating the discovery of a manuscript and vouching for its authenticity: "As an Evidence that 'tis very probable these Memorials were written many Years ago, the Persons now concerned in the Publication, assure the Reader, that they have had them in their Possession finished, as they now-appear, above twenty Years: That they were so long ago found by great Accident, among other valuable Papers in the Closet of an eminent publick Minister, of no less Figure than one of King *William's* Secretaries of State" (*MC*, 1).

Two paragraphs later the editors disclose a further piece of evidence: a memorandum affixed to the manuscript, the contents of which they quote verbatim: "I found this Manuscript among my Father's Writings, and I understand that he got them as Plunder, at, or after, the Fight at *Worcester*, where he served as Major of — — —'s Regiment of Horse on the Side of the Parliament. L. K." (*MC*, 2). With these brief facts of textual transmission, Defoe establishes a chain of ownership: from the Cavalier to the parliamentary cavalry major to his son, L. K., who may also be the secretary of state in whose closet the manuscript is later rediscovered. The manuscript first changes owners in 1651 during or in the immediate aftermath of the Battle of Worcester, which ended Charles II's abortive campaign to retake his father's throne. It resurfaces sometime before 1700 — the editors, writing in 1720, claim to have had it in their possession "above twenty Years" — during the reign of the Protestant King William III and Queen Mary II. Defoe is playing a historical dating game here, one that closely and self-consciously resembles the internal dating of his recent best seller, *Robinson Crusoe*. In a now classic article on that novel's temporal markers, Michael Seidel demonstrates how Defoe aligns the 28 years of Crusoe's island existence, starting in 1659 and ending in 1686–87 when he returns to England, with the 28 years of Stuart rule from the Restoration of 1660 to the Glorious Revolution of 1688–89.[37] In this way, Crusoe's stay on the island becomes at once an exile from and an allegorical figuration of the home left behind, a figuration that assumes a high level of historical specificity and which Defoe clearly intended as a political commentary upon English society. Written over seventeenth century history, Crusoe's life and adventures are also a rewriting of that history, one that connects the *nostos* or homecoming to the new conditions of national possibility and liberal subjecthood under William III. The hero sits out, even as he replicates, the rule of the absolutist Stuart monarchs on an island of his own.

A parallel temporal pattern informs the *Memoirs,* centered not on the autobiographical experiences of its narrator-protagonist, but on the recovery and transmission of his story. For the afterlives granted to both fictional characters, the Cavalier through the chance discovery of his forgotten manuscript, and Crusoe through his fortuitous rescue and return to England after his island exile, are aligned with the forced abdication of James II and the creation of a new English state. In the 28 years between the Restoration and the Glorious Revolution, also the first 28 years of Defoe's — and Friday's — life, Crusoe and the Cavalier's manuscript fall out of national time and history. More striking still, Crusoe's initial departure from England in the autumn of 1651 coincides with the battlefield theft of the Cavalier's manuscript at Worcester, a plot device that recalls the actual seizure of documents, including the royal correspondence between Charles and Henrietta Maria, at the Battle of Naseby some six years earlier.[38] Defoe's protagonists appear born to succeed one another: the textual, if not actual, death of the Cavalier on the English battlefield launches Crusoe on his epoch- and empire-making adventures.

If the preface is read in this way, as a sequence of temporal clues that acquire the force and coherence of political allegory; if it is read also as part of an interlocking design that ties the Cavalier to Crusoe, the old world soldier-of-fortune to the new world mariner and slave merchant, then the scope of Defoe's ongoing ambition, to compose a revisionist history of the seventeenth century, one life at a time, starts to become clear. In the case of the *Memoirs,* however, this ambition is also bound up with the political charges and countercharges over the meaning and significance of the civil war during the first decades of the eighteenth century. Defoe's preface may start out as a historical dating game, but it builds to an attack on Clarendon's

History of the Rebellion, first printed in a three-volume folio set between 1702 and 1704, followed by a more affordable six-volume octavo edition in 1705, and, with reprintings in 1707, 1710, 1712, 1714, 1717, 1719, and 1720–21, by far the most influential account of the English civil wars in circulation during Defoe's lifetime.[39]

Yet if *The History of the Rebellion* proved a runaway best seller, it was also a political product, marketed to the public by a Tory inner circle based at Christ Church, Oxford. After circulating for years in manuscript, its printed release occurred within months of the accession of Queen Anne in March 1702, timed to coincide with the summer elections that returned a Tory majority to Parliament.[40] Readers would have opened all three volumes to find a preface presenting a slate of Tory positions. The first focuses its attention on foreign affairs, arguing in favor of a "blue water" policy and against the buildup of land forces to fight against France.[41] The second and third are shriller, more interested in identifying enemies at home than fighting those abroad. They are also a strictly family affair, written by Clarendon's son, Laurence Hyde, and addressed to his great-niece, Queen Anne, dedicating the *History* to her so that she might apply its political lessons to her own reign: "And now Your Majesty, who succeeds to a Revolution, as well as a Restoration, has the advantage of a retrospect on all these Accidents, and the benefit of reviewing all the failings in those times."[42] The recommendation sounds ominous, and quickly turns to threat. By February 1703, Laurence Hyde had been forced out of Anne's cabinet after clashing with the Duke of Marlborough and the Lord High Treasurer Godolphin over the progress of the war against France, a personal humiliation that may, in part, account for the prefaces' scaremongering tactics and high-handed tone. Appearing at a time when high church Tories were attempting to legislate against occasional conformity (the practice of taking Anglican Communion once a year in order to qualify for civil office), they rail against Dissenters (of whom Defoe, of course, was one), attacking the Nonconformist academies for their "industrious Propagation of the Rebellious Principles of the last Age" and hinting at secret gatherings and republican cabals.[43] Other Tory tracts took up these themes. The high churchman Charles Leslie warned of a coordinated campaign among the latitudinarian clergy, Whig politicians, and Protestant Dissenters in his aptly titled *The New Association of those called Moderate-Church-Man, with the Modern-Whigs and Fanaticks, to Under-mine and Blow-up the Present Church and Government...By a True-Church-Man.* Leslie's hyphenations are truly inflammatory, recalling the (Catholic) Gunpowder Plot that had threatened another newly crowned monarch in 1605. His tract ends with a quotation from, and a recommendation to read, Clarendon's *History.*[44]

In this context, it is worth reconsidering the editorial announcement that prefaces the Cavalier's first-person narrative:

> In a Word, this Work is a Confutation of many Errors in all the Writers upon the Subject of our Wars in *England,* and even in that extraordinary History written by the Earl of *Clarendon;* but the Editors were so just, that when near twenty Years ago, a Person who had written a whole Volume in Folio, by Way of Answer to, and Confutation of *Clarendon's* History of the Rebellion, would have borrowed the Clauses in this Account, which clash with that History, and confront it: We say the Editors were so just as to refuse them. (*MC,* 3)

Needless to say, this editorial boast is part of a larger ruse, establishing the *Memoirs* as a genuine historical document by suggesting how it might call to account other documents less genuine, or less accurate, than itself. It plays its own trick upon readers when, after a crescendo of initial consonants — "Clarendon," "Clauses," "Clash" — the editors pull back from the fight in prospect, declaring it never to have occurred. Earlier, I characterized this passage as a tip-off, a tell-tale clue of the kind that Defoe was fond of giving as an indication of his ulterior motives and intentions. But I think it might equally be characterized as a backdated promissory note, payable now, almost 20 years after the print publication of Clarendon's *History.* For all their third-person pomposity, the editors don't give us a clear sense of how, precisely, the *Memoirs* are to answer the errors of the *History,* but they do refer to an original confuter, "a Person who had written a whole Volume in Folio." Who might this person be?

There's no way of knowing for sure, but I believe Defoe here intends a reference to clergyman and ecclesiastical historian White Kennett, whose anonymous, 900-page contribution to *A Complete History of England* (1706) was perhaps the closest thing to a Whig response to the Tory-sponsored publication of Clarendon's *History.* A collaborative enterprise among 13 booksellers, the funds for which had been raised by public subscription, *A Complete*

History proposed to make available in one multivolume anthology the outstanding works of English history and, by joining them together, to construct a comprehensive account of the nation's past. The first two volumes follow this general strategy, starting out with Milton's *History of Britain* and progressing to the reign of James I through the writings of such estimable and irreproachable authors as Samuel Daniel, Thomas More, Francis Bacon, John Hayward, and William Camden.[45] With the third and final volume, however, the editors took a radically different approach. Rather than combining a series of anthology pieces with prose links and annotations, they commissioned a single stretch of narrative covering the reigns of Charles I, Charles II, James II, and William III. The author's name was withheld, but the narrative was widely — and correctly — reported to be the work of Kennett.

By 1706, Kennett was a marked man, despised in high church Tory circles for having used the anniversary of Charles I's martyrdom, that most sacred of Anglican holy days, to preach a sermon claiming that the civil war was caused by credible fears of popery and of growing French power. Such fears combined to deleterious effect, the sermon concedes, but they also presaged the overthrow of James II later in the century, a political revolution very much in the national interest and one that had taken place without recourse to the bloody crime of regicide. As word of his sermon spread, Kennett put out a printed version, *A Compassionate Enquiry into the Causes of the Civil War* (1704).[46] It immediately ran through four editions, setting off a short-lived but acrimonious pamphlet debate, to which Mary Astell and Defoe contributed.[47] Writing for *A Complete History*, Kennett was able to reprise and extend the scope of his sermon's argument, presenting not one but three Catholicizing Stuart kings taking instruction from France. By framing seventeenth century history as a constant struggle to secure English rights and freedoms against French influence, he offered a defense not just of the Glorious Revolution of 1688–89, but of the costly land war waged in the decade since against Louis XIV.[48]

What was most shocking about Kennett's narrative was not its thesis, however, but its declared reliance upon the "inimitable Clarendon" to advance it. Kennett acknowledges his indebtness in a prefatory address to the reader, claiming, at the same time, to have discovered an intrinsic subversiveness within this most canonical of texts: "A great Regard has been had to the excellent History written by my Lord Clarendon, which," he adds provocatively, "is far from serving any one side only."[49] Quite how bold this raid into enemy territory must have seemed is hard to appreciate without understanding the degree to which the *History of the Rebellion* had given the Tories the final word on the civil war, making it their political issue. "Great was the Consternation the Whigs were thrown into on the formidable Appearance of that History," wrote John Oldmixon many years later. "It had such a Torrent of Currency at first, that it bore down all before it."[50] By 1706, crying Clarendon had become a habit among Tory writers and no one was quite prepared for a Whig historian to try doing the same.

Kennett had put Clarendon's *History* to the test not by plain proof, but by further interrogation, undermining its achieved consensus and reopening its findings to additional argument. By invoking Kennett as a precedent, Defoe hints at his own ambition to reground seventeenth century history along equally alternative lines. Unlike Kennett, however, Defoe offers his confutation in the literary form of biography, stripping away the *History*'s epic note and proportion to leave only the personal-scale drama and self-interpreting worldview of the Cavalier. As noted above, the canonization of Clarendon's *History* takes place within the specific conditions of its print production and reception at the turn of the century. Noted too was the way in which its royalist ideology gets repackaged as political propaganda for a continuing Anglican hegemony and the Tory cause. There is no question that Clarendon consolidated for the eighteenth century a distinctly politicized understanding of the seventeenth century. But it was, perhaps first and foremost, as a biographer that Clarendon represented for Defoe so formidable — and elusive — a political opponent. Exquisitely crafted, dazzling in both their clarity and conviction of judgment, the portraits that punctuate the *History* may ostensibly be about the dirty game of politics, but they appear to advocate for nothing, floating gloriously free of ideological commitment and its heavy-handed terms of expression. Eighteenth century readers were, quite simply, amazed and delighted by them. It is to these embedded biographies, therefore, at least as much as to the *History*'s belligerent sponsors, that we should look in order to understand what Defoe was going up against in his *Memoirs of a Cavalier*.

3

Edward Hyde, later the Earl of Clarendon, composed his *History of the Rebellion and Civil Wars in England* during two periods of political exile: the first in 1646–48 after he had fled with the Prince of Wales (the future Charles II) to the Scilly Isles and then onto Jersey to escape the advancing parliamentary army; the second in 1668–72 after he had fled to France at the end of November 1667, a target of public anger and a political scapegoat for the economic and naval mismanagement of the war against the Dutch. During this second exile, Hyde made numerous additions to the first seven books of the *History* he had completed as a much younger man, interpolating passages from his memoir, the *Life of Himself,* and carrying the narrative forward to the restoration of the Stuart monarchy in 1660.[51] The completed *History* is framed by the deaths of royal favorites: that of George Villiers, Duke of Buckingham, at the beginning of book 1, and those of Cardinal Mazarin and Luis Méndez de Haro, advisors to Anne of Austria during the regency of Louis XIV and Philip IV of Spain, at the end of book 16. While Buckingham's assassination is precipitant to rebellion, the deaths of Mazarin and de Haro are reactionary: aggrieved responses to the Restoration, "as if," writes Clarendon scathingly in his closing sentence, "they had taken it ill that God Almighty would bring such a work to pass in Europe without their concurrence and against all their machinations."[52] Akin to the Olympian blocking figures of classical epic, Mazarin and de Haro at last concede defeat, absenting themselves from a new European order in which England, not France or Spain, will assume imperial dominance. Yet for all its triumphalism, a triumphalism perhaps not without its share of *schadenfreude* since these were politicians with whom he had been forced to negotiate on frustratingly unequal terms throughout the 1650s, Hyde's ending feels meager and only minimally palliative, a turning from home back to the years of exclusion on the continent, which is, of course, where he was, a fallen royal favorite and an exile once more, as he finished the *History.*

By beginning and ending his vast narrative with the deaths of favorites, Hyde hints at ambivalence toward his involvement in the power-brokering and bloodletting at the political center of Europe. The unifying design of the *History* confirms the influence of powerful individuals over even the most momentous events, advancing a conservative rhetoric of character (checked only by divine dispensation) over other modes of historical explanation. Hyde provides an overview of this anti-heroic characterology at the end of the exordium, when he contends that because the war was predictable in principle its causes are possible to explain:

> By viewing the temper, disposition, and habit, of that time, of the court and of the country, we may discern the minds of men prepared, of some to do, and of others to suffer, all that hath since happened: the pride of this man, and the popularity of that; the levity of one, and the morosity of another; the excess of the court in the greatest want, and the parsimony and retention of the country in the greatest plenty; the spirit of craft and subtlety in some, and the rude and unpolished integrity of others, too much despising craft or art; like so many atoms contributing jointly to this mass of confusion now before us. (1.4)

Balanced clauses draw up the future battle lines, diagnosing the split psychology, not, as we might expect, the divided political sympathies, of the English people. A single semi-colon separates their orderly ranks from the ensuing spectacle, when all demarcations break down and the individuated become indistinguishable, "like so many atoms." On this account, the war is the result of a clash of personalities configured into opposing extremes and reduced to a level of quasi-allegorical and mechanistic impersonality.

Noticeably missing from Hyde's dialectical pairings is the representation of actual persons: here are only isolated faults and traits seemingly dependent upon or behaviorally compelled by their equal and opposite partner. This dependence or compulsion is most clearly visible when the habits of mind are ascribed not to unspecified actors (this/that, one/another, some/others), but to particular social groups: the license of the court is produced by scarcity; the frugality of the country by abundance as each internally replicates the dynamics that structure their external relationship. Hyde's gaze is here a panoramic and a totalizing one, a god's-eye view of human conflict. Still, his literal atomization and aggregation of persons into competing drives and contrarieties has the effect of psychologizing, if not also pathologizing, all forms of social, religious, and political struggle. His will be a story of predilections, not principles; of attitudes, not ideas.[53]

Given this understanding of ideological or political difference as arising from natural differences of character, it comes as no surprise that Hyde approaches recent history through the lens of biography. Indeed, there can be little question that, as Martine Watson Brownley writes, the character sketch is "Clarendon's most important literary method for historical explanation."[54] Central to the edifying purpose of the narrative, the sketches also provide its keenest entertainment, offering the lure of aristocratic celebrity, of insider access to a reprobate and chastened governing class. The *History's* first readers tended to agree that Hyde's portraits were the most compelling and colorful aspect of what was, after all, a 16-book slog. "I know very well," declares John Oldmixon, "that a hundred to one of all the Readers of the *Grand Rebellion* admire it most for those very Characters," while James Tyrrell, writing to John Locke, recommends the *History* for "being full of lively (and I believe for the most part) true Characters of the chief persons concerned in the public affairs of that time."[55] When the enterprising Grub Street hack writer Ned Ward set about abridging and versifying the *History* (a project that itself ran to three volumes), he commissioned engravers to produce "a Hundred Heads" of the "Worthy Royalists and other Principal Actors," copied from seventeenth century oil paintings by "Eminent" artists, including Anthony van Dyck, principal painter to Charles I. A list of the "Heads by whom Painted, and who Engrav'd them" appeared at the beginning of the volume, making the plates a key selling point.[56] The project lost money — Ward claims that the expense of the engravings alone left him 500 pounds out of pocket — but its focus on specific artists and printmakers and its curation of an entire sequence of portraits consciously emulated elite practices of collecting and connoisseurship. "Pag'd as the Binders are to place them," the engravings were designed to bookmark the character sketches, enabling readers to skip over the narrative's transitions and focus solely on its gallery of public figures. Thus demarcated, and returned to the company of painting, its rival medium and sister art, the biographical portrait assumes expressive primacy, demoting history to the hook upon which it hangs. At the end of the century, Horace Walpole would quip that "Vandyke little thought, when he drew Sir Edward Hyde, that a greater master than himself was sitting to him."[57]

Ward's illustrated abridgment may have helped Clarendon's *History* appear less intimidating to readers, but its presentation of the portraits as self-contained and without need of contextualization holds true, to a remarkable extent, for the *History* itself. Even those who tackled the work at full length would have been struck by how little the portraits depend for their meaning on the historical plot, which is simply halted to accommodate them. We can see this suspension of the narrative in the opening book when Hyde pauses to offer first a portrait of the Duke of Buckingham (*History,* 1.65–94) and then a series of subordinate portraits, extending for a further 50 paragraphs and introducing one by one the courtiers who compete for the spoils after Buckingham's assassination (1.96–145). Each portrait is an extraordinary piece of character satire, contending for the reader's attention just as the courtiers themselves must vie and jostle for precedence. Their cumulative effect is hard to reproduce in quotation, but here are two examples, from the commendatory description of the unlovable Sir Thomas Coventry, Lord Keeper of England: "But then this happy temper and these good faculties rather preserved him from having many enemies, and supplied him with some well-wishers, than furnished him with any fast and unshaken friends; who are always procured in courts by more ardour and more vehement professions and applications than he would suffer himself to be entangled with. So that he was a man rather exceedingly liked than passionately loved" (*History,* 1:100). And, from the portrait of Thomas Howard, the Earl of Arundel, who, Hyde dryly observes, "was never suspected to love anybody": "He resorted sometimes to the Court, because there only was a greater man than himself; and went thither the seldomer, because there was a greater man than himself" (1:118). Both passages deliver their judgments in a deceptively bland and level tone. The first explains why Coventry's affability has checked his political ambitions; the second why Arundel attends, and does not attend, the royal court, a place to which he exists in a relation of perpetual need and estrangement. The self-repeating quality of Hyde's sentence, with neither clause subordinate to the other, enacts the impasse at the center of Arundel's crippled existence: the desire to see the king as the sole object worthy of his envy, and, because the truly envied cannot be equaled, the opposing desire to avoid him. In the case of Coventry, who declined to cultivate or excite immoderate feelings, the judgment is qualified — not merely liked but "exceedingly liked" — to its own parodic extremity.

Perhaps the most mean-spirited of Hyde's portraits is of Richard Weston, the Earl of Portland and, as Lord High Treasurer from 1628 to 1635, the financial architect of Charles's "personal rule" (that is, the eleven years in which he governed without calling a parliament, from 1629 to 1640). The portrait opposes Weston's imposed austerity on the kingdom, his curtailing of crown expenditure and extracting of revenue from extra-parliamentary taxes and impositions, to his own compulsive prodigality. Not untypically, its final sentence is also the most pitiless.

> After six or eight years spent in outward opulency, and inward murmur and trouble that it was no greater, after vast sums of money and great wealth gotten, and rather consumed than enjoyed, without any sense or delight in so great prosperity, with the agony that it was no greater, he died unlamented by any, bitterly mentioned by most, who never pretended to love him, and severely censored and complained of by those who expected most from him, and deserved best of him; and left a numerous family, which was in a short time worn out, and yet outlived the fortune he left behind him. (1.115)

Working toward and then away from its monosyllabic, two-word center ("he died"), Hyde's sentence disburses and then inexorably withdraws its largesse. The first half describes how Weston dooms himself, while the second devotes itself to the doom he calls down, like an antique curse, on his dependents and descendants, consigned first to penury and only then to oblivion.[58]

The leading terms of the Weston portrait — "outward opulency" and "inward murmur" — turn out to be more consequential than they initially appear, returning at the end of book 1 in a description of the condition of England at the time of the king's coronation progress to Scotland in 1633: "And with this general observation of the outward visible prosperity, and the inward reserved disposition of the people to murmur and unquietness, we conclude this first book" (*History,* 1.213). Drawing his narrative to a temporary close, Hyde dwells upon the disjunction between the objective appearance of plenty and the subjective experience of discontent, a disjunction now no longer particular to one person but escalated into a national grievance. Habits and behavior that had initially been presented as idiosyncratic are now revealed to belong to the English people as a whole, a move that might best be described as the communalization of personal character. Through their sequential rendering, the "murmur and unquietness" of the people can be construed as the *effect* of the "inward murmur and trouble" previously attributed to Weston, but it matters, I think, that Hyde omits any clearer indication of their causal relationship. On the one hand, Hyde is exposing the ideology of social hierarchy, of an elite authority at once indifferent to and dictating the terms — affective as much as they are social or economic or religious — of a broader political culture. On the other, he evinces little sympathy for the people themselves, who are shown not rebelling against their betters, but ignominiously conforming to their behavior, presenting a collective version of Weston's dysphoric singularity.

Strung together in this way, and for a full 80 paragraphs (more than a third of the total number in book 1), Hyde's portrait series does not so much pause or interrupt the unfolding narrative as suspend it indefinitely, eating it up, as it were, from within. One set of readerly expectations — that historical writing is impelled by events and the causal connections it establishes — cedes priority to another — that historical writing, or much the better part of it, has little to do with plot and everything to do with persons and their moral character. We have seen how this shift in priorities is reflected in the work's early reception. Responding to the immediate popularity of the portraits, Ward labored to elevate even higher the cultural status of the *History*. By turning its prose into heroic couplets, by altering still more drastically the proportions of biographical portraiture to narrative action, and by commissioning engravings after seventeenth century paintings of its historical figures, Ward fetishized and sought to enhance the literary and aesthetic qualities of Clarendon's original narrative.

But it is possible to see Ward's efforts in canonizing Clarendon as an intensification of many of Clarendon's own commitments to high culture. By the time of his political disgrace, Clarendon had amassed one of the most impressive art collections in all of Europe. The walls of his newly built palace in Piccadilly were hung with portrait paintings — ill gotten, it was darkly rumored, from the estates of bankrupt royalists. Represented in the collection were "the most Illustrious of our Nation, especially of his Life time and Acquaintance" according to John Evelyn, a not infrequent and always admiring visitor.[59] They included many of the Caroline courtiers whose characters appear in book 1 of the *History,* as though Clarendon were reproducing his lost art collection on the manuscript page. Among those whom Evelyn lists are the courtiers whose verbal portraits we have already encountered: the Earl of Arundel, in a full-length portrait by Anthony van Dyck; the Lord Keeper

Coventry painted three-quarters length by Cornelius Jansen; the Duke of Buckingham in a portrait also by Jansen, originally part of the royal collection sold off by the commonwealth government after Charles's execution; and Richard Weston, painted by van Dyck, standing full length, his white wand of office held loosely in one hand, an unfolded sheet of paper hanging limp in the other.[60]

Hyde assembled his portraits of the Caroline court gradually over many years, and there's no direct evidence that they were ever displayed together as a historical grouping. We do know, however, that during the late seventeenth century, the commissioning and hanging of portraits in sets had become newly fashionable, a practice facilitated by the development of Peter Lely's studio system that not only produced repetitions of portraits to order but reused signature "looks" and poses across multiple sitters.[61] Both as a luxury acquisition and as a decorative scheme, the portrait series was closely associated with Clarendon's daughter, Anne Hyde, the Duchess of York, whose "Windsor Beauties" — ten portraits of court ladies, all by Peter Lely and displayed either at Whitehall or at Saint James's Palace — were the poster girls of Restoration opulence. Anne assembled her female beauties in a spirit of playful competition, emulating her husband's, the Duke of York's, series of naval officers or "flag-men," also painted by Lely, commemorating the English victory at the Battle of Lowestoft in 1665.[62] It was in the spirit of just this precious courtly culture devoted to the commissioning and arrangement of portraits into coteries and cliques that Clarendon found himself assembling, verbally rather than visually, his own series of courtly portraits.

Here I propose that we pause to reconsider the political portraits assembled in book 1 in light of perhaps the most important and interesting thing that we know about them: they were not part of the *History* as Hyde originally conceived and wrote it between 1646 and 1648. Instead, the long character of Buckingham and its sequel, the catalog of Caroline courtiers, were introduced into the manuscript during the second and final stage of its composition between 1671 and 1672. There are, of course, many distinguished precedents for the inclusion of character sketches in historical writing, and these have been amply and expertly documented by scholars of the *History*.[63] Nonetheless, the portraits' addition to and obstruction of the narrative Hyde had crafted 30 years earlier has struck several readers as sufficiently remarkable as to carry some additional burden of explanation. Among these, Charles Firth, the first scholar to look closely at Hyde's Restoration additions to the *History,* proposed that the portraits be excused as a lapse in discipline and judgment. Reworking the manuscript during his second period of exile, Hyde "inserted characters not merely when the incidents of narration demanded but whenever he could find a pretext for indulging his predilection for that particular kind of composition."[64] Some 50 years later, E. M. W. Tillyard hazarded that Hyde may have inserted the portraits not to indulge his creative proclivities but to imitate the structure of the opening books of Homer's *Iliad:* "As Homer began with the origin of the Greeks' trouble in the quarrel of Agamemnon and Achilles, so Clarendon began with the fatal influence of the Duke of Buckingham in getting Parliament dissolved and alienating men's affections from the King. And just as Homer put his catalogue of forces and descriptions of leaders in the pause after the main motivating action had been recounted, so Clarendon introduced his characters of the main actors after he had finished his account of the origin of the rebellion."[65] What, for Firth, was supererogatory decoration becomes, for Tillyard, a deliberate reaching toward the cultural domain and prestige of classical epic.

Tillyard's conjecture has not been taken up by subsequent scholars, in part because Tillyard himself is unwilling to put much weight behind his theory of the *History's* belated Homeric construction.[66] I would suggest, however, that his theory is worth revisiting, in part because we can find a more historically proximate analogue for the biographies that Hyde interpellates in 1671–72, an analogue that offers its own, no less pointed, discourse of weak-mindedness and craven accommodation within a Homeric frame. In the opening books of *Paradise Lost,* Milton presents a biographical catalog "long to tell" of the rebel angels in their future identities as pagan gods.[67] The catalog (1.376–521) is followed by a council of war (2.1–505) during which the angelic leaders debate whether to continue their pursuit of armed warfare against heaven, as Moloch, the first speaker, urges, or whether to remain in hell, as Belial and Mammon recommend. Emptied of initiative, the assembly echoes the positions presented to them, "as when hollow rocks retain / The sound of blust'ring winds" (2.285–86). Both Colin Burrow and David Quint observe how their loss of martial resolve divides the epic form from its traditional contents, diverting it into a world of romance characterized not by fighting but by fraud and cunning. Moreover, and as Quint further notes, Milton inverts the order of the *Iliad's* opening sequence of events. In Homer, the catalog of the ships follows the Greek council in which Odysseus convinces Agamemnon to renew the siege of Troy. In Milton, by contrast, the catalog precedes the council, a martial exhibition that serves no meaningful function except as an ironic prelude to its peacetime talks.[68]

Hyde, too, bends his Iliadic plot to a distinctly unheroic end. The Caroline courtiers are assembled to fill the political — and narrative — space left vacant by the loss of Buckingham, the Achillean favorite. But in their eagerness to make peace with France and Spain and withdraw from any further military involvement in Europe, they more closely resemble Milton's fallen angels, who dread any continuance of the war against heaven, than Homer's Greek warriors, who agree to renew their assault on the city of Troy. "And so they all concurred (though in nothing else)," writes Hyde at the end of the catalog, "in their unanimous advice to the King to put the quickest period he could possibly to the expensive war against the two crowns: and, his majesty following their advice... there quickly followed so excellent a composure throughout the whole kingdom that the like peace and plenty and universal tranquillity for ten years was never enjoyed by any nation" (*History*, 1.146). "Peace and plenty and universal tranquillity" — Hyde's perfectly spaced and laudatory nouns seem to validate a nostalgic view of an idyllic, prewar past. Once read in relation to the Homeric catalog that precedes them, however, they sound a more ambivalent and defeatist note. Rather than spending ten years emulating the Greek warriors of the *Iliad,* heroically defending the cause of Protestantism in Europe (as Defoe's Cavalier is doing), Hyde's devilish courtiers opt for ease, like Belial, and self-enrichment, like Mammon, at home.

We can see Hyde, the exiled architect of the Stuart Restoration, and Milton, the poet of the republican commonwealth, both turning to the same Homeric precedent to write their epic catalogs, or portrait series, of fallen worthies who withdraw ignominiously from heroic action. "O shame to men! Devil with devil damned / Firm concord holds," the Miltonic narrator of *Paradise Lost* interjects at the end of the counsel scene in hell, praising the devils for all agreeing with one another, while men "yet live in hatred, enmity,

and strife / Among themselves, and levy cruel wars" (2.496–501). The animus of this tirade is clearly directed against the members of the human race,
who, alone "of creatures rational" (2.498), prove incapable of living together
without exhaustive argument or violent adjudication. But there is animus
left over for the devils, too, whose agreement is slavish, strategically self-
interested, and so, in its own way, just as damning. Hyde's version of this
Miltonic tirade — "And so they all concurred (though in nothing else)"
(*History*, 1.146) — is more succinct, less inflated with indignation and outrage, but it works the same ironic angles of interpretation. If the swift concurrence of the courtiers ranks them among the diabolical, the parenthetical
aside returns them to the company of the human.

We are now in a better position to see how with his belated introduction
of the political portraits Hyde was not merely satirizing the vices, vanities,
and venalities of particular courtiers, expertly rendered as these are and delivered in some of the seventeenth century's most entertainingly acerbic prose.
For although the portraits appear detachable from the larger narrative, and
were, as we have seen, certainly received in this way as a series of pictures on
view, it is precisely their lack of connection that makes them politically significant for Clarendon's historical analysis of Caroline England. The portraits
interrupt the historical narrative at the very moment at which the narrative
details the takeover of affairs by Charles's courtiers, after the dismissal of a
Parliament that will not convene again for another dozen years. The move
to biographical description, therefore, marks a political and, as we have seen,
antiheroic move away from a narrative account of certain kinds of participatory and outward-looking engagement; a retrenchment to a smaller, less
capacious, unexpansive, and isolated world. It is, thus, as an instantiation,
and indictment, of aristocratic politics that the form of the biographical portrait achieves its ideological effects in the *History*. The portraits that upend
Clarendon's *History* make no attempt to offer an analysis of the rebellion or
its causes. But it is in this very failure, in this occlusion of argument or analysis, that we can see biography emerging as an alternative explanation for why
the rebellion happened.

Turning now from the perspective of the *History* to the analytical perspective of this study, we can see how the biographical portraits that Hyde interpolated into his narrative in 1671–72 are able to stand more generally for

the operations of biography across the late seventeenth century. In pressing himself, at the end of his life, to revise his understanding of the decades leading up to the English civil wars, Hyde found himself galvanized by the same cultural recognition of the capacity of biography to dull the edges of political argument that had first galvanized his contemporary, and old adversary, Milton in 1649. With what degree of irony and self-wounding insight Clarendon may have come to this recognition during his months of exile in Montpelier, months in which he honed and crafted his sequence of political portraits into crystalline brilliance, is of course an unanswerable question and, more properly, a biographical one. It was these portraits that raised his literary stature and secured his reputation as a thrilling prose stylist and pitiless observer of human folly, but they also, I have argued, declare him to be a participant in, and practitioner of, the biographical populism that marked the postwar era.

For whatever powers of insight Clarendon may have commanded, he was still writing from within a culture of biography that had eclipsed open debate and the accepted protocols of political argument. Defoe, by contrast, was writing from outside it. The fictionalized biographies of his pair of seventeenth century Englishmen, Crusoe and the Cavalier, attempt to do more than merely diagnose or contest the occlusion of certain kinds of political activity by biographical storytelling and its privatization of the political within the public political sphere. What they do, in addition and inside the gravitational logic of their own first-person points of view, is to historicize the sociopolitical conditions under which the biography usurped the reign of argument. Theirs is at once a national tale and, inarguably now, a personal one.

AFTERWORD

WRITING IN 1716, in a periodical essay for the Whig-sponsored *Free-holder,* Joseph Addison remarked upon the sudden proliferation of biographers among the hack writers looking to turn a quick profit from their work: "There is a race of Men lately sprung up among this sort of Writers, whom one cannot reflect upon without Indignation as well as Contempt. These are our *Grub-Street* Biographers, who watch for the Death of a Great Man, like so many Undertakers, on purpose to make a Penny of him. He is no sooner laid in his Grave, but he falls into the Hands of a Historian."[1] Addison compares his "Race" of biographers to "so many Undertakers," tradespeople who profited not only from arranging funerals but lavishly furnishing them, renting out cloaks, gloves, drapes, hangings, coats of arms, and carriages. In 1716, this commercial enterprise was comparatively new: the *Oxford English Dictionary* traces to 1698 the narrower use of the term "undertaker" to mean "one who makes a business of carrying out the arrangements of funerals."[2] Yet as we saw in the introduction, the term "biographer" was hardly less novel, entering the English lexicon, initially with very little uptake, in the decade after the Restoration before making its belated literary debut in Dryden's *Life of Plutarch* (1683). Upstarts on the cultural and consumer scene, the biographer and the undertaker ply their money-making trades alongside each other. If death is inescapable, so, too, is being stalked by "our *Grub-Street* Biographers." These are the worms that get you in the end.

Addison presents the biographers as an undifferentiated collective, "a race of Men" whose spontaneous generation recalls the myth of Cadmus and the springing up of dragon's teeth that we saw Milton using some 50 years earlier in his revolutionary tract *Areopagitica* (1644). Their indistinguishable anonymity contrasts with the proper names attached to the most durable collections of lives published in the sixteenth and seventeenth centuries: Foxe's *Book of Martyrs,* Clarke's *Lives,* Fuller's *Worthies,* Walton's *Lives.* These sponsoring names guaranteed the popularity of their serial productions, offering readers the assurance of predictability while expanding the canon of the like-minded. The distinction between the named celebrity of these life writers and Addison's nameless biographical hacks is not simply one of marketability or of temporal chronology, however. For as I discussed in the introduction, the older and looser designation of the "life" is capable of holding in a kind of precritical suspension the relation of the life written to the life lived. A newer and more self-consciously literary term, "biography" picks out only the written life, breaking the unarticulated bond between represented and lived experience. In Addison's characterization, the ideal fiction of a commonality sheltering under the banner of the named life-writer is notably absent. Instead, it is the biographers who are presented as the members of a collectivity that is purely tribal, while it is their victim, a generic or representative "Great Man," who is isolated helplessly in the posthumous singular. Addison speaks his disapproval through the fictional mouthpiece of the Freeholder (an owner of land whose value, of at least 40 shillings, qualifies him to vote), but the public he addresses is conjured by the possessive first-person plural, "*our Grub-Street* Biographers." The pronoun presumes familiarity even as it assumes responsibility: the biographers belong to us however strenuously we disown them.

Throughout this study, I have argued that lives and life stories offered a means to put contentious beliefs beyond variance or debate. This claim may hold true more generally, supporting a broader history of how narratives of people and their lived experiences stand apart from and intersect with an elite or learned culture of argument. But for the later seventeenth century in particular, lives rendered an important cultural service. The traumatic experience of the English civil wars, the alterations in church and state that followed first with the Interregnum and then with the Restoration, and the rapid advance of public political discussion across these middle decades of the century, all urged the need for ways of disarticulating beliefs and convictions from open animosity and full-blown conflict. Interpreting recent history — and intercepting present controversy — the life served as a highly effective vehicle for reinforcing an ideological worldview that was often intolerant or reactionary while avoiding the direct avowal of its divisive political effects. As a successful literary form, it appealed to segments of the population who were wary of the negative effects of the period's political culture: those who felt nostalgia for a simpler, more traditional, world; who found the pace, volume, and intensity of public discussion alienating or overwhelming; or who felt marginalized by or merely indifferent to the rhetorical maneuverings and ponderous obfuscations of disputatious prose. The life's polemical relation to public debate is visible in its celebration of a world that is socially cohesive, bound together by the mutually dependent relations of custom and affection, community and companionship. It is visible, too, in its casting of disagreement as a disreputable act, something that only the people you disagree with would think to do.

This study does not extend its purview to the periodical prose of the early eighteenth century. Still, it is worth pausing to reflect upon Addison's censorious attitude toward contemporary biography, his scorning of it as a demotic and desacralizing exercise, embarked upon for profit and to satisfy public curiosity rather than for any higher or more edifying purpose. It is Addison's indictment, slightly rephrased — "Our Grubstreet *biographers* watch for the death of a great man, like so many undertakers, on purpose to make a penny of him" — that will be included as the sole illustration of usage in Samuel Johnson's entry for "biographer" in *A Dictionary of the English language* (1755), consolidating the status of the biographer as a malign yet relatively minor and uninspiring figure in the construction of national public life.[3]

In his *Freeholder* essay, Addison bases his judgment on the undeniable popularity and competitive success of biography as an ephemeral form of entertainment, a record of the spectacular and scandalous lives of the departed rushed into print in order to capitalize on the newsworthiness of death itself. As he wrote, the fate of his own patron and leading Whig politician, John Somers, was foremost in his mind. Dying just six days after Addison's essay appeared, Somers would become within a matter of months the subject of an anonymous and unauthorized biographical memoir.[4] Attributed by Pat Rogers to John Oldmixon, the memoir is prefaced by a "large introduction, in vindication of the modern biography occasion'd by some general reflections upon it in the Free-holder." Oldmixon would not submit to Addison's displeasure without a fight. Instead, he attacks the fictional persona of the Freeholder for his high-toned elitism, declaring, "a plain, careful, curious Writer, may, tho' he walks a-Foot and writes in a Calico Gown, put facts in as good Order as if he loll'd in his Chariot and wrote in *Brocade*; it ought not to discourage him to undertake a useful and pleasant Work, because his Character does not come up to the *High Idea* some Cricks have conceiv'd of *Biographers*."[5] Through these paired portraits of the perambulatory "Writer" and the indolent "Criticks," Oldmixon implies that the Freeholder's poor opinion is motivated as much by social attitude as by aesthetic taste. The ill will of the gentlemanly essayist toward the self-made writer of biography is symptomatic, he suggests, of a broader class struggle taking place within the realm of letters. Rather than denying the antagonistic relation between the essayist and the biographer, Oldmixon aggressively reinterprets its terms. He transforms Addison's satire of the Grub Street biographers into a competing satire of the cultural aristocracy and their luxurious, unproductive labor of commentary and analysis.

The quarrel between Addison and Oldmixon shows that biography had become a cultural flashpoint, but to understand why it had become so — why, that is, under the disinterested pose of the Freeholder, Addison hides his interest in attacking the genre — we need to meet another polarizing figure, the enterprising, unscrupulous, and indefatigable bookseller Edmund Curll. Starting in 1713, Curll made a specialty of publishing lives of prominent public figures with copies of their last will and testament attached for the world to see.[6] It is this practice to which Addison makes his most strenuous objection. "What can we expect," he complains, "from an Author that undertakes to write the Life of a Great Man, who is furnished with no other Matters of Fact, besides Legacies; and instead of being able to tell us what he did, can only tell us what he bequeathed."[7] It turned out, of course, that how rich somebody was and who they left their money to were precisely the "Matters of Fact" that the reading public most wanted to know. Curll was to prove a lasting arbiter of the public's fascination with the final fortunes of the famous. The *Oxford Dictionary of National Biography* continues to list "wealth at death" in the reference section at the foot of each entry, and it is a disciplined reader indeed who does not sneak a look. (Addison's entry reveals that he left most of his property to his much wealthier wife.)[8]

In constructing his distinction between the stalwart Freeholder, whose civic identity is proudly founded upon land ownership, and the new breed of biographers, who possess no lineage and recognize no fealty, Addison might be seen to embrace the position occupied by the other dissenting commentators of this study: Milton and, more playfully and ironically, Defoe. They, too, had protested the populist energies of the biography and its destructive effects upon the national public life. Like Milton and Defoe, the Whig Addison sees the discursive mode he favored, the disciplined, principled, moderate, and judiciously argued contributions to an open public dialogue, threatened by an insurgent, exploitative, irrational, and unapologetically populist mode of biographical storytelling.[9]

But this opposition is neither as stable nor as absolute as it might initially appear. It is true that there are undeniable structural affinities between the critical stance assumed by Addison, on the one hand, and the seventeenth century Puritan poet he so admired, on the other. It is true, too, that the Grub Street biographers of the eighteenth century, in their avoidance of meaningful critical engagement, have much in common with the anti-intellectual life writers of the earlier period. At the same time, however, it should be possible for us to see that Addison's self-possessing, independently minded essayist finds his profoundest parallel in the seventeenth century writer of lives. We remember how in the hands of Charles I, for example, or of Thomas Fuller or Izaak Walton, the life implicitly declared itself to be distinct from public contentiousness, cultivating a community of readers whose public identity was imaginatively defined by a shared disinclination to join in argument. It is a later iteration of this posture of political disinterestedness that the periodical essayist, in Addison's characterization of the Freeholder, actively and more studiously takes up. The competing alignments and misalignments of biography and criticism in Addison's essay alert us to the complex ways in which, as public discourse proliferated, the life's deflection of argument was appropriated and dispersed among a variety of literary forms, of which the periodical essay was only one. In his fable of the birth of the biographers, Addison, as we have seen, denies to the upstart genre of biography any legitimating affiliation to the early modern life. What his fable also obscures, we might now insist, are the less evident lines of affiliation between the life's depoliticization of the public's imagination and Addison's own understanding of his discursive performance.[10]

Yet these ironies of political alliance are little compared to our own. In the contemporary field of life-writing studies, many have found in the recovery of early modern England's rich archive of unconventional life records something broadly akin to our contemporary memoir culture. We generally feel comfortable assuming that these diverse and unique expressions of personality harbor at their core a progressive politics that joins up with our own. It is my hope that this book, which has focused its attention on some of the mostly widely available, most widely read examples of life narratives (commonly found, as we have seen, in printed collections) has expanded our understanding of the ideological significances that the representation of a life was able, and often typically asked, to sustain. I have tried to show how the life, in its many printed and populist incarnations, was put to specific partisan and illiberal ends, seemingly detached from political conflict but implicated fully in its ideological aims and effects. The enlightened goals of today's field of life-writing studies could not be more opposed to the conservative agenda of much of the period's best-selling works of biography. For all the value of its singular insights and discoveries, the academy's life-writing movement has underestimated the power of these broader, institutionally sponsored, and culturally dominant examples of biographical populism.

How could it be otherwise? We have seen throughout this book the multiple strategies by which the early modern life labors to occlude its deepest political investments. With its wearyingly banal expressions of sanctimony, piety, simplicity, and even simple-mindedness, the life has managed — managed, I think it can said, brilliantly — to make itself invisible to the typical perspectives of critical analysis by which scholars attempt to understand the embedded meanings of a period's written culture. From the royal memoir to the merest minute, the early modern life has always invited misrecognition. It is in this very misrecognition, perhaps, that we can see the clearest sign of its extraordinary success. In a crowded public realm, the stories we tell of ourselves and to ourselves retain their power, for good or ill.

NOTES

NOTES TO INTRODUCTION

1. Thomas Fuller, *Abel redevivus* (London, 1651), 599.

2. Samuel Clarke, *The marrow of ecclesiastical historie, conteined in the lives of the fathers, and other learned men, and famous divines, which have flourished in the Church since Christ's time, to this present age* (London, 1650).

3. Clarke, *A generall martyrologie containing a collection of all the greatest persecutions which have befallen the church of Christ from the creation to our present times* (London, 1651), sig. b4r. Clarke's *Marrow of ecclesiastical historie* was entered into the Stationers' Entry Book of Copies, commonly known as the Stationers' Register (SR), on August 6, 1649, under the title *A tract of the lives of the fathers & other eminent & famous divines which have lived from Christs tyme to this present age.* See *A Transcript of the Registers of the Company of Stationers of London from 1640 to 1708,* 3 vols., ed. G. E. Briscoe Eyre and C. R. Rivington (London, 1913–14), 1:324. There is no entry for Fuller's *Abel redevivus.*

4. The argument that successive editions of the *Acts and Monuments* are better understood as distinctive works, designed for particular publics at particular times, is now widely accepted among early modern scholars. John N. King gives summary accounts of all eight unabridged editions of the text — from the first edition of 1563 to the ninth edition of 1684 — in *Foxe's Book of Martyrs and Early Modern Print Culture* (Cambridge: Cambridge University Press, 2006), 92–161. For the seventh (1632) and eighth (1640) editions of the *Acts and Monuments,* which enlisted Foxe's brand of evangelical Protestantism to intervene in contemporary debates over Charles I's religious and foreign policies, see, in particular, Damian Nussbaum, "Appropriating Martyrdom: Fears of Renewed Persecution and the 1632 Edition of *Acts and Monuments,*" in *John Foxe and the English Reformation,* ed. David Loades, 178–91 (Aldershot: Ashgate, 1997). David Scott Kastan, "Little Foxes," in *John Foxe and His World,* ed. Christopher Highley and John N. King, 117–32 (Burlington, VT: Ashgate, 2002), surveys the early seventeenth century market for (novelty) abridgments of Foxe. In the preface to his *Generall Martyrologie* (1651), Clarke joins the ranks of abridgers, announcing his intention "to contract and methodize" lives "so largely set down" by Foxe himself (sig. a2r).

5. John Fell (attributed), *The Life of that reverend divine, and learned historian, Dr. Thomas Fuller* (London, 1661), 62–63, 27–29.

6. The punchline to Milton's "tailed" sonnet, "On the New Forcers of Conscience Under the Long Parliament," offers perhaps the most famous and certainly the most succinct formulation of the perceived lack of any meaningful distinction between these two rivalrous ecclesiastical regimes, each willing to be underwritten by coercive state power, declaring, "New *Presbyter* is but old *Priest* writ large." All references to Milton's poetry are to *The Complete Poetry and Essential Prose of John Milton,* ed. William Kerrigan, John

Rumrich, and Stephen M. Fallon (New York: Modern Library, 2007); hereafter cited in the text.

7. On ecclesiastical policies and the toleration debates, see John Coffey, "Puritanism and Liberty Revisited: The Case for Toleration in the English Revolution," *Historical Journal* 41, no. 4 (1998): 961–85. Kathleen Lynch, *Protestant Autobiography in the Seventeenth-Century Anglophone World* (Oxford: Oxford University Press, 2012), 121–78, examines the "surge" of printed conversion narratives, sponsored by independently gathered churches, at midcentury.

8. Fuller, *Abel redevivus,* sig. A4v.

9. The Nine Worthies were traditionally composed of three pagan (Hector, Alexander, and Julius Caesar), three Jewish (Joshua, King David, and Judas Maccabaeus), and three Christian (King Arthur, Charlemagne, and Godfrey of Bouillon) heroes, although individuals could always be swapped out and in. During the play of the Nine Worthies in *Love's Labour's Lost,* for example, Costard the clown berates the curate Nathaniel for his timid impersonation of Alexander: "O, sir, you have overthrown Alisander the Conqueror. You will be scraped out of the painted cloth for this. Your lion that holds his pole-axe sitting on a close-stool will be given to Ajax. He will be the ninth Worthy" (5.2.566–69). Costard's penal — and scatalogical — substitution, Ajax for Alexander, makes clear that a finite canon is also a competitive one in which everyone must fight to maintain their place. All references to Shakespeare's plays are to *The Norton Shakespeare,* 2nd ed., gen. ed. Stephen Greenblatt, (New York: Norton, 2008); hereafter cited in the text. Tessa Watt, *Cheap Print and Popular Piety, 1550–1640* (Cambridge: Cambridge University Press, 1991), discusses the Worthies as a subject of artwork and wall hangings — Costard's "painted cloth" (212–14).

10. The distinction between pace of sale (fast sellers) and volume of sale (steady sellers) is taken from John Sutherland, *Bestsellers: A Very Short Introduction* (Oxford: Oxford University Press, 2007), 18. Alan B. Farmer and Zachary Lesser, "What Is Print Popularity?: A Map of the Elizabethan Book Trade," in *The Elizabethan Top Ten: Defining Print Popularity in Early Modern England,* ed. Andy Kesson and Emma Smith, 19–54 (Burlington, VT: Ashgate, 2013), redistribute Sutherland's two categories across four sectors of the early modern book trade — "monopolistic," "mature," "innovative," and "topical" — each possessed of a normative span and pattern of sale.

11. For that purpose, Donald Stauffer's remarkable *English Biography before 1700* (Cambridge, MA: Harvard University Press, 1930) remains an indispensable reference guide.

12. Horace, *Epistle,* 1.16. The line was routinely quoted. It appears on a 1519 bronze medal struck by Quentin Massys for Erasmus and is cited by Montaigne in "That to Philosophize Is to Learn to Die" ("Que philosopher c'est apprendre à mourir"), in *The Complete Essays of Montaigne,* trans. Donald M. Frame (Stanford, CA: Stanford University Press, 1957), 64.

13. In this way, the frontispiece works a variation on the split iconography of medieval *transi* tombs that represented the decomposition of the naked corpse on the bottom level and the fully clothed idealized figure on the level above it. See Kathleen Cohen, *Metamorphosis of a Death Symbol: The Transi Tomb in the Late Middle Ages and the Renaissance* (Berkeley, CA: University of California Press, 1973).

14. Rev. 20:12–15.

15. Ann M. Blair, *Too Much to Know: Managing Scholarly Information before the Modern Age* (New Haven, CT: Yale University Press, 2010), 1.

16. Thomas Fuller, *The History of the Worthies of England, Who for Parts and Learning have been eminent in the several Counties. Together with an Historical Narrative of the Native Commodities and Rarities in each County* (London, 1662), 1. All subsequent quotations are taken from this edition, hereafter cited in the text as *Worthies*.

17. Ian Donaldson, "National Biography and the Arts of Memory: From Thomas Fuller to Colin Matthew," in *Mapping Lives: The Uses of Biography*, ed. Peter France and William St. Clair, 67–82 (Oxford: Oxford University Press for the British Academy, 2002), 74–75.

18. Peter Buck, "Seventeenth-Century Political Arithmetic: Civil Strife and Vital Statistics," *Isis* 68 (1977): 67–84; Joyce Oldham Appleby, *Economic Thought and Ideology in Seventeenth-Century England* (Princeton, NJ: Princeton University Press, 1978), 78–128; Mary Poovey, *A History of the Modern Fact: Problems of Knowledge in the Sciences of Wealth and Society* (Chicago: University of Chicago Press, 1998), 120–38; Steve Pincus, "From Holy Cause to Economic Interest: The Transformation of Reason of State Thinking in Seventeenth-Century England," in *A Nation Transformed: England after the Restoration,* ed. Alan Houston and Steven Pincus, 272–98 (Cambridge: Cambridge University Press, 2001); Andrea A. Rusnock, *Vital Accounts: Quantifying Health and Population in Eighteenth-Century England and France* (Cambridge: Cambridge University Press, 2002), 15–42. Richard Helgerson explores an earlier phase in the political history of mapping the nation in "The Land Speaks: Cartography, Chorography, and Subversion in Renaissance England," *Representations* 16 (1986): 50–85.

19. Samuel Pepys, *The Diary of Samuel Pepys,* 11 vols., ed. Robert Latham and William Matthews (London: G. Bell and Sons, 1974), 3:26 (February 10, 1662); 3:34 (February 23, 1662); 5:118 (April 10, 1664).

20. Ibid., 4:410–11 (December 10, 1663). In his "Naval Minutes," preparatory notes for a maritime history he would never get around to writing, Pepys complains of the paucity of "Dr. Fuller's sea-worthies" in comparison to his "land-ones," vowing to redress the balance in his own research. *Samuel Pepys's Naval Minutes,* ed. J. R. Tanner (London: Navy Records Society, 1926), 266–67, 421.

21. Margaret Canovan, "Populism for Political Theorists?" *Journal of Political Ideologies* 9, no. 3 (2004): 243. Canovan's first definition of populism, the struggle of the people against established power, has been extensively theorized by Ernesto Laclau, *On Populist Reason* (London: Verso, 2005). Against Canovan, Laclau insists that the term "populism" cannot pick out any actual group, ideology, or series of demands; it can only pick out the political logic that subtends them.

22. Raymond Williams, "Popular," in *Keywords: A Vocabulary of Culture and Society,* rev. ed. (New York: Oxford University Press, 1983), 236–38. For more on the political understanding of popularity from the 1580s forward, see Andy Kesson and Emma Smith, introduction to *Elizabethan Top Ten,* 3–4; and Joad Raymond, ed., introduction to *The Oxford History of Popular Print Culture,* vol. 1, *Cheap Print in Britain and Ireland to 1660* (Oxford: Oxford University Press, 2011), 4–7.

23. Peter Lake and Steve Pincus, "Rethinking the Public Sphere in Early Modern England," *Journal of British Studies* 45 (2006): 284; Mark Knights, *Representation and*

Misrepresentation in Later Stuart Britain: Partisanship and Political Culture (Oxford: Oxford University Press, 2005), 3. See also Tim Harris, "Understanding Popular Politics in Restoration Britain," in Houston and Pincus, *A Nation Transformed,* 125–53.

24. *OED Online,* s.v. "life," from Old Saxon *lif,* n., 1a, 13, http://www.oed.com/view/Entry/19219 (accessed May 11, 2016).

25. *OED Online,* s.v. "biography," n., 1, http://www.oed.com//view/Entry/108093 (accessed May 11, 2016). The word "biography" does appear, although infrequently, in Greek in late antiquity and in Latin during the medieval period. For the French equivalents, *biographe* (1721) and *biographie* (1750), see Ann Jefferson, *Biography and the Question of Literature in France* (Oxford: Oxford University Press, 2007), 18.

26. Habermas lays out this account in his seminal 1962 study, *Strukturwandel der Öffentlichkeit,* published in English as *The Structural Transformation of the Public Sphere,* trans. Thomas Burger and Frederick Lawrence (Cambridge, MA: MIT Press, 1991). The essays in *Public and Private in Thought and Practice: Perspectives on a Grand Dichotomy,* ed. Jeff Weintraub and Krishan Kumar (Chicago: Chicago University Press, 1997), analyze public-sphere theory, its uses, limitations, and implications. For historical assessments and applications of Habermas's work within the field of early modern studies, see the essays in *The Politics of the Public Sphere in Early Modern England,* ed. Peter Lake and Steve Pincus (Manchester: Manchester University Press, 2007); and Joseph Loewenstein and Paul Stevens, eds., "Special Issue: When Is a Public Sphere?" *Criticism* 46, no. 2 (2004).

27. Samuel Johnson, *The Rambler,* no. 60 (October 13, 1750); *The Idler,* no. 84 (November 24, 1759), in *The Yale Edition of the Works of Samuel Johnson,* 23 vols., gen. ed. Herman W. Liebert (New Haven, CT: Yale University Press, 1955–), 2:261–64, 3: 318–23.

28. John Dryden, "The Life of Plutarch," in *Plutarch's Lives: Translated from the Greek by Several Hands* (London, 1683), 94.

29. Ibid., 95. John Evelyn the Younger's translation of this same passage for the Tonson edition of Plutarch reads: "sometimes a Matter of less moment, an Expression, or a Jest, informs us better of their Manners, and Inclinations, than the most famous Sieges, the greatest Armies, or the bloudiest Battels whatsoever." "The Life of Alexander the Great," in *The fourth volume of Plutarch's Lives: Translated from the Greek, by several hands* (London: Printed for Jacob Tonson, 1693), 245–46. Roger North makes the same point rather more irreverently: "What signifies it to us, how many battles Alexander fought. It were more to the purpose to say how often he was drunk." Roger North, general preface to "The Life of the Lord Keeper North," qtd. in *Biography as an Art: Selected Criticism, 1560–1960,* ed. James L. Clifford (New York: Oxford University Press, 1962), 31.

30. Michael McKeon, *The Secret History of Domesticity: Public, Private, and the Division of Knowledge* (Baltimore: Johns Hopkins University Press, 2005), 337–41.

31. Fuller, *Worthies,* 8; Fell (attributed), *Life of Fuller,* 105; John Gauden, *The Works of Mr. Richard Hooker* (London, 1662), 2; James Heath, "To the Reader," in *Flagellum; or, The life and death, birth and burial of O Cromwel* (London, 1663), sig. A5v. All of these examples are listed by Stauffer, *English Biography before 1700,* 218–19. The *OED* (s.v. "biographer," n. 1) records an earlier use in John Bulwer's handbook of manual gestures, *Chirologia* (London, 1644): "The *Hand* according to the primitive intention of Nature, having by a necessary consent of Nations beene ever chosen Chronologer of al remarkable actions, hath consequently proved its own Biographer" (82).

32. William Empson, *Some Versions of Pastoral* (London: Chatto and Windus, 1935).

33. To the extent that the modern field of life-writing studies recognizes a founder text, it would be Olaudah Equiano's *Interesting Narrative of the Life of Olaudah Equiano* (1789), published in England just seven years after Rousseau's *Confessions* was published in France (1782), although both works had been circulating in manuscript before they appeared in print. For the disciplinary origins and history of the term "life-writing," see Shirley Neuman, "Life-Writing," in *Literary History of Canada: Canadian Literature in English*, gen. ed. W. H. New (Toronto: University of Toronto Press, 1990), 333–70; and Sidonie Smith and Julia Watson, "Life Narrative: Definitions and Distinctions," in *Reading Autobiography: A Guide for Interpreting Life Narratives* (2001; repr., Minneapolis: University of Minnesota Press, 2011), 1–14.

34. Sidonie Smith, "Narrating Lives and Contemporary Imaginaries," *PMLA* 126, no. 3 (2011): 564–74.

35. Kevin Sharpe and Steven N. Zwicker articulate this historicist concern in their introduction to *Writing Lives: Biography and Textuality, Identity and Representation in Early Modern England* (Oxford: Oxford University Press, 2008): "Our endeavor in this volume is to set aside the dominant Enlightenment model of biography in order to explore the variety and the complexities of all the forms in which early modern lives were written" (4).

36. A critical note that did justice to this archival project of reclamation would be long indeed, but some landmark moments and recent assessments include Mary Prior, ed., *Women in English Society, 1500–1800* (London: Meuthen, 1985); Catherine Gallagher, "Embracing the Absolute: The Politics of the Female Subject in Seventeenth-Century England," *Genders* 1 (1988): 24–39; Elspeth Graham, Hilary Hind, Elaine Hobby, and Helen Wilcox, eds., *Her Own Life: Autobiographical Writings by Seventeenth-Century Englishwomen* (1989; repr., London: Routledge, 2004); Patricia Crawford and Laura Gowing, eds., *Women's Worlds in Seventeenth-Century England* (London: Routledge, 2000); Helen Ostovich and Elizabeth Sauer, eds., "Life-Writing: Non-Fiction and Fiction," in *Reading Early Modern Women: An Anthology of Texts in Manuscript and Print, 1550–1700* (London: Routledge, 2004), 241–315; Michelle M. Dowd and Julie A. Eckerle, eds., *Genre and Women's Life-Writing in Early Modern England* (Aldershot: Ashgate, 2007); Kate Chedgzoy, *Women's Writing in the British Atlantic World: Memory, Place, and History, 1500–1700* (Cambridge: Cambridge University Press, 2007); Ramona Wray, "Autobiography," in *The Cambridge Companion to Early Modern Women's Writing*, ed. Laura Lunger Knoppers, 194–207 (Cambridge: Cambridge University Press, 2009).

37. Margreta de Grazia, Maureen Quilligan, and Peter Stallybrass, eds., *Subject and Object in Renaissance Culture* (Cambridge: Cambridge University Press, 1996); Debora Shuger, "Life-Writing in Seventeenth-Century England," in *Representations of the Self from the Renaissance to Romanticism*, ed. Patrick Coleman, Jayne Lewis, and Jill Kowalik, 63–78 (Cambridge: Cambridge University Press, 2000); Lena Cowen Orlin, *Locating Privacy in Tudor London* (Oxford: Oxford University Press, 2009). Katharine Eisaman Maus adopts a more skeptical stance in *Being and Having in Shakespeare* (Oxford: Oxford University Press, 2013).

38. Adam Smyth, *Autobiography in Early Modern England* (Cambridge: Cambridge University Press, 2011).

39. David Booy, *Personal Disclosures: An Anthology of Self-Writings from the Seventeenth Century* (Aldershot: Ashgate, 2002); Meredith Anne Skura, *Tudor Autobiography: Listening for Inwardness* (Chicago: University of Chicago Press, 2008).

40. Stauffer, *English Biography before 1700;* Allan Pritchard, *English Biography in the Seventeenth Century: A Critical Survey* (Toronto: University of Toronto Press, 2005); *The Rhetorics of Life-Writing in Early Modern Europe: Forms of Biography from Cassandra Fedele to Louis XIV,* ed. Thomas F. Mayer and Daniel R. Woolf (Ann Arbor: University of Michigan Press, 1995).

41. Richard Wendorf, *The Elements of Life: Biography and Portrait-Painting in Stuart and Georgian England* (Oxford: Oxford University Press, 1990); Jessica Martin, *Walton's "Lives": Conformist Commemorations and the Rise of Biography* (Oxford: Oxford University Press, 2001); Ian Donaldson, "National Biography and the Arts of Memory"; Keith Thomas, *Changing Conceptions of National Biography: The Oxford DNB in Historical Perspective* (Cambridge: Cambridge University Press, 2005); Sharpe and Zwicker, introduction to *Writing Lives.*

42. Judith Anderson, *Biographical Truth: The Representation of Historical Persons in Tudor-Stuart Writing* (New Haven, CT: Yale University Press, 1984); Kevin Pask, *The Emergence of the English Author: Scripting the Life of the Poet in Early Modern England* (Cambridge: Cambridge University Press, 1996).

Notes to Chapter 1

1. John Milton, *Eikonoklastes,* in *The Complete Prose Works of John Milton,* 8 vols., ed. Don M. Wolfe et al. (New Haven, CT: Yale University Press, 1953–82), 3:337–38; hereafter cited as YP, followed by volume and page number. All quotations from *Eikonoklastes* refer to this edition.

2. Milton had already used the figure of left and right handedness to organize a discussion of competing modes and strengths. In *The Reason of Church-Government* (1642), he uses it to partition his soaring poetry of the right hand from his comparatively disadvantaged prose, the hurried labor of the left (YP 1:808).

3. Francis F. Madan's *A New Bibliography of the Eikon Basilike of King Charles the First; with a Note on the Authorship,* Oxford Bibliographical Society (Oxford: Oxford University Press, 1950) remains the standard reference work for the *Eikon*'s print history. I have noted Madan's edition numbers where these might be helpful. Thomason's copy, for example, was part of the first edition's third issue, likely the first to be sold in bookshops (no. 1iii).

4. Ibid., no. 1i. For Royston's royalist career during the 1640s and 1650s, see Lois Potter, *Secret Rites and Secret Writing: Royalist Literature, 1641–1660* (Cambridge: Cambridge University Press, 1989), 7–11.

5. Tanner MSS LVII, fol. 453, The Bodleian Library, University of Oxford. Quoted in Madan, *New Bibliography,* 16. The letter is dated February 27, 1649.

6. Madan attributes this sequence of minute editions to the bookseller Henry Seile (*New Bibliography,* nos. 4–10).

7. Kathleen Lynch, "Devotion Bound: A Social History of the *Temple,*" in *Books and Readers in Early Modern England: Material Studies,* ed. Jennifer Anderson and Elizabeth Sauer, 177–99 (Philadelphia: University of Pennsylvania Press, 2001), 184–85.

8. Late in the sequence, two chapters break with this pattern of historical narrative, pivoting at the point of impasse to the special urgency of prayer. Set entirely in italic type, chapter 25 functions as a devotional coda to the preceding chapter, in which Charles protests being denied access to his chaplains. Bereft of their edifying and sustaining ministry, Charles worships alone, improvising additional and original prayers. Chapter 27 makes a stronger break with the volume's expressive protocols. Set entirely in the roman type reserved for narrative prose, it consists of a letter of fatherly advice from the king to his son and political heir, the exiled Prince of Wales, retroactively establishing him as the nominal addressee for the volume's contents.

9. Existing in at least eight separate states, sold as a separate broadside and reworked both on canvas and in needlepoint, Marshall's frontispiece has been compared to religious art showing the Annunciation and Christ's prayers in Gethsemane. Elizabeth Skerpan-Wheeler, "The First 'Royal': Charles I as Celebrity," *PMLA* 126, no. 4 (2011): 912–34, shows how it draws also upon a Protestant, patriotic, and populist tradition of devotional illustration, invoking the prayerful attitudes of the English men and women depicted in the woodcuts of Thomas Cranmer's *Catechismus* (1548) and John Foxe's *Acts and Monuments* (1563).

10. Madan, *New Bibliography,* no. 22. Kathleen Lynch, *Protestant Autobiography in the Seventeenth-Century Anglophone World* (Oxford: Oxford University Press, 2012), 106. Charles's last utterance, according to witnesses, was "Remember." For Dugard's turncoat career, see Lynch, *Protestant Autobiography,* 108–10, and Leona Rostenberg, "Republican Credo: William Dugard, Pedagogue, and Political Apostate," in her *Literary, Political, Scientific, Religious, and Legal Publishing, Printing, and Bookselling in England, 1551–1700: Twelve Studies,* 2 vols. (New York: Burt Franklin, 1965), 1:130–59.

11. Madan documents the retrospective incorporation of Dugard's additions in copies of 12 of the 21 prior editions (*New Bibliography,* nos. 3, 8, 10, 12, and 14–21, respectively). The additions were also included in Samuel Browne's second and third English language editions published at The Hague in the spring of 1649 (nos. 38–39).

12. The newsbook *The Moderate* (March 13–20, 1649) reports that "Mr. Cranford (the Minister and reputed penner of the black book called the King's Meditations) Ordered upon that accompt, and some others scores, to be disabled Licensor of any books hereafter"; quoted in Madan, "Appendix III," *New Bibliography,* 169. Appointed as a divinity licensor after the collapse of Laudian press controls in June 1643, Cranford used his tenure to advance an unapologetically Presbyterian agenda. Ann Hughes, "*Gangraena*" *and the Struggle for the English Revolution* (Oxford: Oxford University Press, 2004), 138–41, and Jason Peacey, *Politicians and Pamphleteers: Propaganda during the English Civil Wars and Interregnum* (Aldershot: Ashgate, 2004), 131–62, offer further details of Cranford's colorful licensing career.

13. *Journal of the House of Commons, Volume 6, 1648–1651* (London: His Majesty's Stationery Office, 1802), 165–66. Nicholas McDowell, "Milton, the *Eikon Basilike,* and

Pamela's Prayer: Re-Visiting the Evidence," *Milton Quarterly* 48, no. 4 (2014): 225–34, posits an alternative narrative of events. He points out that the unnamed printer, whose arrest and press seizure is noted in the *Commons Journal* on March 17, may not be Dugard. He further suggests that Dugard's expanded edition of the *Eikon Basilike* may not have been the target of the commonwealth's search; that the edition may, in fact, have not been published until the following month, after a stand-alone edition of the king's prayers had already been printed, in late April 1649.

14. Laura Lunger Knoppers, "Material Legacies: Family Matters in *Eikon Basilike* and *Eikonoklastes*," in her *Politicizing Domesticity from Henrietta Maria to Milton's Eve* (Cambridge: Cambridge University Press, 2011), 68–93.

15. Knoppers, *Politicizing Domesticity,* 90, 92–93.

16. Ibid., 8, 68–70.

17. Ibid., 93.

18. On the transformation of political communication after 1640 — a process that the *Eikon* confirms by contestation — see David Zaret, *Origins of Democratic Culture: Printing, Petitions, and the Public Sphere in Early-Modern England* (Princeton, NJ: Princeton University Press, 2000).

19. *Eikon Basilike, with selections from Eikonoklastes,* ed. Jim Daems and Holy Faith Nelson (Peterborough, Ontario: Broadview, 2006), 61. All quotations from the *Eikon Basilike* refer to this edition.

20. YP 3:393. *OED,* s.v. "demagogue," n., 1–2, http://www.oed.com//view/Entry/49573 (accessed May 17, 2016); s.v. "patriot," n., 1, http://www.oed.com/view/Entry/138899 (accessed May 17, 2016). "Patriot" is not a native English word but is borrowed from French, a point that Milton conspicuously neglects to mention.

21. Katharine Eisaman Maus, *Inwardness and Theater in the English Renaissance* (Chicago: University of Chicago Press, 1995), 2; On the *Eikon*'s deployment of the language of conscience, and of conscientious objection, see Sharon Achinstein, "Milton Catches the Conscience of the King: *Eikonoklastes* and the Engagement Controversy," in *Milton Studies,* vol. 29, ed. Albert C. Labriola, 143–63 (Pittsburgh: University of Pittsburgh Press, 1992). On its use of the tragic soliloquy, see Paul Stevens, "Milton's Janus-Faced Nationalism: Soliloquy, Subject, and the Modern Nation State," *Journal of English and Germanic Philology* 100, no. 2 (2001): 247–68. Richard C. McCoy, *Alterations of State: Sacred Kingship in the English Reformation* (New York: Columbia University Press, 2002), explores Milton's polemical construction of the *Eikon Basilike* as a royalist tragedy of revenge, paralleling the executed Charles I with the ghost of Hamlet's father (104–05).

22. I'm indebted here to two sharp formulations by Lauren Berlant in her preface to *The Female Complaint: The Unfinished Business of Sentimentality in American Culture* (Durham, NC: Duke University Press, 2008): "Yet the autobiographical isn't the personal.... The personal is the general" (vii).

23. Barbara Kiefer Lewalski, *Protestant Poetics and the Seventeenth-Century Religious Lyric* (Princeton, NJ: Princeton University Press, 1979), 39–53, 231–45; Ramie Targoff, *Common Prayer: The Language of Public Devotion in Early Modern England* (Chicago: University of Chicago Press, 2001), 65–84.

24. The Athanasius passage appears in Matthew Parker, *The whole Psalter translated into English Metre* (London, 1567), sig. Civ; the Bernard passage is in *Davids Musick;*

or, Psalmes of that royall prophet, once the sweete singer of that Israel... by R. B. and R. A. (London, 1616), sig. A2v. Both passages are quoted by Targoff, *Common Prayer,* 66–67.

25. John Calvin, *The Psalmes of David and Others. With M. John Calvins commentaries,* trans. Arthur Golding (London, 1571), sig. *6ᵛ; quoted by Lewalski, *Protestant Poetics,* 43.

26. For one such consideration of Psalm 51, see Hannibal Hamlin, *Psalm Culture and Early Modern English Literature* (Cambridge: Cambridge University Press, 2004), 192–95.

27. Steven N. Zwicker, *Lines of Authority: Politics and English Literary Culture, 1649–1689* (Ithaca, NY: Cornell University Press, 1993), 50.

28. My categories of parenthetical example follow John Lennard's study, *But I Digress: The Exploitation of Parentheses in English Printed Verse* (Oxford: Oxford University Press, 1991). See esp. 5–7, 20–21, 44–46.

29. Lynch, *Protestant Autobiography,* 108. Thomas Corns explains the inclusion of the chapter headings on more pragmatic grounds as part of a textual apparatus designed to make the *Eikon* as "user-friendly" as possible. As he remarks, "no-one was ever sacked for underestimating the intelligence of mid-century royalists." Thomas N. Corns, "The Early Modern Search Engine: Indices, Title Pages, Marginalia and Contents," in *The Renaissance Computer: Knowledge Technology in the First Age of Print,* ed. Jonathan Sawday and Neil Rhodes, 93–102 (London: Routledge, 2000), 101.

30. Herbert Marks, ed., "Introduction: The Book of Psalms," in *The English Bible: King James Version,* vol. 1, *The Old Testament* (New York: Norton, 2012), 955–56. The Hebrew subtitle, *mizmor l'david* (a song of David), is the most frequently used ascription. As John Hollander points out in "Hearing and Overhearing the Psalms," in his *Work of Poetry* (New York: Columbia University Press, 1997), 113–28, the grammar of this subtitle is "enigmatic," being capable of supporting a range of meanings: is this "a song about, or by, or to, or for David the shepherd and/or king?" (120).

31. Beth Quitslund, *The Reformation in Rhyme: Sternhold, Hopkins and the English Metrical Psalter, 1547–1603* (Aldershot: Ashgate, 2008), 209, 215–16. Quitslund shows how the arguments in the Geneva Bible were themselves indebted not only to Calvin's *Commentaries* but to the metrical Psalter *One and Fiftie Psalmes of David in Englishe Metre* (Geneva: J. Crespin, 1556) produced by the Anglo-Genevan community (190–92).

32. *The whole booke of Psalmes, collected into Englysh metre by T. Starnhold I. Hopkins, & others* (London: J. Day, 1562), 4.

33. "Penitential Psalms," in *Collected Poems of Sir Thomas Wyatt,* ed. Kenneth Muir and Patricia Thomson (Liverpool: Liverpool University Press, 1969). Line numbers refer to this edition, which uses Egerton MS 2711, a collection of fair copies of poems written out in Wyatt's hand, as its copy text. Readings of Wyatt's sequence include: James Simpson, *The Oxford English Literary History, Volume 2, 1350–1547: Reform and Cultural Revolution* (Oxford: Oxford University Press, 2002), 322–29; Brian Cummings, *The Literary Culture of the Reformation: Grammar and Grace* (Oxford: Oxford University Press, 2002), 223–31; Stephen Greenblatt, "Power, Sexuality, and Inwardness in Wyatt's Poetry," in his *Renaissance Self-Fashioning: From More to Shakespeare* (Chicago: University of Chicago Press, 1980), 115–28; and Lynn Staley, "The Penitential

Psalms: Conversion and the Limits of Lordship," *Journal of Medieval and Early Modern Studies* 37, no. 2 (2007): 221–69.

34. Rivkah Zim, *English Metrical Psalms: Poetry as Praise and Prayer, 1535–1601* (Cambridge: Cambridge University Press, 1987), compares Wyatt's narrator to a preacher delivering a sermon or series of devotional lessons on the psalms that David sings (69). He is more persuaded than I am of the narrator's reliability (and dramatic consistency).

35. Henry Lawes, *Choice Psalmes put into musick, for three voices* (London, 1648), sig. A3ᵛ. Frontispiece to *Il Davide perseguitato, David persecuted* (London, 1647); reproduced in Margery Corbett and Michael Norton ed., *Engraving in England in the Sixteenth and Seventeenth Centuries: A Descriptive Catalogue with Introductions,* 3 vols. (Cambridge: Cambridge University Press, 1964), 3:171. Both works were printed for the bookseller Humphrey Moseley.

36. The *Tenure* argues for a natural right to confer and revoke power, making both the election and deposing of the king a subjective preference of the people, who may "*as oft as they shall judge it for the best,* either choose him or reject him, retaine him or depose him though no Tyrant, meerly by the liberty and right of free born Men, to be govern'd *as seems to them best.*" John Milton, *Political Writings,* ed. Martin Dzelzainis (Cambridge: Cambridge University Press, 1991), 13, my emphasis.

37. Thomas N. Corns, *The Development of Milton's Prose Style* (New York: Oxford University Press, 1982), is just one of many critics who have remarked upon the fact that Milton's prose style changes abruptly in the regicide tract of early 1649 when the poet replaces "what was possibly the most exhilarating and inventive prose style of the seventeenth century" with a "spare functionalism" (101–02). The scholarship on the subject of Milton's authorial self-production is vast and growing. See, for example, Kevin Dunn, "Humanist Individualism and the Puritan Polity in Milton's Antiprelatical Tracts," in his *Pretexts of Authority: The Rhetoric of Authorship in the Renaissance Preface* (Stanford, CA: Stanford University Press, 1992), 51–75; Leah S. Marcus, "John Milton's Voice," in her *Unediting the Renaissance: Shakespeare, Marlowe, Milton* (New York: Routledge, 1996), 177–227; Brooke Conti, "'That Really Too Anxious Protestation': Crisis and Autobiography in Milton's Prose," in *Milton Studies,* vol. 45, ed. Albert C. Labriola (Pittsburgh: University of Pittsburgh Press, 2006), 149–86; and Stephen M. Fallon, *Milton's Peculiar Grace: Self-Representation and Authority* (Ithaca, NY: Cornell University Press, 2007).

38. Daniel Shore, *Milton and the Art of Rhetoric* (New York: Cambridge University Press, 2012), 85.

39. Thomas Morley, *A plaine & easie introduction to practicall musicke set downe in forme of a dialogue* (London, 1597), 70. *OED,* s.v. "descant," v., def. 1, http://www.oed .com/view/Entry/50699 (accessed May 17, 2016).

40. Nicholas Temperley, *The Music of the English Parish Church,* 2 vols. (Cambridge: Cambridge University Press, 1979), 1:73–76. Timothy Duguid, *Metrical Psalmody in Print and Practice: English "Singing Psalms" and Scottish "Psalm Buiks," c. 1547–1640* (Aldershot: Ashgate, 2014), agrees with Temperley's characterization of congregational psalm singing in England, although he notes that in Scotland, as on the Continent, psalms were sung to a wider repertoire of tunes (189).

41. Barbara Lewalski, *The Life of John Milton* (Oxford: Blackwell, 2000), 3. Ravenscroft's *Whole booke of psalmes* remained popular throughout the seventeenth century, with a second edition appearing in 1633. Samuel Pepys recalls singing "Ravenscroft's four-part psalms, most admirable music" with his friends and neighbors, Mr. Andrews and Mr. Hill, and the chorister Thomas Edwards, on a Sunday evening in November 1664. The company sang again, with Mr. Andrews's wife Hester, "a well-bred and a tolerable pretty woman," taking the treble part of Thomas Edwards, on another Sunday two weeks later, although this time Pepys was critical of the collection's limited repertoire of tunes: "It is a little strange how these psalms of Ravenscroft, after two or three times singing, prove but the same again, though good — no diversity appearing at all almost." *The Diary of Samuel Pepys,* 11 vols., ed. Robert Latham and William Matthews (London: G. Bell and Sons, 1974), 5:332, 342.

42. Helen Darbishire, ed., *The Early Lives of Milton* (London: Constable, 1932), 6, 32. The first quotation is from John Aubrey; the second from Cyriack Skinner (although attributed by Darbishire to John Phillips).

43. *Choice Psalmes,* sigs. Cc^r–Dd4^v. One of the elegies is written by John Wilson, the future composer of the *Psalterium Carolinum* (London, 1657), a musical setting of the *Eikon's* prayers reworked into a variety of verse forms by Thomas Stanley.

44. Titled "To my Friend Mr. Henry Lawes," the sonnet is the third of four commendatory poems (Lawes, *Choice Psalmes,* sig. a^v). It was likely to have been written to accompany a presentation copy of Milton's 1645 *Poems,* which used Lawes's name and title, "Gentleman of the Kings Chappel, and one of his Majesties Private Musick," on its title page.

45. John Milton, *Poems, &c. upon several occasions* (London, 1673), 143.

46. Zwicker, *Lines of Authority,* 59. Richard Helgerson, "Milton Reads the King's Book: Print, Performance, and the Making of a Bourgeois Idol," *Criticism* 29, no. 1 (1987): 1–25, anticipates Zwicker in focusing critical attention upon what Milton learned (but in another, more powerful sense earned), from his punitive encounter with the King's Book.

47. William Shakespeare, *Richard III,* in *The Norton Shakespeare,* 2nd ed., gen. ed. Stephen Greenblatt (New York: Norton, 2008), 1.1.27. All references to Shakespeare's plays are to this edition, hereafter cited in the text.

48. Nicholas McDowell, "Milton's Regicide Tracts and the Uses of Shakespeare," in *The Oxford Handbook of Milton,* ed. McDowell and Nigel Smith, 252–71 (Oxford: Oxford University Press, 2009), 270–71.

49. Thomas Blount, *Glossographia; or, A dictionary, interpreting all such hard vvords, whether Hebrew, Greek, Latin, Italian, Spanish, French, Teutonick, Belgick, British or Saxon; as are now used in our refined English tongue* (London, 1656), sig. M7r.

50. *Journal of the House of Lords: Volume 3, 1620–1628* (London: His Majesty's Stationery Office, 1767–1830), 811–20. BHO: British History Online, http://www .british-history.ac.uk/lords-jrnl/vol3/pp811-820 (accessed September 25, 2015).

51. Here Milton taps into a long tradition of aristocratic standards of public speaking, stretching back at least as far as Homer's *Iliad,* in which the commoner Thersites, he "of the endless speech," threatens not only the military hierarchy of the Greek army

but the progress of the epic itself. *Iliad of Homer,* trans. Richmond Lattimore (Chicago: University of Chicago Press, 1951), 2.212.

52. Anonymous, *An appeal to the men of New-England* (Boston, 1689), 1; Michael Warner, *The Letters of the Republic: Publication and the Public Sphere in Eighteenth-Century America* (Cambridge, MA: Harvard University Press, 2009), 36.

53. Chaucer, "The Prologue of the Nonnes Preestes Tale," in *The Riverside Chaucer,* 3rd ed., gen. ed. Larry D. Benson, 252–53 (Boston: Houghton Mifflin, 1987), lines 2767–70, 2788–802.

54. Paul Strohm, "Chaucer's Fifteenth-Century Audience and the Narrowing of the 'Chaucer Tradition,'" *Studies in the Age of Chaucer* 4 (1982): 3–32. *De casibus* tales are narrated by the Wife of Bath, by Chauntecleer, in the Nun's Priest's Tale, and by the Pardoner.

55. The *Mirror* was originally commissioned by Wayland as a supplement to his new edition of Lydgate's *Fall of Princes.* Its printing was suppressed in 1554/55, however, and it did not appear for another five years. For the early publication history of *A Mirror,* see Lily B. Campbell's introduction to her edition of *The Mirror for Magistrates, Edited from Original Texts in the Huntington Library* (Cambridge: Cambridge University Press, 1938), 3–60.

56. Ibid., 69.

57. Baldwin dedicates the 1559 edition "To the nobilitye and all other in office" (ibid., 63). Political readings of *A Mirror* include Paul Budra, "The *Mirror for Magistrates* and the Politics of Readership," *Studies in English Literature* 32, no. 1 (1992): 1–13; Andrew Hadfield, *Literature, Politics, and National Identity: Reformation to Renaissance* (Cambridge: Cambridge University Press, 1994), 81–107; and Jessica Winston, "A *Mirror for Magistrates* and Public Political Discourse in Elizabethan England," *Studies in Philology* 101, no. 4 (2004): 381–400.

58. The 1559 *Mirror* was reprinted in an expanded version in 1563. Subsequent reprintings took place under the direction of four different editors — William Baldwin, John Higgins, Thomas Blennerhasset, and Felix Kyngston — in 1571 (rev.), 1574 (rev., enlarged, and retitled), 1575 (rev. and enlarged), 1578 (rev. and enlarged), 1587 (rev. and enlarged), and 1610 (rev., enlarged, and retitled). The 1610 *Mirror* was reissued in 1619, 1620, and 1621. Campbell, "Appendix A," *Mirror for Magistrates,* 515–21.

59. Campbell, *Mirror for Magistrates,* 81.

60. Meredith Anne Skura, "Autobiography: History or Fiction?; William Baldwin Writing History 'Under the Shadow of Dreames and Visions' in *A Mirror for Magistrates* (1559)," in her *Tudor Autobiography: Listening for Inwardness* (Chicago: Chicago University Press, 2008), 73–97.

61. In winter's tedious nights, sit by the fire / With good old folks, and let them tell thee tales / Of woeful ages long ago betid; / And ere thou bid good night, to quit their griefs / Tell thou the lamentable fall of me" (5.1.40–44). Richard goes on to describe how the tears of these superannuated listeners will find reciprocation in the burning logs of the fire that turn to coal and ash and put themselves out with weeping (5.1.45–50).

62. *The Religious & Loyal Protestation of John Gauden Dr. in Divinity; Against the present Declared Purposes and Proceedings of the Army and others; About the trying and*

destroying our Soveraign Lord the King (London, 1649), sig. A2ᵛ. Gauden's tract appears to have sold well; a second edition was printed in 1649 and a third in 1660.

63. Campbell, *Mirror for Magistrates,* 181.

64. *The Works of John* Milton, 20 vols., gen. ed. Frank Allen Patterson (New York: Columbia University Press, 1923–40), 7:8–9.

65. John Milton, *Samson Agonistes,* line 1181, in *The Complete Poetry and Essential Prose of John Milton,* ed. William Kerrigan, John Rumrich, and Stephen M. Fallon (New York: Modern Library, 2007); hereafter cited in the text.

66. The scene recalls, too, Achilles's brazen survey of Hector, "joint by joint" and "limb by limb" in Shakespeare's *Troilus and Cressida* (4.7.115–22).

67. Sharon Achinstein, *Literature and Dissent in Milton's England* (Cambridge: Cambridge University Press, 2003), 49.

68. Linda Charnes, *Notorious Identity: Materializing the Subject in Shakespeare* (Cambridge, MA: Harvard University Press, 1993).

69. Geoffrey Chaucer, "The Wife of Bath's Prologue and Tale," in Benson, *Riverside Chaucer,* lines 682–85.

70. For a different reading of the interpretative traditions that Milton places at odds with one another in Manoa's final speech, see Joseph Wittreich, "Samson among the Nightingales," in his *Interpreting "Samson Agonistes"* (Princeton, NJ: Princeton University Press, 1986), 285–92.

Notes to Chapter 2

1. "Walton's Book of Lives," Sonnet 3.5, in William Wordsworth, *The Ecclesiastical Sonnets,* ed. Abbie Findlay Potts (New Haven, CT: Yale University Press, 1922); hereafter cited in the text by sonnet and line number.

2. For Walton as "virtuoso," see Marjorie Swann, "*The Compleat Angler* and the Early Modern Culture of Collecting," *English Literary Renaissance* 37, no. 1 (2007): 100–17.

3. Izaak Walton, *The Life of Dr. Sanderson* (London, 1678), sig. i3v.

4. Izaak Walton, *The Compleat Angler, 1753–1676,* ed. Jonquil Bevan (Oxford: Oxford University Press, 1983), 83. Following Horace's Ode 1.9, Lovelace "poises" an overflowing wineglass and glowing hearth to the floods and frosts of the polity: "We will create / A Genuine Summer in each others breast; / And spite of this cold Time and frosen Fate / Thaw us a warme seate to our rest." Richard Lovelace, "The Grasse-hopper. To my Noble Friend, Mr. Charles Cotton. Ode," lines 21–24, in *Lucasta: Epodes, Odes, Sonnets, Songs, &c.* (London, 1649). John Milton also adapts the Horatian ode to the political upheavals of the Protectorate in two sonnets, "Lawrence of virtuous Father virtuous Son," and "Cyriack, whose Grandsire on the Royal Bench," first published in 1673.

5. Raoul Granqvist, "Izaak Walton's *Lives* in the Nineteenth and the Early Twentieth Century: A Study of a Cult Object," *Studia Neophilologica* 54, no. 2 (1982): 247–61. For the repeal legislation, see *English Historical Documents, 1783–1832,* ed. Arthur Aspinall and E. Anthony Smith (London: Eyre and Spottiswoode, 1959), 671–75, 687–89.

6. Diarmaid MacCulloch, "Richard Hooker's Reputation," *English Historical Review* 117, no. 473 (2002): 783, 799–800. Hanbury is severe: "The *naïveté* and garrulity of Walton impart a fascination to his narrative which will not bear the touch of the disenchanter's rod; for when the veil is withdrawn, and the smoke of the incense is dissipated, we see nothing left but the dregs of credulity and intolerance. But for the party purpose it was designed to serve, is this such a Life of such a man as his country owes him?" Benjamin Hanbury, *The "Ecclesiastical Polity" and Other Works of Richard Hooker: With His "Life" by Izaak Walton,* 3 vols. (London: Holdsworth and Ball, 1830), 1:lvii.

7. MacCulloch, "Richard Hooker's Reputation," 773–74; Peter Lake, *Anglicans and Puritans?: Presbyterianism and English Conformist Thought from Whitgift to Hooker* (London: Unwin Hyman, 1988), 227.

8. Sharon Achinstein, "Reading George Herbert in the Restoration," *English Literary Renaissance* 36, no. 3 (2006):447.

9. David Novarr, *The Making of Walton's "Lives"* (Ithaca, NY: Cornell University Press, 1958).

10. John Spurr, "Morley, George (1598?–1684)," *Oxford Dictionary of National Biography,* http://www.oxforddnb.com/view/article/19285 (accessed May 31, 2016). For Morley's ecclesiastical career after the Restoration and Walton's relations with him, see also Novarr, *Making of Walton's "Lives,"* 226–28, 389–90.

11. The phrase "happy affinity" comes from Walton's introduction to *The Life of Mr. Rich. Hooker* (London, 1665), 3.

12. John Spurr, *The Restoration Church of England, 1646–1689* (New Haven, CT: Yale University Press, 1991), 48–49; Mark Goldie, "Danby, the Bishops, and the Whigs," in *The Politics of Religion in Restoration England,* ed. Tim Harris, Paul Seaward, and Mark Goldie, 75–105 (Oxford: Blackwell, 1990).

13. Walton, *Life of Hooker,* 59–60.

14. Samuel Clarke, *A collection of the lives of ten eminent divines* (London, 1662), 210.

15. My ideological grouping of the churchmen in Clarke's collection follows that of Peter Lake in "Reading Clarke's *Lives* in Political and Polemical Context," in *Writing Lives: Biography and Textuality, Identity and Representation in Early Modern England,* ed. Kevin Sharpe and Steven N. Zwicker, 293–318 (Oxford: Oxford University Press, 2007), 303–04.

16. Clarke, *Ten eminent divines,* "To the candid reader," sig. A4r–v.

17. Samuel Clarke, *The lives of sundry eminent persons* (London, 1683), 11. Equivalent religious policies were pursued in Ireland and (with fiercer resistance) in Scotland, where episcopacy was also restored. For the legislating and enforcing of the new settlement, see Paul Seaward, *The Cavalier Parliament and the Reconstruction of the Old Regime, 1661–1667* (Cambridge: Cambridge University Press, 1989); also John Spurr, "Later Stuart Puritanism," in *The Cambridge Companion to Puritanism,* ed. John Coffey and Paul C. H. Lim, 89–105 (Cambridge: Cambridge University Press, 2008).

18. Lake, "Reading Clarke's *Lives*," 305.

19. Barksdale, *Memorials of worthy persons, two decads* (London, 1661), sig. A2v–3r.

20. *OED Online,* s.v. "decad," n., http://www.oed.com/view/Entry/47965 (accessed May 18, 2016); Thomas Stanley, *The History of Philosophy, the Third and Last Volume* (London, 1660), 56–57.

21. Richard Hooker, *The Works of Mr. Richard Hooker,* ed. John Gauden (London, 1662), title page. A second edition of the first four books appeared in 1604, prepared by Hooker's literary executor, John Spenser, with further editions appearing in 1611, 1616, 1622, 1631–32, and 1638–39. Book 8 and the surviving portions of book 6 of the *Polity* were eventually published in 1648. Book 7 remained in manuscript until Gauden's edition of 1662. For an overview of the *Polity*'s complex seventeenth century manuscript circulation and reception history, see Conal Condren, "The Creation of Richard Hooker's Public Authority: Rhetoric, Reputation, and Reassessment," *Journal of Religious History* 21, no. 1 (1997): 35–59; MacCulloch, "Richard Hooker's Reputation," 773–812; and Michael Brydon, *The Evolving Reputation of Richard Hooker: An Examination of Responses, 1600–1714* (New York: Oxford University Press, 2006), 45–80.

22. John Gauden, "The Life and Death of Mr. Richard Hooker," in Hooker, *Works of Richard Hooker,* 1.

23. Novarr, *Making of Walton's "Lives,"* 220–22, Appendix C, 507–09..

24. Richard Hooker, *Of the Laws of Ecclesiastical Polity, Books VI–VIII,* ed. P. G. Stanwood (Cambridge, MA: Harvard University Press, 1981), 167.

25. Gauden, "Life," in *Works of Richard Hooker,* 4.

26. Thomas Fuller, *Church-History of Britain* (London, 1656), book 9, 216–19; Robert Greene, *A Notable Discovery of Coosenage* (London, 1591), sigs. Dr–D4v; Gauden, "Life," in *Works of Richard Hooker,* 13–14, 30, 32–33.

27. Thomas Fuller, *The History of the Worthies of England* (London, 1662), 264.

28. Walton, *Life of Hooker,* 42–44.

29. Ibid., "An Appendix to the Life of Mr. Richard Hooker," 155–74.

30. The monument was erected in 1635. An English translation of the monument's Latin epitaph follows the conclusion to Walton's *Life of Hooker* (153–54).

31. Walton, *Life of Hooker,* 130–31.

32. For the early history of communion kneeling and its disputed place in religious and political argument, see Lori Anne Ferrell, "Kneeling and the Body Politic," in *Government by Polemic: James I, the King's Preachers, and the Rhetorics of Conformity, 1603–1625* (Stanford, CA: Stanford University Press, 1998), 140–66.

33. The 1662 rubric was based on the "Black Rubric" inserted in the 1552 *Book of Common Prayer* but omitted from the 1559 version. Although the main text of the prayerbook revisions had been agreed upon by December 20, 1661, the rubric on kneeling was not written into the manuscript until the end of February 1662, perhaps as a last-minute conciliatory gesture toward the Presbyterian party. *The Book of Common Prayer: The Texts of 1549, 1559, and 1662,* ed. Brian Cummings (Oxford: Oxford World Classics, 2011), 399, 407, 773–74.

34. Walton, *Life of Hooker,* 132.

35. Debora Shuger, "Life-Writing in Seventeenth-Century England," in *Representations of the Self from Renaissance to Romanticism,* ed. Patrick Coleman, Jayne Lewis, and Jill Kowalik, 63–78 (Cambridge: Cambridge University Press, 2000), 67–68.

36. Richard Hooker, *The Works of Mr. Richard Hooker* (London, 1666), title page.

37. Walton, *Life of Sanderson,* sigs. g1v–g2v.

38. Edward Coke, "Of Theft or Larceny by the Common Law," in his *Third Part of the Institutes of the Laws of England* (London: W. Clarke and Sons, 1817), 110. In his

Commentaries on the Laws of England, 4 vols. (London, 1765–69), eighteenth century jurist William Blackstone restates Coke's ruling: "if any one in taking up the dead body steals the shroud or other apparel, it will be felony; for the property thereof remains in the executor, or whoever was at the charge of the funeral" (2:429). Although there could be no property interest in a dead body, there could still be a penal interest. Corpses could be subject to disinterrment and desecration as punishment for the crimes of the decedent.

39. Keith Thomas gives a narrative overview of Protestant casuistry and its foremost practitioners and detractors in "Cases of Conscience in Seventeenth-Century England," in *Public Duty and Private Conscience in Seventeenth-Century England: Essays Presented to G. E. Aylmer,* ed. John Morrill, Paul Slack, and Daniel Woolf, 29–56 (Oxford: Oxford University Press, 1993). A more analytic treatment, exploring the connections between casuistry and philosophy, is offered by Margaret Sampson, "Laxity and Liberty in Seventeenth-Century English Political Thought," in *Conscience and Casuistry in Early Modern Europe,* ed. Edmund Leites, 72–118 (Cambridge: Cambridge University Press, 1988).

40. Walton, *Life of Sanderson,* sigs. d6r–d7r.

41. Ibid., sigs. d3v.

42. The study carries different titles in different manuscript versions. An alternative title, "Dr. Sanderson's Answer to a Case of Conscience, proposed in the time of the War, 1652, about reading or omitting the forms in our Liturgy," emphasizes the case's historical occasion and its wartime conditions. William Jacobson gives all of these variant titles in *The Works of Robert Sanderson, D.d., Sometime Bishop of Lincoln,* 6 vols., ed. William Jacobson (Oxford: Oxford University Press, 1854), 5:37. For extant manuscript versions of Sanderson's casuistical writings and Walton's probable connections to their owners, see Novarr, *Making of Walton's Lives,* 426–31.

43. *Works of Robert Sanderson,* 5:47–48. For the controversy surrounding Sanderson's pragmatic approach, see Peter Lake, "Serving God and the Times: The Calvinist Conformity of Robert Sanderson," *Journal of British Studies* 27, no. 2 (1988): 81–116; and Isabel Rivers, "Prayer-Book Devotion: The Literature of the Proscribed Episcopal Church," in *The Cambridge Companion to Writing of the English Revolution,* ed. N. H. Keeble, 198–214 (Cambridge: Cambridge University Press, 2001), 202.

44. *Works of Sanderson,* 6:457–58.

45. Edward Vallance, "The Dangers of Prudence: *Salus populi suprema lex,* Robert Sanderson and 'The Case of the Liturgy,'" *Renaissance Studies* 23, no. 4 (2009): 538, notes that an abrogated version had previously appeared under the title "The Case of Scandal," in the anonymously published *Fives Cases of Conscience: Occasionally determined by a late Learned Hand* (London, 1666). Another unauthorized version, *The Case of using or forbearing the establish'd liturgie, during the late troublesome times, and prohibition of it by the then usurpers* (London, 1672), also appeared anonymously, with neither printer nor bookseller registering their identity on its title page. Its title is closer to the one carried by the octavo pamphlet published by Richard Marriot and adjoined to Walton's *Life of Sanderson* in 1678.

46. "Debates in 1677: March 27th–29th," in *Grey's Debates of the House of Commons, vol. 4,* ed. Anchitell Grey (London: T. Becket and P. A. De Hondt, 1769), 315–34. *British History Online,* http://www.british-history.ac.uk/greys-debates/vol4/pp315-334

(accessed March 20, 2016). Andrew Marvell, *An account of the growth of popery and arbitrary government in England. More particularly, from the long prorogation of November, 1675, ending the 15th of February, 1676, till the last meeting of Parliament, the 16th of July, 1677* (Amsterdam, 1677), 89–100.

47. My summary of these political developments follows Goldie, "Danby, the Bishops, and the Whigs," 83–90. For the 1677 parliamentary session, see also Spurr, *Restoration Church of England,* 67–75.

48. Walton, *Life of Sanderson,* sigs. h3v.

49. G. A. Starr, *Defoe and Casuistry* (Princeton, NJ: Princeton University Press, 1971); J. Paul Hunter, *Before Novels: The Cultural Contexts of Eighteenth-Century English Fiction* (New York: Norton, 1990), 288–94.

50. Walton, *The Lives of Dr. John Donne, Sir Henry Wotton, Mr. Richard Hooker, Mr. George Herbert* (London, 1670), 10.

51. Thomas North, *The lives of the noble Grecians and Romanes* (London, 1579), 718. New editions of North's Plutarch appeared in 1595, 1603, 1612, and 1631. For Walton's relation to Plutarch, see Jessica Martin, *Walton's Lives: Conformist Commemorations and the Rise of Biography* (Oxford: Oxford University Press, 2001), 32–41.

52. Walton, *Lives,* 11.

53. *OED,* s.v. "officiously," adv., def. 1–3, http://www.oed.com//view/Entry/130680 (accessed May 14, 2016); John Milton, *Areopagitica,* in *The Complete Prose Works of John Milton,* 8 vols., ed. Don M. Wolfe et al. (New Haven, CT: Yale University Press, 1953–82), 2:506–07; hereafter cited as YP, followed by volume and page number.

54. *A Directory for the publique worship of God throughout the three kingdoms of England, Scotland, and Ireland* (London, 1645), 35; Rivers, "Prayer-Book Devotion," 206.

55. For the Laudian championing of prayers for the dead, see Peter Marshall, *Beliefs and the Dead in Reformation England* (Oxford: Oxford University Press, 2002), 180–87. The label "avant-garde" is Peter Lake's: "Lancelot Andrewes, John Buckeridge, and Avant-Garde Conformity at the Court of James I," in *The Mental World of the Jacobean Court,* ed. Linda Levy Peck, 113–33 (Cambridge: Cambridge University Press, 1991).

56. Walton, *Lives,* 75, 78. Richard Wendorf, *The Elements of Life: Biography and Portrait-Painting in Stuart and Georgian England* (Oxford: Oxford University Press, 1990), 46–48; and Rami Targoff, *John Donne: Body and Soul* (Chicago: University of Chicago Press, 2008), 180–83, offer appreciative accounts of Walton's rendering of this final sitting.

57. The phrase is taken from Donne's Holy Sonnet 3, "This is my play's last scene." John Donne, *The Divine Poems,* ed. Helen Gardner (Oxford: Oxford University Press, 1978), 7, 67n.

58. *Poems, by J. D. With Elegies on the Authors Death* (London, 1633), sig. A2v. Walton's elegy is grouped with others at the end of the volume (382–84).

59. Margaret Whinney, *Sculpture in Britain, 1530–1830* (New Haven, CT: Yale University Press, 1982), 80–83.

60. *Poems by J. D. with Elegies on the Authors Death* (London, 1635), title page. The differences between the 1633 and 1635 editions, together with Marriot's dedicatory epigram and Walton's epigraph, are discussed by Leah Marcus, *Unediting the Renaissance:*

Shakespeare, Marlowe, Milton (New York: Routledge, 1996), 192–98; and by Kevin Pask, *The Emergence of the English Author: Scripting the "Life" of the Poet in Early Modern England* (Cambridge: Cambridge University Press, 1996), 113–18. Pask notes how Walton's *Life*, by appearing at the head of Donne's sermons, aligns itself with the tradition of ecclesiastical biography and not with the "lives of the poets," further subordinating the literary to the religious dimensions of Donne's personal history and public career (122).

61. Joseph Roach, *It* (Ann Arbor: University of Michigan Press, 2007), 47.

62. The letters are given their own title page, but they start in the middle of a gathering and continue the pagination of the *Life*, suggesting that the volume was designed as an integral unit. Novarr argues persuasively that this separate publication predates the joint publication of the *Lives*, although both share the same imprimatur (see Appendix D in Novarr, *Making of Walton's "Lives*,*"* 510–12). For Walton's development of Magdalen Herbert as a biographical character and parallel to Augustine's mother, Monica, see Clayton D. Lein, "Art and Structure in Walton's *Life of Mr. George Herbert*," *University of Toronto Quarterly* 46, no. 2 (1976/77), 167–68.

63. Barnabus Oley, *Herbert's Remains; or, sundry pieces of that sweet singer of the temple, Mr. George Herbert, sometime orator of the University of Cambridg. Now exposed to publick light* (London, 1652); Novarr, *Making of Walton's "Lives*,*"* 309; also, Elizabeth Clarke, "The Character of a Non-Laudian Country Parson," *Review of English Studies* 54, no. 216 (2003): 479–96. For Herbert's career before Bemerton, see Michael C. Schoenfeldt, *Prayer and Power: George Herbert and Renaissance Courtship* (Chicago: University of Chicago Press, 1991), 25–37.

64. Achinstein, "Reading George Herbert," 431–33. On Herbert's seventeenth century reception, see also, for example, Robert H. Ray, "Herbert's Seventeenth-Century Reputation: A Summary and New Considerations," *George Herbert Journal* 9, no. 2 (1986): 1–15; Daniel W. Doerksen, "The Laudian Interpretation of George Herbert," *Literature and History* 3, no. 2 (1994): 36–54; and Achinstein, *Literature and Dissent in Milton's England* (Cambridge: Cambridge University Press, 2003), 200–09.

65. Izaak Walton, *The Life of Mr. George Herbert* (London, 1670), 10–11.

66. Matthew does not identify the woman who is named only in the Gospel of John as Mary, sister of Martha and Lazarus. The episode is recounted in all four of the Gospels: Matthew 26:6–13, Mark 14:3–9, Luke 7:36–50, and John 11:1–2 and 12:1–8, although with some variation. In Luke, for example, the Pharisee's objection to the anointing is not the waste of scarce resources, but the woman's sinfulness, which pollutes her touch. Luke's emphasis is also Herbert's in his single poem on the saint's legend, titled "Mary Magdalene."

67. We know from Donne's will that a "Picture of Marie Magdalene" hung in his bedchamber. Donne bequeathed it to George Garrard, his "kynde Frend" and coterie reader of his verses. R. C. Bald, *John Donne: A Life* (Oxford: Oxford University Press, 1970), Appendix D, 563. Walton was admitted into Donne's bedchamber during his final days and would have seen it there.

68. Walton, *Life of Herbert*, 64. Herbert's poem, from which Walton paraphrases, is a meditation on the Pauline verse, "For we are unto God a sweet savour of Christ" (2 Cor. 2:15). George Herbert, "The Odour," in *The Works of George Herbert*, ed.

F. E. Hutchinson (Oxford: Clarendon Press, 1941), 174–75. All quotations from Herbert's poetry are taken from this edition and identified by title rather than by page number. For the importance of "sweetness" to the associated realms of feeling and knowing in medieval devotional practice, see Mary Carruthers, "Sweetness," *Speculum* 81, no. 4 (2006): 999–1013; and Rachel Fulton, "'Taste and See That the Lord Is Sweet' (Ps. 33:9): The Flavor of God in the Monastic West," *Journal of Religion* 86, no. 2 (2006): 169–204.

69. Walton, *Compleat Angler*, 111–12.

70. William Shakespeare, *Hamlet*, in *The Norton Shakespeare*, 2nd ed., gen. ed. Stephen Greenblatt (New York: Norton, 2008), 5.1.227.

71. These echoes are given by Russell Fraser, "George Herbert's Poetry," *Sewanee Review* 95, no. 4 (1987): 580. Christopher A. Hill, "George Herbert's Sweet Devotion," *Studies in Philology* 107, no. 2 (2010): 236–58, charts Herbert's use of the term "sweet" through *The Temple*, noting that "around fifty of the poems...include some form of the word" or its cognates (236).

72. Walton, *Life of Herbert*, 34–35, 92–93; *The lives of Dr. John Donne, Sir Henry Wotton, Mr. Richard Hooker, Mr. George Herbert* (London, 1675), 274–75. In the 1670 text, Walton dates the confrontation with Melville to Herbert's tenure as university orator at Cambridge, after 1620. This dating is revised in the 1675 text, which relocates their confrontation to Herbert's school days at Westminster. Novarr conjectures that Walton learned that Melville was imprisoned from 1607 until 1611 and living abroad after his release, from 1611 until his death in 1622. The episode, if it were to be retained, would need to happen before Herbert's fourteenth year (*Making of Walton's "Lives,"* 344–46). The amended date strengthens the parallel between the child Herbert and the child Jesus, providing an additional, perhaps more compelling, reason for the change.

NOTES TO CHAPTER 3

1. John Aubrey, *Brief Lives with an Apparatus for the Lives of Our English Mathematical Writers*, 2 vols., ed. Kate Bennett (Oxford: Oxford University Press, 2015), 1:259. All quotations from the *Brief Lives* refer to this edition unless otherwise indicated and are cited parenthetically in the text. I have not reproduced all of the nonverbal markings recorded so painstakingly in Bennett's edition, except in cases where they are relevant to my analysis.

2. *Sequitur celebritas & pompa funeris* (London, 1588), popularly known as "Lant's roll" after the herald Thomas Lant, who collaborated with the Dutch engraver Theodor de Brii to produce it. The plates and accompanying text, in both Latin and English, are reproduced in *John Nichols's "The Progresses and Public Processions of Queen Elizabeth,"* 3 vols., ed. Jayne Elisabeth Archer, Elizabeth Clarke, and Elizabeth Goldring (Oxford: Oxford University Press, 2013), 3:283–340. For readings of the *Sequitur celebritas* as a work of political and religious propaganda, see Ronald Strickland, "Pageantry and Poetry as Discourse: The Production of Subjectivity in Sir Philip Sidney's Funeral," *English Literary History* 57, no. 1 (1990): 19–36; Elizabeth Goldring, "'In the cause of his God and true religion': Sir Philip Sidney, the *Sequitur celebritas,* and the Cult of the Protestant

Martyr," in *Art Re-formed: Re-assessing the Impact of the Reformation on the Visual Arts,* ed. Tara Hamling and Richard L. Williams, 227–42 (Newcastle: Cambridge Scholars, 2007); and Alan Stewart, *Philip Sidney: A Double Life* (London: Random House, 2011), 1–8.

3. See, for example, Aubrey's famous account of the crepuscular storytelling of maids and nurses in an era before popular literacy: *Three Prose Works: Miscellanies; Remaines of Gentilisme and Judaisme; Observations,* ed. John Buchanan-Brown (Fontwell, Sussex: Centaur Press, 1972), 289–90.

4. John Aubrey to Anthony Wood (hereafter A–W), February 21, 1680, Bodleian MS Ballard 14, fol. 127; qtd. in Maurice Balme, *Two Antiquaries: A Selection from the Correspondence of John Aubrey and Anthony Wood* (Edinburgh: Durham Academic Press, 2001), 87.

5. A–W, March 27, 1680, Bodleian MS Ballard 14, fol. 131; A–W, May 22, 1680, Bodleian MS Wood F39, fol. 340; both qtd. in Balme, *Two Antiquaries,* 89, 91.

6. A–W, December 20, 1681, Bodleian MS Ballard 14, fol. 134; qtd. in Balme, *Two Antiquaries,* 102. Aubrey interviewed Beeston at his house in Shoreditch sometime after December 20. He also made a note of Beeston's death, perhaps with the intention of hunting down his papers: "Old Mr Beeston (whom Mr Dreyden calles the Chronicle of the Stage) died at his house in Bishops-gate-street without, about Bartholomew-tyde 1682. Mr. Shipey in Somerset-house hath his papers" (*Brief Lives,* 1:447, 2:1256).

7. Andrew Hadfield, *Edmund Spenser: A Life* (Oxford: Oxford University Press, 2012), 6.

8. Kate Bennett, "John Aubrey and the 'Lives of our English Mathematical Writers,'" in *The Oxford Handbook of the History of Mathematics,* ed. Eleanor Robson and Jacqueline Stedall 329–52 (Oxford: Oxford University Press, 2009), 339.

9. One possible candidate is the anonymous *Art and Science of Arismetique,* a practical handbook for merchants, translated from the French and published in London by Richard Faques in 1526. For Faques's career, see Peter W. M. Blayney, *The Stationers' Company and the Printers of London, 1501–1557* (Cambridge: Cambridge University Press, 2013).

10. The only work Aubrey saw into print during his lifetime was a volume titled *Miscellanies* (London, 1696), devoted to supernatural happenings and the occult.

11. MS Aubrey 8, fol. 27r.

12. "He had a trick sometimes to goe into Westminster-hall in a morn: in Terme-time and tell some strange False story (Sham) and would come thither again about 11, or 12: to have the pleasure to heare how it spred; and sometimes it would be altered, with additions, he could scarce know it to be his owne" (*Brief Lives,* 1:480).

13. Bennett prefers "shamed" to "shammed," offering the explanation of May's disinterred corpse (*Brief Lives,* 1:573, 2:1520). In "Tom May's Death," Andrew Marvell imagines Spenser and "reverend Chaucer" expelling May, an apostate from poetry, from his resting place in the abbey beside them (85–90), in *The Poems of Andrew Marvell,* ed. Nigel Smith (Harlow, England: Pearson Longman, 2007); hereafter cited in the text. Chaloner had made the arrangements for May's burial in Westminster Abbey in 1650, securing his temporary place in the national shrine. The life of May is adjacent to the life of Chaucer in Aubrey's manuscript.

14. Aubrey went back and inserted an anecdotal note, attributed to Charles I's court painter, Emmanuel de Critz, reporting the long discussion that took place at the "parting" of May and Fanshawe "before Sir Richard went to the King" (*Brief Lives,* 1:573).

15. Christopher Ricks, "The Wit and Weight of Clarendon," in *Augustan Studies: Essays in Honor of Irvin Ehrenpreis,* ed. Douglas Lane Patey and Timothy Keegan, 65–78 (Newark, NJ: Associated University Presses, 1985), 65–66.

16. John James Purdon, "John Aubrey's 'Discourse in Paper,'" *Essays in Criticism* 55, no. 3 (2005): 229–30.

17. Kate Bennett, "Editing Aubrey," in In *Ma(r)king the Text: The Presentation of Meaning on the Literary Page,* ed. Joe Bray, Miriam Handley, and Anne C. Henry, 271–90 (Aldershot: Ashgate, 2000), 276.

18. Bennett, *Brief Lives* (1:xci); *OED Online,* s.v. "minute," n. 1, esp. III.8a–b, http://www.oed.com/view/Entry/118997 (accessed June 5, 2016).

19. A–W, October 23, 1688, Bodleian MS Tanner 456a, fol. 34; qtd. in Balme, *Two Antiquaries,* 115.

20. A–W, February 21, 1680, Bodleian MS Ballard 14, fol. 127; qtd. in Balme, *Two Antiquaries,* 87.

21. Thomas Birch, *The History of the Royal Society of London for Improving of Natural Knowledge from Its First Rise,* 4 vols. (London, 1756–57), 2:5 (January 11, 1665); 2:40 (April 26, 1665); 2:236 (January 2, 1668).

22. *OED Online* s.v. "peruse," v., http://www.oed.com/view/Entry/141653 (accessed June 4, 2016). This early modern use of "peruse" to describe a thoroughgoing and critical examination is distinct from the verb's later sense of browsing or skimming, a more leisurely or superficial practice of reading. The formalized routine of presentation and perusal at the Royal Society is vividly described by Adrian Johns, *The Nature of the Book: Print and Knowledge in the Making* (Chicago: University of Chicago Press, 1998), 482–91.

23. For these salutations, see Balme, *Two Antiquaries,* 44, 49, 62, 87, 89, 103, and so on.

24. Bennett notes that Aubrey lifts his distinctive adverb "tumultuarily" from a letter he received from John Evelyn: "Sir, my hasty writing will require your pardon. I have sett things downe tumultuarily, as they came into my suddaine thoughts" (*Brief Lives,* 1:xxxi).

25. *OED Online,* s.v. "minium," n., http://www.oed.com/view/ (accessed June 5, 2016).

26. James Noel Adams, *The Latin Sexual Vocabulary* (Baltimore: Johns Hopkins University Press, 1982), 55.

27. Rader's 1599 volume acquired an immediate notoriety in England, provoking anti-Catholic attacks by Ben Jonson and John Donne, both of whom use castration as a metaphor to characterize its radical removals, and running through some 22 editions before the Restoration. Aubrey may be thinking of one particularly notorious epigram by Martial, left out of Rader's school edition, in which the poetic speaker pleads with Cornelius the censor not to cut off his priapic pleasure-giving verses: "sed hi libelli / tamquam coniugibus suis mariti, / non possunt sine mentula placere" (but these little books are like husbands with their wives — they cannot please without a cock). Martial, *Epigrams I,* ed. and trans. D. R. Shackleton Bailey (Cambridge, MA: Harvard University Press, 1993), 1.35.3–5.

28. This practice began with the Bodleian's first librarian, Thomas James, who compiled his *Index generalis liborum prohibitorum a pontificiis* (Oxford, 1627) as a guide to collecting. Jennifer Summit, *Memory's Library: Medieval Books in Early Modern England* (Chicago: University of Chicago Press, 2008), 222.

29. *The Early Lives of Milton,* ed. Helen Darbishire (London, 1932).

30. "The early lives that ultimately shape the version of Milton that has come down to us are the early lives he wrote himself." Thomas N. Corns, "The Early Lives of John Milton," in *Writing Lives: Biography and Textuality, Identity and Representation in Early Modern England,* ed. Kevin Sharpe and Steven N. Zwicker, 75–89 (Oxford: Oxford University Press, 2008), 87.

31. For the Ranelagh circle and its connections to the Hartlib circle, see Catherine Gimelli Martin, *Milton among the Puritans: The Case for Historical Revisionism* (Aldershot: Ashgate, 2010), 184–85. For the attendees at the Rota Club discussions, see Aubrey's life of James Harrington (*Brief Lives,* 1: 318–19).

32. I am grateful to Edward Jones for bringing this note to my attention.

33. "A True and Perfect Inventory of yᵉ Goods & Chattels of late Mrs. Eliz. Miltton," qtd. in *The Life Records of John Milton,* 5 vols. (New York: Gordian Press, 1966), 5:328–31. French's list of items is not complete. The original document is in the Chester Record Office. For a discussion of the inventory's items in relation to the domestic economy of the Milton household, see Laura Lunger Knoppers, *Politicizing Domesticity from Henrietta Maria to Milton's Eve* (Cambridge: Cambridge University Press, 2011), 142–45.

34. For Ashmole's collection, see Ann Geneva, *Astrology and the Seventeenth Century Mind: William Lilly and the Language of the Stars* (Manchester: Manchester University Press, 1995), 158–59. In book 4 of *Paradise Regained,* Satan, uninvited, casts the horoscope of the Son, reading the "starry rubric" in what is clearly a parody of contemporary astrological practices (4.380–93). *The Complete Poetry and Essential Prose of John Milton,* ed. William Kerrigan, John Rumrich, and Stephen M. Fallon (New York: Modern Library, 2007); hereafter cited in the text. See also Harry Rusche, "A Reading of John Milton's Horoscope," *Milton Quarterly* 13, no. 1 (1979): 6–11. Celebrity and astrology still go together. Magazine horoscopes, organized by the signs of the zodiac, invariably give the birthday of a famous person who shares this month's astral fate with you.

35. William Kerrigan, *The Sacred Complex: On the Psychogenesis of "Paradise Lost"* (Cambridge, MA: Harvard University Press, 1983), 11.

36. Ibid., 179–80; Aubrey's own father suffered with eye problems, what Aubrey describes as "a pinne and Webbe in the Eie (a pearle)." His interest in Milton's blindness as a familial inheritance, and, particularly, in determining whose side of the family he inherited it from, was likely motivated by his own anxiety about going blind.

37. Homer, *The Iliad,* translated by Robert Fitzgerald (New York: Farrar, Straus and Giroux, 2004), 19.417, 426.

38. Stanley Fish, *Surprised by Sin: The Reader in "Paradise Lost"* (New York: Saint Martin's, 1967), 25.

39. The genre of the character book derives from the classical model of Theophrastus. Popular English character collections include Joseph Hall's *Characters of Virtues and Vices* (1608); *A Wife Now the Widow of Sir Thomas Overbury* (1614), attributed to Overbury and containing 22 prose characters; and John Earle's *Micro-cosmographie; or, A Peece of*

the world discovered in essayes and characters (1628). The latter may well have given Hooke the idea of writing up his experimental observations in the "micro-" genre of the character; it went through ten editions before 1665.

40. Hooke, *Micrographia* (London, 1665), 211.

41. In *The Blazing World* (1666), Margaret Cavendish hybridizes Hooke's insects with their human counterparts: "some were bear-men, some worm-men,…some bird-men, some fly-men, some ant-men, some geese-men, some spider-men, some lice-men,…and many more, which I cannot all remember; and of these several sorts of men, each followed such a profession as was most proper for the nature of their species." When the "lice-men" are summoned to perform before the Empress, they "endeavored to measure all things to a hair's breadth," another humorous turn on Hooke's drawing. Margaret Cavendish, *The Blazing World and Other Writings,* ed. Kate Lilley (London: Penguin Classics, 1992), 133–34, 159.

42. Hooke, *Micrographia,* 211, 198, 175. Janice Neri, *The Insect and the Image: Visualizing Nature in Early Modern Europe, 1500–1700* (Minneapolis: University of Minnesota Press, 2011), observes how the clean frame and controlled lines of the drawing occlude the violent decapitation that makes it possible: "an atmosphere of calm and quiet prevails as the insect serenely presents itself to the viewer for study and contemplation" (120). In *The Prose of Things: Transformations of Description in the Eighteenth Century* (Chicago: University of Chicago Press, 2006), Cythnia Wall observes a tension between the "magnificent still lifes" of Hooke's insect portraits and the animation of his narrative prose: "in the text, they [the insects] scuttle and scud and lurk and intrude and trample and spring" (76).

43. John Aubrey, *The Life of Thomas Hobbes,* in *John Aubrey: Brief Lives,* ed. John Buchanan-Brown (London: Penguin Classics, 2000), 443. All quotations from the *Life of Hobbes* refer to this edition, hereafter cited as *Hobbes.* Bennett does not include Aubrey's *Life of Hobbes* in her edition, treating it as a "separate, if closely related, work" (*Brief Lives,* 1:cxli).

44. William Poole, *John Aubrey and the Advancement of Learning* (Oxford: Bodleian Library, 2010), 97.

45. Lisa Jardine, *The Curious Life of Robert Hooke: The Man Who Measured London* (New York: HarperCollins, 2004), dates Hoskins's visit to the autumn of 1647 when Charles I was in residence at Carisbrooke Castle, a closely guarded guest of the island's governor, Robert Hammond. Charles's departure from the Isle of Wight the following October coincided with the death of Hooke's father, leading Hooke, too, to depart for London. He would have arrived in the capital, Jardine notes, in time for the execution of Charles I, which took place outside the Banqueting House in Whitehall, a short distance from Lely's studio in Covent Garden and from the school gates of Westminster (47–53).

46. In the *Life of Hobbes,* Aubrey twice refers to Cooper. He is "our common friend" who drew Hobbes's portrait "as like as art could afford, and one of the best pieces that ever he did, which his Majestie, at his returne bought of him, and conserves as one of his great rarities in his Closet at White-hall." Aubrey also describes how Hobbes worked his way back into Charles II's favor by diverting the king while he sat for Cooper soon after the Restoration (*Hobbes,* 431–33).

47. Richard Wendorf, *The Elements of Life: Biography and Portrait-Painting in Stuart and Georgian England* (Oxford: Oxford University Press, 1990), 108–34.

48. John Murdoch, *The English Miniature* (New Haven, CT: Yale University Press, 1981), 110.

49. The birding story follows immediately upon the report of Hobbes's schoolboy nickname, "His haire was black, and his schoolefellowes were wont to call him Crowe" (*Hobbes*, 425).

50. A–W, March 7, 1680; Bodleian MS Tanner 456a, fol. 23; qtd. in Balme, *Two Antiquaries*, 88.

51. A–W, March 27, 1680; Bodleian MS Ballard 14, fol. 131; qtd. in Bennett, *Brief Lives*, 1:xc–xci.

52. A–W, May 22, 1680; Bodleian MS F 39, fol. 340; qtd. in Bennett, *Brief Lives*, 1:xci.

53. MS Aubrey 9, fol. 28.

54. Richard Garnett, "John Aubrey," in *The Dictionary of National Biography*, ed. Sir Leslie Stephen and Sir Sidney Lee (London: Smith, Elder, 1885), 2:245.

55. Lytton Strachey, *Portraits in Miniature and Other Essays* (New York: Norton, 1931), 29.

56. Both passages are quoted from *The Norton Shakespeare*, 2nd ed., gen. ed. Stephen Greenblatt (New York: Norton, 2008). The passage from *Troilus and Cressida* also supplies the refrain line for Virginia Woolf's novel *Between the Acts* (1941).

57. What Aubrey had managed to accomplish by a kind of alchemical inadvertence, Strachey presents himself performing flagrantly in the preface to *Eminent Victorians* (1918), abandoning "the direct method of a scrupulous narration" in favor of more cowardly but also more efficacious military tactics, falling "upon the flank, or the rear." Lytton Strachey, *Eminent Victorians*, ed. John Sutherland (Oxford: Oxford World Classics, 2003), 5.

Notes to Chapter 4

1. Daniel Defoe, *Robinson Crusoe*, ed. John Richetti (London: Penguin, 2003), 5.

2. For the symbolic implications of Crusoe's original surname, see Robert W. Ayers, "*Robinson Crusoe*: 'Allusive Allegorick History,'" *PMLA* 82, no. 5 (1967): 404–05n28; and David Marshall, "Autobiographical Acts in *Robinson Crusoe*," *ELH* 71, no. 4 (2004): 901–02.

3. The third provision of the act stipulates "that in case the Crown and Imperiall Dignity of this Realm shall hereafter come to any Person not being a Native of this Kingdom of England this Nation be not obliged to ingage in any Warr for the Defence of any Dominions or Territories which do not belong to the Crown of England without the Consent of Parliament." "An Act for the further Limitation of the Crown and better securing of Rights and Liberties of the Subject," http://www.legislation.gov.uk/aep/Will3/12-13/2/section/III (accessed May 28, 2016).

4. John J. Murray, *George I, the Baltic, and the Whig Split of 1717: A Study in Diplomacy and Propaganda* (London: Routledge and Kegan Paul, 1969); and Jeremy

Black, *The Continental Commitment: Britain, Hanover and Interventionism, 1714–1793* (London: Routledge, 2005), 48–58, discuss George I's foreign policy and its domestic ramifications.

5. James Joyce, "Daniel Defoe," trans. and ed. Joseph Prescott, *Buffalo Studies* 1 (1964): 24–25. Written to answer John Tutchin's poem "The Foreigners" (1700), Defoe's verse satire "The True-Born Englishman" (1701) ridiculed English distrust of foreign immigrants and of their foreign king, William III. It proved an improbable hit, running through ten editions as well as numerous pirated copies to become the best-selling poem of the reign of Queen Anne.

6. Crusoe's cultural identification with European imperialism has provoked powerful postcolonial rewritings of his story, including those by Derek Walcott in his poetry collection *The Castaway* (1965) and stage play *Pantomime* (1978); and J. M. Coetzee in his novel *Foe* (1987).

7. Defoe, *Robinson Crusoe*, 7.

8. In his pioneering study published over 50 years ago, *The Rise of the Novel: Studies in Defoe, Richardson, and Fielding* (Berkeley, CA: University of California Press, 1957), Ian Watt proposes that the decline of feudalism and the growth of individualism, both socioeconomic and political-philosophical, provided the cultural conditions for the new form of the novel to develop in England. Watt's thesis has been subject to frequent and important reassessment, most comprehensively by Michael McKeon, who, taking issue with its Whig methodology, replaced signs of progress (the development of capitalism, the growth of a reading public) with sites of contention (the ideological struggle between conservative and progressive ideologies and the epistemological struggle between romance idealism and a skeptical empiricism). But Watt's essential point, that the rise of new social formations coincided with and contributed to the rise of the novel, continues to receive general acceptance across the disciplines of literary studies. Michael McKeon, *The Origins of the English Novel, 1600–1740* (Baltimore: Johns Hopkins University Press, 2002). See also Lennard J. Davis, *Factual Fictions: The Origins of the English Novel* (New York: Columbia University Press, 1983); Nancy Armstrong, *Desire and Domestic Fiction: A Political History of the Novel* (New York: Oxford University Press, 1987); J. Paul Hunter, *Before Novels: The Cultural Contexts of Eighteenth-Century English Fiction* (New York: Norton, 1990); and for a non-Anglocentric view, David Quint, *Cervantes's Novel of Modern Times: A New Reading of "Don Quijote"* (Princeton, NJ: Princeton University Press, 2003). On the interdependence of historiography and the early novel, see Everett Zimmerman, *The Boundaries of Fiction: History and the Eighteenth-Century British Novel* (Ithaca, NY: Cornell University Press, 1996); and Robert Mayer, *History and the Early English Novel: Matters of Fact from Bacon to Defoe* (New York: Cambridge University Press, 1997). On the vogue for the memoir novel in late seventeenth and early eighteenth century France, see Philip Stewart, *Imitation and Illusion in the French Memoir-Novel, 1700–1750: The Art of Make-Believe* (New Haven, CT: Yale University Press, 1969).

9. Jonathan Swift, *Gulliver's Travels*, ed. Robert DeMaria Jr. (London: Penguin Classics, 2003), 172. The king of Brobdingnag may have reacted so violently to Gulliver's summary of recent European history because his own grandfather had to fight a civil war to secure his reign (129).

10. Hyde was given the title Earl of Clarendon in 1661. I am using the name "Hyde" and title "Clarendon" interchangeably throughout this chapter.

11. Daniel Defoe, *Memoirs of a Cavalier,* ed. James T. Boulton (Oxford: Oxford University Press, 1972), 3; hereafter abbreviated as *MC* and cited in the text. The full title to the 1720 first edition (the only edition to appear in Defoe's lifetime) is *Memoirs of a Cavalier; or, A Military Journal of the Wars in Germany, and the Wars in England; from the Year 1632, to the Year 1648. Written Threescore Years ago by an English Gentleman, who served first in the Army of Gustavus Adolphus, the Glorious King of Sweden, till his Death; and after that, in the Royal Army of King Charles the First, from the Beginning of the Rebellion, to the End of That War.* Defoe's name does not appear on the title page. Beginning with the second edition of the *Memoirs,* printed by James Lister (n.d.) in Leeds, and continuing with the eighteenth and nineteenth century editions that followed, the Cavalier is positively identified as Andrew Newport, second son of Sir Richard Newport, a Shropshire gentleman who gave money to the king in exchange for a barony in 1642.

12. "The Preface to the Reader," in *The Swedish Intelligencer, The first part,* comp. William Watts (London, 1632). Arthur W. Secord discusses Defoe's stitching together of this and other sources in "The Origins of Defoe's *Memoirs of a Cavalier,*" in his *Robert Drury's Journal and Other Studies* (Urbana: University of Illinois Press, 1961), 72–133. For the reception of military news from abroad, see David Randall, *Credibility in Elizabethan and Early Stuart Military News* (London: Pickering and Chatto, 2008).

13. Philip Vincent, *The Lamentations of Germany* (London, 1638), 29.

14. Ibid., 27.

15. John Aubrey, *Three Prose Works: Miscellanies; Remaines of Gentilisme and Judaisme; Observations,* ed. John Buchanan-Brown (Fontwell, Sussex: Centaur Press, 1972), 250–51.

16. Mark Stoyle, *Soldiers and Strangers: An Ethnic History of the English Civil War* (New Haven, CT: Yale University Press, 2005), surveys the numbers and nationalities of foreign fighters, including Irish, Welsh, and Scottish soldiers, who served in the royalist and parliamentary armies between 1642 and 1644.

17. Anonymous, *A Copie of the Kings Message sent by the Duke of Lenox* (London, 1644), 1; cited by Tamsyn Williams, who notes the visual allusion to *Lamentations,* "'Magnetic Figures': Polemical Prints of the English Revolution," in *Renaissance Bodies: The Human Figure in English Culture, c. 1540–1660,* ed. Lucy Gent and Nigel Llewellyn (London: Reaktion Books, 1990), 91–93.

18. *OED,* s.v. "plunder," v. 2, def. 1a, http://www.oed.com/view/Entry/146166 (accessed May 27, 2016); *The Swedish Intelligencer, The second part* (London, 1632), 179.

19. Thomas May, *The history of the Parliament of England, the third Booke* (London, 1647), 3.

20. John Taylor (?), *A dog's elegy; or, Rupert's tears* (London, 1644), 8, quoted in T. N. Corns, W. A. Speck, and J. A. Downie, "Archetypal Mystification: Polemic and Reality in English Political Literature, 1640–1750," *Eighteenth Century Life* 7, no. 2 (1982): 5. The tagging of Rupert's black mongrel Boy as a "shagg'd *Cavalier*" (3) makes play with the common identification of the king's supporters by their long hair. On the politics of hair length, see Will Fisher, *Materializing Gender in Early Modern English Literature and Culture* (Cambridge: Cambridge University Press, 2007), 142–44.

21. The rise of large-scale mercenarism in Europe is usefully summarized by Janice E. Thomson in *Mercenaries, Pirates, and Sovereigns: State-Building and Extraterritorial Violence in Early Modern Europe* (Princeton, NJ: Princeton University Press, 1996), 26–32. Michael Howard, *War in European History* (Oxford: Oxford University Press, 1976), 58, notes that at the time of Gustavus Adolphus's death in 1632, less than 10 percent of his army were Swedish nationals, the majority being local recruits or foreign fighters.

22. The character of Wellbred from Ben Jonson's *Every Man in His Humour* (1598) wonderfully defends the prerogatives of the irascible aristocrat, declaring, "Anger costs a man nothing: and a tall man is never his own man, till he be angry" (4.6.7–9), in Ben Jonson, *Every Man in His Humour,* ed. Martin Seymour-Smith (New York: Hill and Wang, 1968).

23. For Samuel Pepys's transcription of the king's Newmarket account, see *Charles II's Escape from Worcester: A Collection of Narratives Assembled by Samuel Pepys,* ed. William Matthews (Berkeley, CA: University of California Press, 1966), 34–84. John Ogilby's coronation entertainment and other triumphal renderings of Charles's escape from Worcester are discussed by Harold Weber, *Paper Bullets: Print and Kingship Under Charles II* (Lexington: University of Kentucky Press, 1996), 25–49.

24. Thomas Blount, *Boscobel; or, The history of His Sacred Majesties most miraculous preservation after the battle of Worcester* (London, 1660), 41.

25. Elliott Visconsi, "A Degenerate Race: English Barbarism in Aphra Behn's *Oroonoko* and *The Widow Ranter,*" *ELH* 69, no. 3 (2002): 673–701, 684–85.

26. Aphra Behn, *Oroonoko and Other Writings,* ed. Paul Salzman (Oxford: Oxford University Press, 1994), 39.

27. Anonymous, *An exact narrative and relation of his Most Sacred Majesties escape* (London, 1660), 6.

28. David H. Solkin, "Isaac Fuller's *Escape of Charles II:* A Restoration Tragicomedy," *Journal of the Warburg and Courtauld Institutes* 62 (1999): 199–240, shows how Fuller combines the low humor of Dutch and Flemish peasant scenes with the more elevated gestures and poses of royal portraiture and devotional painting. This mix of pictorial genres, he suggests, dramatizes the inherent contradictions between the figure of the "peasant king" and his embrace of and by the people.

29. Anonymous, *An exact narrative,* 8.

30. William Shakespeare, *1 Henry IV,* in *The Norton Shakespeare,* 2nd ed., gen. ed. Stephen Greenblatt (New York: Norton, 2008), 2.5.9.

31. McKeon, *Origins of the English Novel,* 212–14, discusses the royal escape narratives in relation to romance conventions.

32. Maximillian E. Novak, *Daniel Defoe, Master of Fictions: His Life and Ideas* (Oxford: Oxford University Press, 2001), 591.

33. Ibid., 82–85, 181–83. Queen Anne ignored the suggestion, sentencing Defoe to the pillory and jail time instead.

34. Paula R. Backscheider, *Daniel Defoe: Ambition and Innovation* (Lexington, KY: University of Kentucky Press, 1986), 123–35; Sharon Alker, "The Soldierly Imagination: Narrating Fear in Defoe's *Memoirs of a Cavalier,*" *Eighteenth Century Fiction* 19, nos. 1–2 (2006): 43–68.

35. Backscheider, *Daniel Defoe,* 124.

36. Daniel Defoe, *Memoirs of a Cavalier* (Edinburgh, 1766), vi–vii. In a footnote, the unnamed editors advise the reader to stop "at the bottom of page 305 of this edition," where they consider the genuine portion of the *Memoirs* to have concluded (vii). Backscheider, *Daniel Defoe*, 124; Boulton, *MC*, xxxvi; Alker, "Soldierly Imagination," 66–67.

37. Michael Seidel, "Crusoe in Exile," *PMLA* 96, no. 3 (1981): 363–74. The temporal parallel is earlier noted by J. Paul Hunter, *The Reluctant Pilgrim: Defoe's Emblematic Method and Quest for Form in "Robinson Crusoe"* (Baltimore: Johns Hopkins University Press, 1966), 204.

38. Richetti (*Robinson Crusoe*, 248n6) notes that the first edition gave 1661 as the date of Crusoe's original departure from England. This date was amended in the second and subsequent editions, suggesting that its accuracy mattered to Defoe.

39. Philip Hicks, *Neoclassical History and English Culture: From Clarendon to Hume* (New York: St. Martin's Press, 1996), 67–68, estimates that close to 16,000 copies of the *History* were printed in Oxford between 1702–04 and 1731–32, the majority distributed wholesale by Thomas Bennet, the university's press agent in London, to over 78 booksellers.

40. Clarendon's *History* was advertised in the issue of the *London Gazette,* dated July 2–6, 1702, that announced the general election, leaving little doubt as to the political intentions of its sponsors. Mark Knights, "The Tory Interpretation of History in the Rage of Parties," *Huntington Library Quarterly* 68, nos. 1–2 (2005), 357n20.

41. How can it be, it asks, "that, whereas the Fleet of England hath been renown'd, through so many Ages, for the honour and security of this Kingdom, in these latter days, by an unaccountable improvidence, our care has been more industriously applied to the raising great Numbers of Land Forces." Edward Hyde, Earl of Clarendon, *The History of the Rebellion and Civil Wars in England… Volume the first* (Oxford, 1702), ix.

42. Laurence Hyde, "To the Queen," in *The History of the Rebellion and Civil Wars in England… Volume the third* (Oxford, 1704), sig. b1r.

43. Laurence Hyde, "To the Queen," in *The History of the Rebellion and Civil Wars in England… Volume the second* (Oxford, 1703), sig. b1v. Tory bills against occasional conformity were thrown out of the 1702, 1703, and 1704 sessions of Parliament, but a Whig-supported bill was passed in 1711. The Schism Act of 1714 further discriminated against Dissenters by banning their schools and academies from meeting, although its measures were never systematically enforced.

44. Charles Leslie, *The New Association* (London, 1702), 18.

45. *A Complete History of England: With the lives of all the Kings and Queens thereof* (London, 1706). The names of the 13 booksellers are given on the title page to volume 1, while those of the more than 700 subscribers are listed alphabetically, covering four closely printed folio pages. Joseph M. Levine, *The Battle of the Books: History and Literature in the Augustan Age* (Ithaca, NY: Cornell University Press, 1991), 309–19, examines the contents and historiographical aims of *A Complete History.* G. V. Bennett's biography, *White Kennett, 1660–1728* (London: SPCK, 1957), 94–97, 168–74, offers the shrewdest account of Kennett's contribution.

46. On the page, the historical parallel between the execution of Charles I and the abdication of his son James II is emphasized through italicized demonstratives: "An unhappy Suspicion of contrary Measures did sadly help to accomplish the *Evil of this* Day

[i.e., January 30, 1649]. We of yesterday remember, that when an Arbitrary Executive Power was much more effectually set up in a later Reign, it broke short *that* Reign." White Kennett, *A Compassionate Enquiry into the Causes of the Civil War, in a sermon preached in the Church of St. Botolph Algate* (London, 1704), 12.

47. Mary Astell, *An Impartial Enquiry into the Causes of Rebellion and Civil War in this Kingdom; in an Examination of Dr. Kennett's Sermon* (London, 1704); Daniel Defoe, *Moderation Maintain'd, in Defence of a Compassionate Enquiry into the Causes of the Civil War* (London, 1704). Astell feigns ignorance of the controversy, accusing Kennett of self-publicity: "To his Person and Character I am utterly a Stranger...nor had I so much as known that his Sermon occasion'd any *Noise*, or *Stories*, or *unreasonable Scandal*, had not he himself been pleas'd to *Advertise* the World of it" (3).

48. Geoffrey Holmes, *British Politics in the Age of Anne* (Ronceverte, WV: Hambledon Press, 1987), 64–68; See also Steve Pincus, *1688: The First Modern Revolution* (New Haven, CT: Yale University Press, 2009), 305–65, for the anti-French foreign policy of William III.

49. White Kennett, "To the Reader," *A Complete History of England: Volume 1* (London, 1706), sig. br.

50. John Oldmixon, *Memoirs of the Press... 1710 to 1740* (London, 1742), 35–36; qtd. in Levine, *Battle of the Books,* 316.

51. C. H. Firth enumerates Hyde's additions in three articles that appear under the same title — "Clarendon's 'History of the Rebellion'" — in consecutive issues of the *English Historical Review* 19, no. 73 (1904): 26–54; 19, no. 74 (1904): 246–62; 19, no. 75 (1904): 464–83.

52. Edward Hyde, Earl of Clarendon, *The History of the Rebellion and Civil Wars in England,* 6 vols., ed. W. Dunn Macray (Oxford: Clarendon Press, 1888), book 16, paragraph 247. All references are to this edition and are cited parenthetically in the text by book and paragraph number.

53. With its elision of long-term structural or institutional causes, *The History of the Rebellion* has plausibly been crowned the first revisionist history of the English revolution, anticipating by 300 years the revisionist turn of the 1970s when scholars, taking issue with earlier Whig and Marxist accounts, explained the crises of the 1640s and 1650s in terms of local grievances, political contingencies, and the mistaken, but not premeditated, actions of courtly and landed elites. Conrad Russell is generally considered one of the foremost architects of revisionism; his publications include *The Causes of the English Civil War* (Oxford: Oxford University Press, 1990), and *Unrevolutionary England, 1603–1642* (London: Hambledon Press, 1990).

54. Martine Watson Brownley, *Clarendon and the Rhetoric of Historical Form* (Philadelphia: University of Pennsylvania Press, 1985), 168.

55. John Oldmixon, *The Critical History of England, Ecclesiastical and Civil,* 2 vols. (London, 1730), 2:184. Despite acknowledging their popular appeal, Oldmixon objects to the character portraits as extraneous to, and commonly extricated from, the historical narrative: "I take the Liberty to add here, that if every one of the Characters were still to be imagin'd, the History wou'd be the same; and when they are detach'd so from the Subject, they are like vicious Episodes in an *Epick* Poem" (2:184). Dated February 15, 1703, James Tyrrell's letter is one of 63 he wrote to Locke, now housed in the Lovelace

Collection in the Bodleian Library, Oxford. It is quoted by J. W. Gough, "James Tyrrell, Whig Historian and Friend of John Locke," *Historical Journal* 19, no. 3 (1976): 604n106.

56. Edward (Ned) Ward, *The History of the Grand Rebellion…Digested into Verse* (London, 1713), title page, sig. a1r–a3r.

57. Horace Walpole, *A Catalogue of the Royal and Noble Authors of England* (London, 1796), 136.

58. For less prejudicial portraits of Arundel and Weston, two in a series of portraits tacitly modeled upon those in Clarendon's *History*, see Kevin Sharpe, *The Personal Rule of Charles I* (New Haven, CT: Yale University Press, 1992), 145–50. The classic study of the transformation of an autonomous aristocratic class into dependent courtiers is Lawrence Stone's *The Crisis of the Aristocracy, 1558–1641* (Oxford: Oxford University Press, 1965). For an opposing view, focused on the collaboration between Arundel and the king in reforming the honors system, see Richard Cust, *Charles I and the Aristocracy, 1625–1642* (Cambridge: Cambridge University Press, 2013).

59. Letter to Samuel Pepys, dated August 26, 1689; quoted in *Particular Friends: The Correspondence of Samuel Pepys and John Evelyn,* ed. Guy de la Bédoyère (Rochester, NY: Boydell Press, 1997), 194.

60. Theresa Lewis, *Lives of the Friends and Contemporaries of the Lord Chancellor Clarendon: Illustrative of Portraits in his Gallery,* 3 vols. (London: John Murray, 1852), 3:251–60, catalogs all the pictures listed by Evelyn and gives a short description of each. Those of Buckingham, Weston, Arundel, and Coventry are numbers 17, 21, 38, and 44, respectively.

61. Catharine MacLeod, "'Good, but not like': Peter Lely, Portrait Practice and the Creation of a Court Look," in *Painted Ladies: Women at the Court of Charles II,* ed. Julia Marciari Alexander and Catharine MacLeod, 50–61 (London: National Portrait Gallery; New Haven, CT: Yale Center for British Art, 2001), explains the studio system that an entrepreneurial Lely put in place.

62. The publicity these "his and hers" series excited made them immediately subject to satirical reinterpretation, most notably in a series of "painter" poems that circulated in manuscript and, eventually, in print during 1666 and 1667. For the "Windsor Beauties," see Catharine MacLeod and Julia Marciari Alexander, "The 'Windsor Beauties' and the Beauties Series in Restoration England," in *Politics, Transgression, and Representation at the Court of Charles II,* ed. Julia Marciari Alexander and Catharine MacLeod, 81–120 (New Haven, CT: Yale University Press, 2007); and Michael Wenzel, "The *Windsor Beauties* by Sir Peter Lely and the Collection of Paintings at St. James's Palace, 1674," *Journal of the History of Collections* 14, no. 2 (2002): 208–09. On their repurposing in the "painter poems" and, especially, in Marvell's *Last Instructions to a Painter,* see Annabel Patterson's *Marvell and the Civic Crown* (Princeton, NJ: Princeton University Press, 1978), 111–67.

63. The most exhaustive discussion of Hyde's models and sources, including Thucydides, Tacitus, Sallust, Plutarch, and Livy among classical writers, and William Camden, Francis Bacon, Paolo Sarpi, Philippe de Commynes, and Enrico Caterino Davila, among early moderns ones, is given in Brownley, *Clarendon and Rhetoric,* 147–52. See also Hicks, *Neoclassical History,* 55–62; Nigel Smith, *Literature and Revolution in England, 1640–1660* (New Haven, CT: Yale University Press, 1997), 345–52; Kevin

Sharpe, *Reading Revolutions: The Politics of Reading in Early Modern England* (New Haven, CT: Yale University Press, 2000), 300–06; and Paul Seaward, "Clarendon, Tacitism, and the Civil Wars of Europe," *Huntington Library Quarterly* 68, nos. 1–2 (2005): 289–311. In a letter he wrote to his friend and fellow royalist John Earles in the winter of 1647, Hyde depreciates the English chroniclers, Raphael Holinshed, John Stow, and Richard Baker among whom he fears to be ranked, declaring his desire to match the standard of the ancient historians Livy and Tacitus: "I am contented you should laugh at me for a fop in talking of Livy and Tacitus; when all I can hope for is to side Hollingshead, and Stow, or (because he is a poor Knight too, and worse than either of them) Sir Richard Baker." *State Papers Collected by Edward, Earl of Clarendon, Commencing from the year 1621.* (Oxford, 1773), 2:386.

64. Firth, "Clarendon's 'History,'" 256.

65. E. M. W. Tillyard, *The English Epic and Its Background* (London: Chatto and Windus, 1954), 450.

66. The discussion concludes on a note of regret: Clarendon "showed epic promise" but failed to follow through on his epic ambitions (ibid., 451). Ultimately, for Tillyard, the epic is a literary standard to be met rather than a set of materials to recast and imagine anew.

67. John Milton, *Paradise Lost,* in *The Complete Poetry and Essential Prose of John Milton,* ed. William Kerrigan, John Rumrich, and Stephen M. Fallon (New York: Modern Library, 2007), 1.507; hereafter cited by book and line number in the text.

68. Colin Burrow, *Epic Romance: Homer to Milton* (Oxford: Oxford University Press, 1993), 263–68; David Quint, "Milton's Book of Numbers: Book 1 of *Paradise Lost* and Its Catalogue," *International Journal of the Classical Tradition* 13, no. 4 (2007): 528–49.

NOTES TO AFTERWORD

1. Joseph Addison, *The Freeholder,* no. 35 (Friday, April 20, 1716), qtd. in *The Freeholder,* ed. James Leheny (Oxford: Clarendon Press, 1979), 195. The *Freeholder*'s run of 55 issues lasted from December 23, 1715, until June 29, 1716, overlapping with the Jacobite rebellion of 1715–16.

2. *OED Online,* s.v. "undertaker," n., def. 5b, http://www.oed.com/view/Entry/ 212144 (accessed May 27, 2016). In *Some considerations offered relating to our present trade* (London, 1698), one T. T. Merchant attacks the undertakers for driving down the cost of funerals, undercutting the "Weavers, Drapers, Taylors, Glovers, &c." who, since "one Cloak and other necessaries do serve several Years, and furnish some hundred Funerals," had lost much of their traditional trade (6–7). Thomas Laqueur quotes Merchant alongside other hostile eighteenth century commentators in "Bodies, Death, and Pauper Funerals," *Representations,* no. 1 (1983): 109–31.

3. Samuel Johnson, *A Dictionary of the English language; in which the words are deduced from their originals and illustrated in their different significations by examples from the best writers* (London, 1755), s.v. "bio'grapher."

4. The *Memoirs of the life of John Lord Somers* were advertised in the London newspaper, the *Post Man,* July 10–12, 1716; Addison's essay appeared on April 20, 1716. Addison, *Freeholder,* 195n5.

5. [John Oldmixon], *Memoirs of the life of John Lord Somers* (London, 1716), 3. Pat Rogers, "The Memoirs of Somers and Wharton: Authorship and Authority in Eighteenth-Century Biography," *Bulletin of the New York Public Library* 77 (1974): 465–86.

6. *The lives and characters of the most illustrious persons British and Foreign. Who died in the year 1711* (London, 1713); *The lives and characters of the most illustrious persons British and Foreign. Who died in the year 1712* (London, 1714); *The lives and characters of the most illustrious persons, who died in the years, 1713, 1714, and 1715* (London, 1716). Biographical appraisals of the dead — what we would now call obituaries — had earlier appeared in Robert L'Estrange's newspaper, the *Intelligencer* (1663–66), celebrating the royalist departed, and, more scurrilously, in John Dunton's periodical, the *Post-Angel* (1701–02), which specialized in spilling lurid details of lives ignominiously lived. Nigel Starck, *Life after Death: The Art of the Obituary* (Carlton, Victoria: Melbourne University Press, 2006), 1–11, dates the earliest newspaper obituaries to the corantos or foreign newsletters of the 1620s. For Curll's promotion of his yearly volumes, see Paul Baines and Pat Rogers, *Edmund Curll, Bookseller* (Oxford: Oxford University Press, 2007), 52, 71–72.

7. Addison, *Freeholder,* 195.

8. "Summary Notes for Contributors," *Oxford Dictionary of National Biography,* https://global.oup.com/oxforddnb/fdscontent/oxforddnb/pdf/odnb/ODNB_summary_Notes_for_Contributors.pdf (accessed May 17, 2016); Pat Rogers, "Addison, Joseph (1672–1719)," *Oxford Dictionary of National Biography* (Oxford: Oxford University Press, 2004), http://www.oxforddnb.com/view/article/156 (accessed May 31, 2016).

9. Scholars have developed an extensive vocabulary for describing the conservative program of periodical prose writing — civility, politeness, sociability, gentlemanliness, and the reformation of manners. There is a large literature devoted to the periodical essay. With regard to its ambiguous relationship to an expanding political culture, see, especially, Brian Cowan, "Mr. Spectator and the Coffeehouse Public Sphere," *Eighteenth-Century Studies* 37, no. 3 (2004): 345–66; and Sophia Rosenfeld, *Common Sense: A Political History* (Cambridge, MA: Harvard University Press, 2011), 17–55.

10. Addison, it might also be noted, passes over the complicity of the periodical press in feeding the growing demand for lives of the fallen and famous. The increasingly collaborative relationship between periodical publications and popular biography is exemplified by the contents of the *Gentleman's Magazine,* founded in 1731 under Edward Cave to provide a monthly digest of metropolitan news and commentary aimed at the provincial reader. It was here that Samuel Johnson got his start, penning, anonymously, a series of abridged lives for the magazine between 1738 and 1744. J. D. Fleeman, *A Bibliography of the Works of Samuel Johnson,* 2 vols. (Oxford: Clarendon Press, 2000), 1:37, 48, 55, 58–59, 83.

Index